The Coast Blockade

THE COAST BLOCKADE

The Royal Navy's War on Smuggling in Kent & Sussex 1817-31

ROY PHILP

COMPTON PRESS

To Margaret and Mark
for their help
and support

Published by Compton Press,
150 Comptons Lane, Horsham,
West Sussex, RH13 6DA
Tel/fax: 01403 252838

A catalogue record for this book is
available from the British Library.

ISBN 0 9536022 0 6

Cover illustration 'Smugglers attacked'
reproduced courtesy of Alan Hay.

Design and typesetting by John Saunders
Printed and bound in Great Britain by
Biddles Ltd., Guildford and King's Lynn

CONTENTS

Royal Naval Coast Blockade Stations in 1825

The six large arrows indicate Divisional Offices

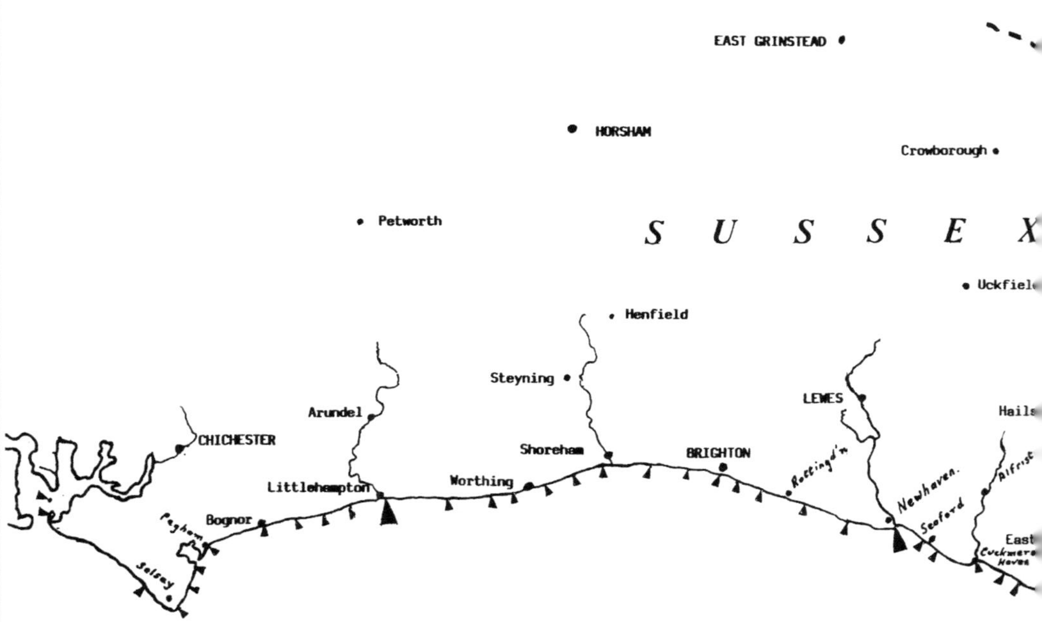

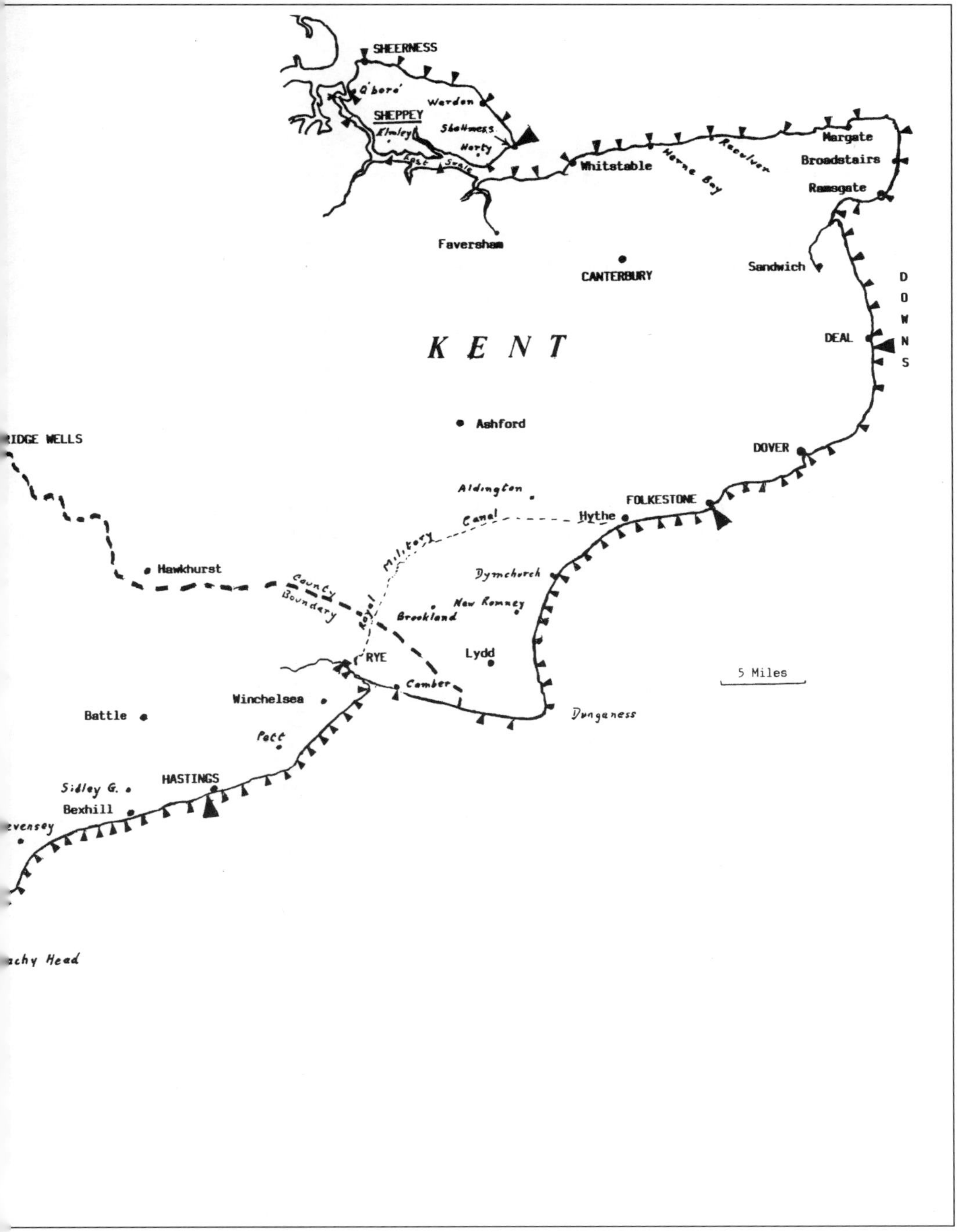

SHEERNESS
Q'boro'
Warden
SHEPPEY
Elmley
Shellness
Harty
East Swale
Faversham
Whitstable
Herne Bay
Reculver
Margate
Broadstairs
Ramsgate
Sandwich
CANTERBURY
DOWNS
DEAL
KENT
Ashford
DOVER
FOLKESTONE
Aldington
Royal Military Canal
Hythe
Dymchurch
New Romney
Brookland
Lydd
County Boundary
Hawkhurst
RYE
Camber
Dungeness
5 Miles
Winchelsea
Battle
Pett
HASTINGS
Sidley G.
Bexhill

ACKNOWLEDGEMENTS

I am grateful for the help provided by:

Members of staff at the Public Record Office, Kew, the Record Offices and various museums in Kent, East Sussex and West Sussex, the National Museum of Customs and Excise and that department's staff newspaper "Portcullis".

David Hewer,
Betty Toovey,
Ted Murray,
Alan Hay.

Finally my particular thanks for the assistance given by Dr. Chris Howard Bailey, Keeper of Records and Director of Publications and her staff at the Royal Naval Museum, Portsmouth.

A contribution from the proceeds of this book will go to the Vigilant Trust, an independent charity formed by volunteers from Customs & Excise to rescue and restore the Customs cruiser 'Vigilant' built in 1901, for preservation in the Historic Dockyard, Portsmouth (see page 179).

INTRODUCTION

The full history of the Royal Naval Coast Blockade for the Prevention of Smuggling, as it was officially known has remained untold since the Blockade was abolished in 1831. Described by some authors as the bloodiest period in the long war against smuggling the full details have, until now, remained buried in naval archives.

At the end of the Napoleonic wars in 1815 both the workers in the industrial north of England and the rural poor in the south were suffering badly. There was more than a whiff of insurrection in the air and many men were coming back to their homes in the south after discharge from the Army or Navy. Many remembered the massive scale of smuggling some 30 or so years before and it was certain to start again in Kent and Sussex - the front line counties that straddled the shortest routes between the suppliers across the Channel and the London markets.

In 1816 the government, desperate to counter the threat, transferred the large fleet of revenue cruisers from Customs to Admiralty control and placed the Preventive Waterguard under the direct management of the Treasury. But the Waterguard was already in a poor state and its efficiency would decline still further over the next six years due to Treasury neglect.

Coming as it did at this anxious time the proposal by Captain J.W.McCulloch R.N. to combat smuggling with a permanent beach cordon of armed naval men ('sentinels') was welcomed by ministers keen to show they could act decisively. The idea was positive and aggressive; it was also expensive, but so too was the loss if anarchy returned to the coasts of Kent and Sussex - a loss not only of revenue but government authority in general. Within five years the initial cordon of some 80 men for a few miles either side of Deal had grown to an unbroken Blockade Line stretching 200 miles from Sheerness to Chichester Harbour with over 3000 naval officers and men.

The Royal Naval Coast Blockade Service was not an auxiliary force but a command, within the Royal Navy, reporting through a C-in-C to the Admiralty and the Navy Board. Later it divided into two commands, one for Kent the other for Sussex. As a preventive campaign against smuggling the Coast Blockade Service could be confused in the public mind with the near contemporary Coast Guard which from 1822 operated, under Customs management, on all other parts of Britain's coasts. Men from both were labelled 'preventives' but, as this book shows, the Royal Naval Coast Blockade Service was very different from any preventive force used in this country, before or since, if only for the rigid naval discipline imposed and the many bitter fights with smuggling gangs during the fourteen year campaign - 'attacks on the Line' in which the naval men were always heavily outnumbered perhaps by as much as forty to one.

In that first half of the nineteenth century the Coast Blockade was a rare instance where a regular naval command was formed as a law enforcement force on shore in Britain. But in all other respects it followed true naval tradition with its heroes and tragedies and perhaps more than its share of offenders.

Stationed amongst coastal communities where any resolute 'preventive' was an enemy the Blockade sentinels stood watch every night on open shores and cliffs perhaps a quarter mile from their nearest colleagues and always in danger of being attacked. And yet, as shown in Chapter Seven, there were many instances where, in atrocious weather, Blockade officers and men risked their lives time and time again to save those from wrecked ships who would have otherwise perished in the raging surf.

This is essentially the Navy's view of that intensive campaign being compiled mainly from the reports of its officers and men. As such the Coast Blockade would never presume to rank with the great naval achievements but it was a campaign in which the Royal Navy did succeed, against much local hatred and an often hostile magistracy, in eventually defeating the large smuggling gangs. The loss in revenue because of smuggling was of relatively minor importance compared to the need to prevent the two counties - particularly their coastal areas - from becoming ungovernable.

The Coast Blockade was a unique campaign, fought the naval way, and as such the story deserves its own, albeit modest, niche in the history of the Royal Navy.

CHAPTER ONE

Smuggling: The National Evil

'Will Washington take America or the smugglers England first? The bet will be a fair and even one.' By posing the question in 1781 Lord Pembroke demonstrated only too well the desperate situation facing the government at home. When the answer came, less that two years later, it was a close finish at least for those who lived in South East England. George Washington had won independence for the colonists but in Kent and Sussex – the front line in the war against smuggling – private armies of smugglers operated virtually unopposed by any government force. In Parliament it was said that 'because of this National Evil . . . the very fabric of society is being torn apart.'

Gangs of men, commonly a hundred or more and many of them armed, were regularly unloading immense quantities of tea, brandy, geneva (gin), fine fabrics and many other varieties of merchandise at various spots on the coasts of the two counties from where they were carried, without hindrance by the authorities, to local towns or on to commercial distribution centres on the outskirts of London. In a typical instance on the morning of Sunday 6 December 1778 a band of one hundred and ninety mounted men, their horses laden with bags of tea and bales of cloth, rode through the main street of Henfield. With them, as captives, were seven revenue officers who were later released unharmed. They were fortunate; some officers were killed in fights where they were always hopelessly outnumbered whilst some were found dead after unexplained falls from cliff tops. Others, after capture were shipped over to France on the vessel that had brought the contraband and left to make their way home back across the Channel.

Organised smuggling in Kent and Sussex had roots running back to the thirteenth century when raw wool was first smuggled out to the Continent to avoid an export duty imposed to protect English weavers. During the following three centuries wool smuggling, or 'owling' as it was known, was the main illegal trade. There was some smuggling of goods, mainly brandy and silks, into this country but the import duties and thus the illegal profits, were too low to create serious problems.

Between 1660 and 1720, however, the situation changed drastically as first import duties rose and then the demand for English wool declined. With years – perhaps generations – of experience in handling heavy and bulky woollen fleeces the smugglers in Kent and Sussex switched easily to 'running' large quantities of contraband, mainly tea and spirits at first, into England. The eighteenth century saw import duties continue to rise, the flow

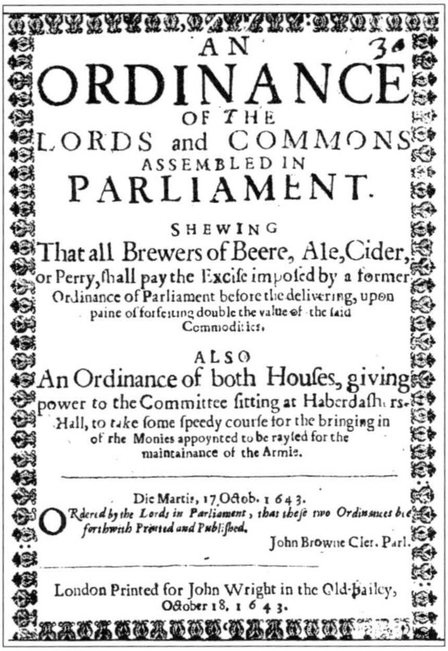

AN 3

ORDINANCE

OF THE

LORDS and COMMONS

ASSEMBLED IN

PARLIAMENT.

SHEWING

That all Brewers of Beere, Ale, Cider, or Perry, ſhall pay the Exciſe impoſed by a former Ordinance of Parliament before the delivering, upon paine of forfeiting double the value of the ſaid Commodities.

ALSO

An Ordinance of both Houſes, giving power to the Committee ſitting at Haberdaſhers-Hall, to take ſome ſpeedy courſe for the bringing in of the Monies appoynted to be rayſed for the maintainance of the Armie.

Die Martis, 17 Octob. 1643.

ORdered by the Lords in Parliament, that theſe two Ordinances be forthwith Printed and Publiſhed.

John Browne Cler. Parl.

London Printed for John Wright in the Old-baily, October 18. 1643.

Excise duty was first imposed by Parliament in 1643 as a 'temporary measure' to help fund its army in the Civil War – and is still with us today!

of illegal imports turned into a flood and the range of contraband evolved from a few commodities into a long list of sophisticated merchandise.

One important contributory factor to this surge in smuggling was the frequency with which the country was at war. Successive governments, needing finance for these wars, were forced to increase revenue duties and thus the profits in smuggling. More and more men were then attracted to the illegal trade to such an extent that the increase in smuggling reduced the revenue yield expected by the government and it was compelled to impose even higher rates of duty – a truly vicious circle. And when the country was at war the revenue authorities could expect little or no help from the Army or Navy in the fight against smuggling.

The revenue authorities themselves were divided into two separate bodies, the Board of Customs and the Board of Excise, both responsible to the Treasury for the collection of their separate duties. Customs duties had been imposed on many imported goods for centuries but duties of Excise (surely the worst choice ever for a tax title!) were introduced by Parliament in 1643 to help finance its army in the Civil War. Charged at first only on goods made here such as spirits, cider, beer and soap, by the 1690s the excise tariff had been extended to cover a wide range of imported goods, all of which were already liable to customs duties. The extra burden of tax brought even more profit for the smuggler.

Up to 1783 most of this profit came from tea. Made popular by the East India Company after it was founded in 1601 by the end of that century tea was one of the most heavily taxed imports and one for which the Company had the monopoly – at least for legitimate trade! Good money could be made running brandy and geneva but the profits in tea were enormous.

High in value for its bulk, and easy to handle, varieties such as Hyson, Bohea and Singlo were shipped from China to France and the Netherlands where they were packed, usually into 28lb bags made of oilskin, for smuggling into England. Bohea at 6d per lb in the Netherlands could sell here at 4s per lb when the lowest duty paid price was 5s. Cargoes of two or three tons were common and on one occasion a gang was said to have landed 11½ tons near Sandwich which needed 330 horses to carry it way inland.

Geneva (gin) and brandy came just below tea in the list of popular items of contraband. Although they were more difficult to handle the profits were good. Legally these spirits had to be imported in casks of forty gallons or more but the smuggling trade used small barrels, holding about four gallons, known variously as ' half ankers', 'tubs', or 'kegs', which could be supplied, ex-distillery already roped together in pairs for carrying across the shoulder. Spirits came from the distillery 'over proof' with an alcohol level well above the prudent drinker's limit and on arrival here had to be diluted or 'let down' with water and, for brandy, some caramel colouring. In this way a half anker of spirits costing £1 at the distillery would fetch £4 or more in England.

'Letting down' brandy was quite a craft and a good practitioner, who usually ran an unlicensed beer house, was well patronised. A Kent correspondent noted that, in five parishes near Maidstone there were not only 11 licensed public houses but another 41 unlicensed beer houses, most of whom sold smuggled spirits. On a sunny Sunday afternoon in Sussex it was said the most popular establishments could be easily identified by the numbers of drunks sitting or sleeping in nearby lanes and hedgerows!

Geneva, introduced into England by William III's courtiers in 1689, was soon being produced here with a tax so light at first that it became the favourite drink of the poor and lowly paid. But the widespread drunkenness brought serious social problems and a drastic remedy had to be found. In 1736 the duty was raised from 2s to 20s a gallon which priced it beyond the reach of the poor but placed it well and truly on the smuggler's list. In the Netherlands a distillery at Schiedam, near Rotterdam, produced geneva exclusively for English smugglers and for many years thereafter the spirit was often described, even in official reports, simply as 'Hollands' or 'Schiedam'.

Rum, not as popular as the other two spirits, was smuggled from time to time being brought from the West Indies by French and Dutch ships to Guernsey which, from the mid eighteenth century, flourished as a major entrepot for English smugglers. The list of popular items of contraband also lengthened during a war with France because many of the goods from there were banned as imports. Smuggling continued unabated during such a war, usually with the active encouragement of the French.

Not all consignments of contraband came direct from the other side of the Channel. Some came from French vessels that hove-to off the English coast and sold to anyone who came alongside. Some was purchased by going alongside East Indian and other merchant ships as they sailed through the

Just two of many casualties in the smuggling war. Daniel Skayles, a smuggler, was 'unfortunately shot' in 1796 and is buried at Patcham. Thomas Fletcher, an Excise man, whose body was found below some cliffs in 1750, was interred at Friston.

Channel. The word 'contraband', incidentally, did not find favour with many revenue officers in those days, probably because of its French origin. Instead their reports referred to 'run goods' such as 'run tea' or 'run Schiedam'.

Various official attempts were made throughout the eighteenth century to estimate the numbers of men engaged in smuggling. In 1745 a House of Commons Committee believed there were over 20,000 in Kent and Sussex and in the same year Admiral Vernon, from the Naval Fleet in the Downs off Deal, reported '. . . . there are said to be . . . .two hundred men in Deal, four hundred in Dover and three hundred in Folkestone . . . getting their living living by smuggling . . . .' At Hawkhurst it was said five hundred men could be raised in an hour. By 1773 an official in the London Custom House believed there might be 15,000 engaged in smuggling in the county of Kent alone and coastal towns such as Margate, Deal, Dover, Folkestone, Lydd, Rye and Hastings were now said to be wholly in the hands of the smugglers.

A typical gang running tea and spirits would have a small core of full time members who could raise many local helpers quickly and easily. The pay was good for one night's work – half a guinea (10s6d) as a labourer or 'tubman' unloading cargo plus a dollop of tea (about 5lbs) or as much spirit as he could drink. This in a poor rural economy where a labourer might earn 1s a day when he could find work.

The immense profits from running tea inevitably attracted the worst villains within an already brutal society and three major gangs came to the fore between 1720 and 1740 with the finance, ability – and ruthless determination – to operate anywhere in the South East. The first came from Mayfield then later another from Groombridge and finally the most infamous from Hawkhurst. With a core of some 20 full time members and the ability, already mentioned, to raise another 500 men the Hawkhurst Gang would often work with local smaller gangs but were always ready to kill anyone – helper, informer or revenue man – who stood in their way. For fifteen years or more this gang ran large consignments of tea at various spots on the coast from the Thames to Hampshire. In their spare time they robbed houses, inns and carrier wagons and so terrorised the coast and countryside throughout the South East. The leading members of the Hawkhurst and some other smaller gangs were finally caught in 1749 but only after three particularly dreadful murders had prompted the Duke of Richmond, a leading opponent of smuggling, to press the government for urgent action. In Sussex alone that year 35 convicted smugglers were hanged whilst some leading members of the Hawkhurst gang perished on the gallows at Tyburn.

The despatch of these villains brought an end to the wanton brutality but the smuggling trade continued to increase through the 1760s. The savagery was gone but local gangs in Kent and Sussex were still more willing than their counterparts elsewhere to stand and fight if need be. To this end they hired guards known as 'scouts" or, more often 'batmen' because of their long wooden clubs or 'bats', explicitly to fight off any attack by revenue officers. The continued use of batmen in Kent and Sussex, on what was essentially the front line in the war against smuggling, would remain an evil feature well into the next century.

A smuggling run needed a fair degree of organisation. Some gangs were wealthy enough to finance their own operations but others had to seek local backers and shareholders although this was never a problem. One or two trusted men then crossed the Channel to buy the cargo and hire a ship. Experienced mariners were very much in demand particularly those masters who had already proved they could bring a vessel to a chosen landing spot, even in foul weather and on the darkest of nights.

When a voyage had been arranged and the landing spot chosen the tubmen and batmen would be told to stand by for the signal to muster at a certain place. Many were the devices and ploys used to give the signal – the pattern of cows tethered in a sloping field, the position of windmill sails when locked at night or certain windows shuttered in a cottage – are just a few examples to say 'the run is tonight'. Horses were then 'borrowed' from nearby farmers and woe-be-tide any who demurred! – he might soon find his barn on fire. After the run the animals would be returned together with a tub or two of spirits or a dollop of tea.

To try to justify this illegal industry some smugglers claimed they were 'free traders' or often just 'in the Trade'. They said the goods they bought were theirs and theirs alone, not to be taxed or seized in the name of the king. The last thing they wanted, however, was for the country to adopt a free trade policy because then their Trade would have collapsed.

During the 1770s smuggling became so prevalent in Kent and Sussex that, in addition to the many organised gangs, there were now entrepreneurs in virtually every village and many more in the towns. Some organised their own runs whilst others were wholesalers or middle men taking deliveries and breaking the bulk into retail orders for regular customers. At this stage spirits were 'let down' and often stored in containers made of pigs bladders. Otherwise respectable tradesmen such as butchers, builders, broom makers and hurdle makers made deliveries by cart with the bladders of gin and brandy hidden beneath their normal wares. Other men thrived without any apparent means of financial support and some of the handsome Georgian houses built during this era in many otherwise poor areas of the two counties testify to the wealth brought to some by the smuggling industry.

Finding suitable hiding places in which to store contraband was a constant problem and many inns, beer houses and shops had secret passages, cellars or rooms. Churches, graveyards and vaults often contained quite tangible spirits! The vicar of Preston and Hove preached in each of these two small villages on alternate Sundays but then came the day when he forgot and went to the wrong church only to find it locked. When eventually a red faced verger opened the door the aisles were seen to be stacked high with tubs of spirits!

If the goods were destined for London then the forests of the Weald were just a few hours on horseback from the coast and provided many temporary hiding places halfway on the journey. Any local prying eyes were frightened away by tales of the dragons, demons and headless spectres that were said to haunt the dark depths of woodlands.

By the 1770s the booming Trade was no longer confined to the old favourites of tea and spirits, but had become truly sophisticated in catering for the customer's requirements. Some idea of the range of goods available is shown in the list of merchandise seized and sold at Sussex Custom Houses in 1779. This included not only 80,000 lbs of tea and 24,000 gallons of spirits but consignments of 'dry goods' such as tobacco, coffee, chocolate and currants together with 'fine goods' like neckcloths, counterpanes, ribbons, hats, caps, lappets (hat bands), and bales of nankeen cloth, lace and calico.

This peak flood of illegal merchandise and the consequent massive loss in revenue came during the years when the country was fighting an expensive war with the American colonists and the government, already hard pressed for finance, was unable to add to the meagre resources used to fight smuggling. For their part the revenue boards produced some alarming estimates. The Customs Board believed smuggling had increased threefold nation-wide between 1780 and 1783 whilst the Excise estimated that in 1780 an average of 1,500 gallons of geneva, 450 gallons of brandy and almost 4½ tons of tea were smuggled through Kent and Sussex *per day*. The tea alone represented three quarters of that imported illegally into the whole country.

The resources available to fight smuggling were not only meagre but divided because the two boards had their own separate national organisations which even extended to separate fleets of coastal patrol vessels, known as 'cutters'. This dichotomy inevitably caused friction at times particularly when local staff were chasing the same smugglers; there was a long list of imported goods liable to both customs and excise duties.

Both boards arranged their national organisations into Collections headed by Collectors. The Excise were centred generally in inland areas where two or three officers would cover a town and some nearby districts. Customs Collections were arranged around the coast and based at towns or ports such as Chichester, Arundel, Shoreham, Newhaven, Hastings, Rye, Dover, Deal, Margate and Whitstable. Each Collector had a deputy, known as a Comptroller, a Tide Surveyor and typically one or two land waiters to examine cargo and one or two tide waiters to search ships. Each Customs Collector also had a team of riding officers to cover the coast between ports. At Chichester, for example, in the 1780s there were seven riding officers and their supervisor to patrol the coast from Emsworth to Climping.

These riding officers were members of a Customs branch known as the Land Guard formed in 1698 to suppress smuggling by patrolling the coast on horseback. Along the coasts of Kent and Sussex each man had to patrol a 'guard' of some four miles whilst elsewhere around Britain it was ten miles. Each officer normally patrolled alone, and if he needed help in tackling smugglers, he could perhaps call on his supervisor and one or two colleagues from adjacent guards. Any revenue officer could legally ask for assistance, in advance, from the Armed Forces but in practice this usually meant a small local unit of dragoons – regular mounted soldiers. But these men had volunteered for the Army to fight the nation's foes, not chase smugglers, and many resented taking orders from a revenue man. Some dragoon officers refused any written request for assistance demanding it be made in person which meant perhaps a round trip of some miles. Even when the dragoons were available a typical encounter might involve two or three riding officers and a handful of troopers attacking perhaps a hundred or more smugglers and their batmen.

In such unequal circumstances those who attempted the attack could be overwhelmed and killed or savagely beaten and it is not surprising to find that many riding officers chose to keep out of the way whenever they knew that a run was being made. Corruption was endemic with many officers taking bribes to ensure a smooth passage for the contraband before collecting perhaps a few tubs of spirits from the consignment to be handed in as a seizure to keep the Collector happy.

At sea the story was so often a repeat of that on shore, with the odds heavily in favour of the smuggler. In the many fights between vessels in the Channel there were successes for revenue cutters – most of the goods mentioned above being sold from Sussex Custom Houses in 1779 came from these encounters – but the revenue craft were too often inferior in size and firepower to their English and French opponents.

The sailing rig favoured by both sides in this war was that of the cutter. Using the 'fore and aft' rig first developed by the Dutch more than a hundred years before, the cutter had evolved into the most efficient vessel for both the smuggler and the revenue boards. Fast and manoeuvrable in all but the most adverse weather it had a single mast and carried a long bowsprit that could slide in or out to enable the foresails to take best advantage of the wind. So popular was the cutter with the smuggling fraternity that an Act of 1789 required all vessels, other than those in naval or revenue fleets , to have fixed bowsprits not more than two-thirds the length of the

A small Excise cutter carrying a long bowsprit.

hull. But as with so many of the laws introduced against smuggling in those days, this had no real impact on the Trade.

At sea the odds were also in favour of the smuggler when it came to the calibre of the crews. Those on a smuggling vessel, spurred on by good pay and the urge to avoid capture, were willing to take chances when the weather was bad whereas many a revenue commander had to be cautious knowing he might have men who simply wanted to avoid trouble. It was difficult to attract good seamen with pay of around £15 a year when they could earn £35 on a merchantman and even more on a smuggling cutter.

Another vessel popular with some seamen was the lugger which carried four-cornered lug sails hung from oblique yards on one, two or three masts. Small and medium luggers, although not as fast as cutters, were good working boats needing fewer crew. As such they were popular at Deal where 'hovellers' – local boatmen and unlicensed pilots – provided supplies and ferry services to the many merchant ships that anchored in the Downs. And, of course, Deal luggers were equally popular for the short smuggling trip over to France and back. Large luggers were favoured by many French seamen and by the end of the eighteenth century one version had developed into a fully decked, three masted vessel known as a 'chasse-marée'. Fast and well armed with crews of up to 70 these craft were efficient for smuggling and privateering and more than a match for many naval or revenue cutters.

No official estimates were made of the number of vessels engaged in smuggling on the Kent and Sussex coasts in this heyday of the Trade but one Customs report in 1777 said that no fewer than forty five cutters were believed to be running goods into the many creeks just around the Thames Estuary. Fifteen of these were said to be large, ranging in size from 110 to 150 tons, whilst two more were even bigger each carrying 70 men and 20 guns. Against them in the Thames Estuary were three or four revenue cutters, each below 100 tons and carrying ten to twelve guns.

Well armed and with up to 70 crew, the French lugger known as a chasse-marée was more than a match for many revenue cutters.

Stationed around the coasts of Kent and Sussex were, at the most, two Excise and six Customs cutters based at ports where Collectors often complained the vessels were too few and too small. In reply the Commissioners of Customs insisted they provided '. . . vessels of the very best and expensive construction . . .' Furthermore they placed ' . . . the want of success in checking this National Evil . . .on the sad lack of diligent and vigorous exertions by the cutter officers and crews . . .' Later the Commissioners did provide a few larger vessels such as the *Despatch* (138 tons) at Newhaven and the *Tartar* (194 tons) at Dover. But, as with their riding officers, the Board of Customs was so often demanding too much of its staff and providing too little.

As well as the cutters Customs also used stout rowing boats, with four or six oars and a small auxiliary lug sail, to patrol some creeks and harbours. These boats were useful in busy ports as well as in the quiet reaches of the Swale and Chichester Harbour but did not patrol the open coasts. Within the Customs service the cutters and rowing boats were known collectively as the waterguard.

Throughout much of the eighteenth century successive governments, frustrated by their continuing failure to find the ways and means to curb smuggling, resorted to a flood of legislation. Brandy carried in vessels under 15 tons was liable to seizure as were all ships under 50 tons found 'hovering' within six miles off the coast (1718). Rowing boats with more than four oars found on the coasts off Kent would be seized and burnt (1721). Ships under 200 tons carrying illegal cargo would be seized together with rowing boats with more than six oars found on any part of the coast (1779). No clinker built vessels (with hulls of overlapping planks) over 60 tons could be built without Admiralty approval (1784). These were just a few of the laws against smuggling vessels and their cargoes.

Those against the smuggler himself were much more draconian. Any man who refused to plead was liable to transportation (1717). Convicted smugglers were to be transported for seven years (1721). The death penalty was introduced in 1736 for wounding or taking up arms against revenue officers and between 1746 and 1753 this penalty was extended to running contraband, assembling to do so or harbouring smugglers. Information leading to the capture of a gazetted smuggler could bring a £500 reward – twenty five years pay for a labourer! In 1779 there were heavy penalties for any gaoler who was judged to have allowed smugglers to escape.

By that year the accumulated legislation on smuggling had become so complex the government took the unusual step, for those days, of publishing a pamphlet entitled 'Advice to the Unwary'. This attempted to explain the laws and warned everyone that '. . . the illegal trade pervades every city, town and village and brings distress and ruin to the honest trader'. But the legislation and publicity had little or no effect on the smuggling trade and indeed the death penalties had contributed to an escalation in violence in the 1740s as villains not only fought harder to avoid capture but sought to terrorise or eliminate possible informers. In 1783 the Customs Board admitted, with great frustration, '. . . the smugglers carry on a system of business which sets all laws at defiance . . .'

Even when the government resorted to a military strike against a community the results were unsatisfactory. By 1781 Deal had become the most notorious smuggling centre in the South East. In addition to the well known luggers – and despite the legal limits on the size of rowing boats imposed two years earlier – local boatyards also built craft, known as galleys, up to 40 feet long with perhaps ten or more oars, ostensibly for hovelling. It seems local Customs staff had been completely cowed or corrupted into ignoring all illegal activities in and around the town and the government decided some drastic action was needed to set an example to other towns along the coast.

One morning in October 1781 three hundred cavalry and infantry were sent to ransack Deal in a search for contraband but little was found because the townsfolk had somehow received advance warning. After coming to office as First Minister late in 1783 William Pitt waited a while and then ordered another strike in February 1784 when all local boats were drawn up on the town's beach because of a lengthy storm. On the pretext of a mock military exercise a combined force of army units and naval ships arrived and burnt every boat on the shore. The punishment was dire but it failed to bring any lasting curb on local smuggling. Some local boat builders moved their workmen across the Channel to welcoming French ports and were soon, once again, supplying galleys for the Trade.

When the American War of Independence came to an end in 1783 it left Britain with a heavy national debt. Faced with the urgent need to raise yet more revenue, and devoid of further policies to defeat the National Evil, a beleaguered government under Lord North had resorted to forming yet another Select Committee of Inquiry into Smuggling – one of many that century. This produced a comprehensive report in November just after Pitt came to office and, acting on the main recommendation, he reduced tea duty drastically making good the deficit by increasing window tax. Virtually all the profits in smuggling tea were swept away and whilst small amounts of choice tea were brought in during the next few decades it never again featured prominently on the smuggler's list. But the wealth brought by

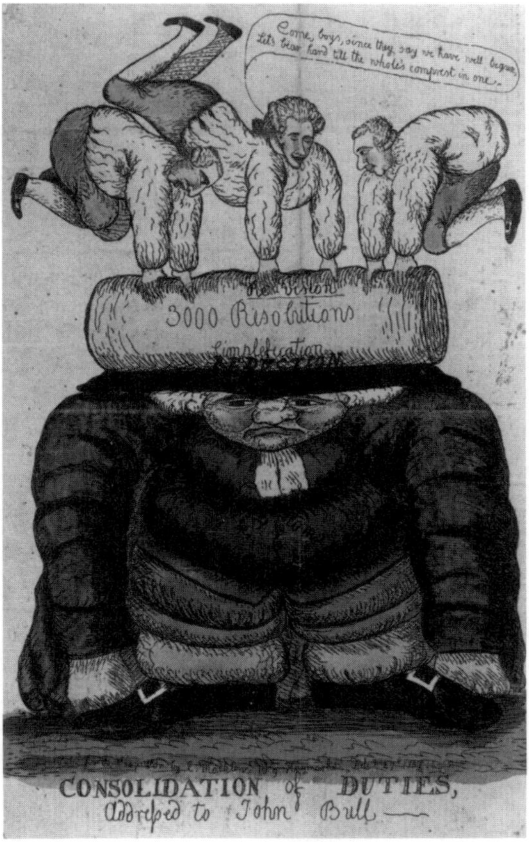

By 1781 revenue duties had become so complicated than an attempt was made to simplify them. Customs & Excise National Museum.

smuggling tea had created a surging black economy that had diversified into many other lines of merchandise and the Trade as a whole was able to take the loss of tea profits in its stride and continue to flourish.

William Pitt, perhaps the most innovative tax gather this country has ever known, introduced a wide range of new taxes and refined old ones. He also attacked the high level of fraud in the legitimate tobacco trade within Britain where, although some raw tobacco leaf was smuggled in, the real illegal profits had been made in the warehouses and factories. Pitt brought in new controls to combat the fraud but this opened up further profitable opportunities to smuggle manufactured tobacco. Although the demand for tobacco, and consequently any profits in smuggling, was low for some years it eventually became a popular item of contraband from the 1820s onwards.

The long expensive wars against Napoleon began in 1793 and, as in past conflicts with the French, smuggling continued with their active support; they even set up a camp near Gravelines to accommodate some five hundred English smugglers. A new item, gold coin for export, now entered the list of contraband. The Revolution in 1789 had brought a financial crisis in France and a gold guinea worth 21s in London fetched 30s in Paris. Many smugglers, accustomed to shipping gold coin over to France to pay for their goods, took readily to the new trade. But the bankers in London and Paris who provided the finance wanted an express service and so even larger galleys were built in France, many by the Deal men who had moved over a few years before, to operate on the shortest Channel crossing. Up to 70 feet long, with perhaps 20 oars and mixed crews of English and French, it was said these craft could make the crossing to Deal, Dover or Folkestone in four or five hours. The 'Guinea' boats as they became known were difficult to spot at night with their low profile and if pressed could dodge a revenue cutter by pulling into the wind. Nevertheless there were dangers in the darkness for those rowers, not only from heavy seas but from merchantmen running without lights up Channel before a westerly wind – they only showed lights when close enough inshore to take soundings.

Years later, after his capture, Napoleon acknowledged that the smuggled gold, which was often as much as 10,000 guineas a week, provided valuable support for his armies. It was said the galleys also ferried spies, intelligence papers and even delivered English newspapers! And of course, they returned to England laden with brandy and other prohibited French goods. Apart from the occasional naval sloop or cutter on patrol in the Channel the galleys had little or no cause to fear detection during the years up to 1805 because many revenue cutters had been taken into naval service.

At the start of the nineteenth century invasion scares were rife throughout Kent and Sussex and the counties were hosts to newly constructed barracks and camps full of regular army and militia units. Sea Fencibles (akin to a naval Home Guard) were formed using licensed fishing boats to guard harbours and creeks, but many of them also found time for a spot of smuggling. Revenue duties were still high and up to 1805 there was still some organised smuggling going on – not at the levels of 20 years before because many men were now in the armed services, but there was plenty of cheap French brandy available in London.

After Nelson's victory at Trafalgar in 1805 many revenue cutters were transferred back to the revenue boards and assigned to their old patrol areas. Fears of invasion, which reached a peak around 1803, had induced the government to order the Board of Ordnance to build a line of Martello Towers (described in Chapter Three) along the beaches and low levels of the Kent and Sussex coasts. The work took from the spring of 1805 to 1810 and for similar strategic reasons the Royal Military Canal was built in 1806 from Seabrook to Pett Level, thereby separating Romney Marsh from the rest of Kent.

All this construction activity along the coast brought problems for any would-be smugglers and their activities eased off during the years up to 1815 although there were occasional bursts of action, particularly in 1807. In June the revenue cutter *Mosquito* made three seizures in the Downs, totalling 1,020 kegs whilst in March two revenue cutters, *Tartar* and *Lively*, seized a smuggling vessel off Folkestone and landed the crew, under arrest, at Dover. A large mob had gathered at the quay and, despite a military escort, two of the crew slipped away during the march to Dover Gaol. Later when the trial was held in Dover two or more men escaped in the midst of mob action; prudently the remaining four prisoners were taken under strong escort, for trial in London. Captain William (Hellfire Bill) Lilburn of the *Lively* would well remember this episode when a similar fracas took place, again in Dover, some thirteen years later.

Late in 1809 the Board of Customs obtained government approval, long overdue, to strengthen their preventive forces. The poor standard of many riding officers had given concern for years; some were said to be idle dodderers, some effectively part time employees with other jobs and others 'mere agents for the smugglers'. Substantial changes were needed and in July 1810 a 'new' revenue force was formed as the Preventive Waterguard which in essence was the fleet of revenue cutters and locally operated rowing boats now expanded and brought under centralised control within the Customs.

The coasts of England and Wales were divided into three districts each supervised by Inspecting and District Commanders recruited from the Navy. In the Southern District, which stretched from North Foreland to Lands End, there were 23 cutters and 42 preventive boats (never known as galleys); the latter to patrol inshore waters, including stretches of open coasts, that were too shallow for the cutters. Recruits for the preventive boats were supposed to come from ex-naval men and the intention was to send them to stations well away from home to prevent collusion with any family or friends who might be smugglers; men from Shoreham, for instance, were sent to Cardiff. But it seems few were willing to transfer in the opposite direction and into the front line against smuggling in Kent and Sussex. Consequently stations there often had to take local men, with all the potential that meant for collusion and bribery.

In a further effort to minimise the corrupting influence of local folk, watch houses combined with living quarters were planned at remote vantage points along the coast, but some landowners were reluctant to lease or sell sites and progress was slow. So too was the construction of these watch houses, even when the site was acquired, which meant that some preventive stations only had tents – a cold prospect in the depths of winter.

One important task for the preventive boats was to combat the increasingly popular method of smuggling whereby a vessel would sink or 'sow' a line of tubs, roped together, off shore to be retrieved at some later opportune time. Perhaps 20 or more tubs would lie on the sea bed, tied like a weighted necklace, and the preventive boat had to be rowed slowly, towing a grapnel on a long line, to 'creep' them up – another cold task in the winter.

Peace came in 1815 but the country's finances were again low, duties were high, the poor in the South were suffering and large numbers of ex-servicemen were about to return home. Over the past one hundred years, despite all efforts to suppress it, smuggling had flourished, going from strength to strength to reach those boom years of the 1780s. The traditions of smuggling in Kent and Sussex were centuries old and that anarchic heyday of thirty to thirty five years ago was well within the memories of many. All the factors were there for the National Evil to flourish again – with a vengeance.

CHAPTER TWO

The Navy Intervenes – On Shore

On land a revenue officer could ask the Army for help in advance if he knew there would be a fight with smugglers. At sea, however, there were few chances to make plans in advance because any fight between a revenue cruiser and a smuggling vessel usually came after a lengthy chase and then it would be rare to find a naval warship near enough to give any help. When naval ships made patrols around the coasts their prime task was to intercept any privateers who might attack our merchant ships.

Nevertheless some attempts were made by the government to encourage a greater naval interest to preventive work. For many years the Navy had paid its officers and men prize money when an enemy ship was taken and in 1757 this was extended to the capture of any vessel caught smuggling. Eight years later the Board of Customs issued special commissions to commanders of all naval ships authorising them to instantly seize a smuggled cargo. But, in reality, these measures had little impact and although there were occasional seizures the Navy, in general, made no substantial contribution to the fight against smuggling, not even in peacetime. No doubt many naval commanders had the same attitude as their army contemporaries – they were there to fight the enemy not gangs of free traders.

There were times when naval officers and men had opportunities to indulge in a spot of smuggling themselves when their ship returned from a foreign station. Even warships on station in the English Channel could visit the Channel Islands and take on tubs of spirits to smuggle into England. Such a consignment may have been that landed by the 18 naval seamen seen by a Buxted correspondent in October 1783. The men, mounted and armed with carbines, cheerfully explained they had 'just been carrying our fleet safely through the Ashdown Forest.'

Guernsey, in particular, was a major entrepot for anything destined to be smuggled into England and Wales. The Channel Islands came under British Customs control in 1805 but some years passed before that control became effective.

With victory at Waterloo in June 1815 the Napoleonic wars were over, wars that had been the most demanding in the history of the Royal Navy. Napoleon had been the master of continental Europe but the Navy had dominated the high seas. The victories of Howe, Jervis and – most of all – Nelson culminated with his triumph at Trafalgar in 1805 and thereafter Collingwood had defended the Mediterranean against French military expansion. There had been naval victories in places as far apart as

Montevideo and Senegal whilst the Caribbean, already a war-torn sphere, saw even more action when Britain was at war with the United States from June 1812 to December 1814.

When the long period of warfare finally came to an end it inevitably brought substantial changes in the role of the Navy. Over the next thirty years it would change from being the great defender of Britain more towards that of a maritime police force keeping the world's sea lanes – the routes to the Empire – free of marauders. More attention was also given to anti-slavery patrols off the West African coast, Britain having abolished the slave trade in 1807. That the Navy could undertake these new roles successfully with far fewer ships and set up a blockade in Britain against smuggling, using some 3000 officers and men, owed much to the quality of it's central administration.

Since the days of Samuel Pepys the administration of the Navy had been divided between separate boards. From their office in Whitehall the Lords of the Admiralty deployed the ships and fleets and appointed all commissioned officers. The subordinate but larger Navy Board, from the Navy Office in Somerset house, controlled finance and shipbuilding, appointed many warrant officers and dealt with naval supplies other than food (Victualling Board) and armament (Board of Ordnance). During the Napoleonic wars and for some time thereafter the Board of the Admiralty and the Navy Board benefited from the work and influence of two highly esteemed administrators, John Croker and John Barrow, both of whom were knighted during their time in office.

John Wilson Croker (1780–1857) was the son of the Surveyor – General for Customs in Ireland. After training as a lawyer he spent his early years working on Customs briefs in Ireland, thanks largely to his father's influence. Elected as Member of Parliament for Downpatrick he became First Secretary to the Admiralty in 1808, at the age of twenty eight, with a salary of £4,000, which dropped to £3,000 when peace came. John Croker served in this post for twenty two years but remained an MP establishing a reputation not only as a good debater in the House but also as a fine Secretary to the Admiralty. On one occasion in the House he remarked that he was merely the servant of the Board, but Sir Joseph Yorke, a former Lord of the Admiralty, responded that when he was on the Board it was precisely the other way! John Croker did much to re-shape the Service and the rules he laid down were acknowledged to be the foundation of the Navy's organisation for the remainder of that century.

John Barrow (1764–1848) came from humble origins in Ulverston to spend his early years as an administrator, first in China and later in the Cape of Good Hope. Through his friendship with the influential Dundas family he was appointed Second Secretary to the Admiralty and thus Secretary to the Navy Board in 1804, with a salary that was half of that for John Croker. John Barrow proved to be a first class administrator and for the next forty years was responsible for civil administration in the Navy. From 1830 to 1832 he was engaged in arranging the merger of the Admiralty and the Navy Board.

Neither of these excellent administrators could have made the progress and changes they achieved in the Navy without the support of Lord Melville, the First Lord of the Admiralty and long time friend of John Barrow. Robert Saunders Dundas (1771–1851) was a Tory MP until 1811 when , on the death of his father, he inherited the title of Viscount Melville. Lord Liverpool made him First Lord of the Admiralty in 1812 and, except for one brief break, he served until 1830.

During the years they were in office together these three men, Melville, Croker and Barrow, were at the centre – in essence they formed the centre – of a naval administration that extended to many parts of the globe. In this context the Naval Coast Blockade of Kent and Sussex was a minor affair at first, instigated by one Captain. But it could never have started, let alone expanded, without the support of these three men.

In July 1815 Britain commenced the drastic demobilisation of her Armed Forces. In 1814 almost a half million men were under arms, but by 1818 some 330,000 had been discharged, with the Navy's strength in men, but not officers, dropping from 140,000 to 20,000. There were 310 ships in commission in 1815, including 90 ships of the line; by 1818 these numbers had fallen to 122 and 22. But the drastic drop in naval ratings (petty officers and below) was not matched in the ranks of commissioned officers whose numbers rose from around 4,800 in 1813 to over 5700 in 1818. The reasons for this disparity lay in the structure of naval hierarchy and the long established Admiralty policy on employment of officers.

The careers of many commissioned officers alternated between spells of perhaps three years active service on full pay and periods at home on half pay. The brightest juniors might be on near continuous active service but for many others it was a part time occupation wherein as they became older and less competent so they spent more time at home, on half pay, until the day they died. Promotion was by merit – 'catching the selector's eye' – up to post Captain but having 'made post' the officer then moved up through the higher (flag) ranks entirely on seniority for as long as he lived, unless found guilty of some grave transgression such as cowardice. Anyone judged unfit for command remained on half pay but still ascended the promotion ladder. To keep some movement in the promotion system many Captains, on promotion to flag rank, were placed on permanent half pay 'without squadron' attracting the nickname of 'yellow admirals'. Further details of naval ranks are given in Appendix A.

Any commissioned or warrant officer permanently injured on active service received a wound pension, in addition to full or half pay, but apart from this no other form of pension was paid to officers and another four decades would pass before the Navy introduced the modern provision of retirement pensions after full time service.

Although the term 'half pay' was a misnomer, being well over half of full pay, it nonetheless meant a poor income for Lieutenants (the lowest commissioned rank) and between 1815 and 1820 the Admiralty tried to ease the problems by some accelerated promotions. Below commissioned officers and warrant officers there were, in descending order, Masters Mates and

Midshipmen, neither of whom were entitled to half pay. Many Midshipmen who had already passed the Lieutenant's examination years before sought to improve their lot by taking the test for Masters Mate with the risk of being left in the dead-end rank of Master. As it happened so many took this path to promotion that it soon became the recognised route to Lieutenant. Many years later, in 1860, the Masters Mate was re-named 'Sub-Lieutenant' and became the most junior of the commissioned ranks.

In principle Masters Mates and Midshipmen were petty officers but they were recognised as potential commissioned officers and permitted to walk the quarter deck. Below them ,on board ship, came the other petty officers and then, in descending order Able Seamen, Ordinary Seamen and Landsmen. Prior to 1815 some in those lower ratings were volunteers but many would have been victims of impressment or 'pressing', – taken by force by the dreaded press gangs to serve on a man-of-war. Convicted criminals could also be pressed men with a sentence of perhaps five years service in the Navy instead of transportation to the colonies. On board a man-of-war (usually a ship of the line) all pressed men were virtually imprisoned and allowed ashore only during visits to distant ports overseas. The use of press gangs ceased in 1815 but impressment remained a punishment for criminals and many convicted smugglers spent what seems to have been a standard sentence of five years in one of His Majesty's ships.

Unlike their officers, some petty officers and seamen were given pensions when they finished a period of naval service. The pensions were arranged by Greenwich Hospital, a body independent of the Navy Board, for which each man contributed sixpence a month from his pay. Commissioned officers were appointed to a ship by the Admiralty and many warrant officers by the Navy Board or Victualling Board. But all ratings were 'rated' (recruited and placed in a rate on ship) by the Captain, who would also 'disrate' if need be; his authority was supreme. The grant of a Greenwich pension depended on a report of good conduct and the length of time served. A small number of men went into Greenwich Hospital as 'In Pensioners' but far more became 'Out Pensioners' and they were often still young enough to find employment elsewhere – even back in the Navy. In 1817, for example, there were 32,000 Out Pensioners of whom nearly 15,000 were deemed capable of further service afloat.

In many towns, including those in Ireland, the Greenwich pension was paid by local Collectors of Customs or Excise because they were often the only government finance officers available. It was possible for Out Pensioners to return to the Navy but normally the pension then lapsed until they were discharged. As will be seen in a later chapter one of the exceptions to this rule was made for pensioners who joined the Royal Naval Coast Blockade Service. They were allowed to keep the pension, in addition to full pay, as an incentive against taking bribes from smugglers and recruitment posters to this effect were sent to the offices where pensions were paid.

When ex-servicemen returned to their homes after the war they found a country beset with unemployment, debt and crime. In Kent and Sussex the distinctions between rich and poor were greater than ever. Speculators and landowners had made fortunes during the wars. The building of barracks and camps, the provision of land and supplies and the increased production of food had brought handsome returns for those either directly involved or with money to invest. Similarly the burgeoning popularity of fashionable resorts, which had started in the 1780s, was continuing to bring wealth to some areas.

Brighton, then known as Brightelmstone, became popular when the Prince of Wales occupied his Marine Pavilion in 1787. From then the town enjoyed mushroom growth; the number of houses doubled between 1775 and 1800 and then almost trebled again by 1820. Major developments had also commenced at Worthing whilst along the coast at Bognor, between 1787 and 1799 Sir Richard Hotham constructed 'an extensive assemblage of brick built villas plus hotel, library, warm baths and subscription room.' A contemporary guide exclaimed that all three resorts 'now had lodging houses and bathing machines to satisfy the greater influx of fashionable company that arrived every season.'

Margate, for many years the recognised landing place for passage to and from Holland, was also being developed as a bathing place; the first bathing machines in England are said to have opened there in 1790. But in Kent the real magnet for 'fashionable company' was still Royal Tunbridge Wells, second only to Bath as the oldest spa in Britain. Here, keeping pace with the newcomers such as Brighton and Bognor, there was also considerable new development around the turn of the century. All of these resorts brought some local prosperity not the least to the smuggling fraternity who could supply fashionable visitors with luxury merchandise such as fine fabrics, silks, gloves and jewellery – with new customers arriving every 'season'.

Much of the development in the resorts came after the extensive provision of turnpike roads in the latter half of the eighteenth century. Stage coach operators were able to set up a system of routes that reached its peak of efficiency in the 1820s when a journey from London took six hours to Brighton and around eight to Dover. But although the turnpikes opened up access into London and between large towns there were no such roads close to the coast between, say, Bognor and Brighton or Eastbourne and Rye. Away from the resorts many roads, particularly in East Sussex and West Kent, were described in a contemporary guide book as still narrow and sandy. Eastbourne and Bexhill were said to be 'neat villages, each with a bathing room and a barracks capable of holding a troop of horse.'

Apart from any money earned by smuggling the prosperity at the resorts never filtered down to the ordinary people in the rural areas that dominated Kent and Sussex. Neither were those folk too occupied with the war and invasion scares being far more concerned with more mundane matters such as the poor rate and the price of bread.

Due to poor harvests and wartime restrictions on imports the price of bread, the essential food for many, had risen sharply during the wars. The poor and lowly paid depended for subsistence on parish relief paid out of the poor rate levied in the parish in which they lived. Worthy but misguided arrangements were made in some areas to link the rise in bread prices with increases in parish relief but the further rate demands were too much for many ratepayers who were themselves struggling to stay out of debt. As a result many rural parishes were unable to provide adequate relief and their labourers and farm workers became paupers.

A report to the House of Commons told of 'thousands throughout the country who are living on 2½d a day, many parishes being unable to provide even basic relief.' This at a time when officers of Customs or Excise were paid around 25s to 30s a week. The agricultural workers in Kent and Sussex were the worst paid, fed and housed of all classes and it is no surprise to find that in 1815 Sussex was spending more on the poor than any other county.

Such desperate social conditions inevitably bring violent reactions and a rise in crime. Kent and Sussex were in an unsettled state but so too were other parts of the country. There were widespread riots in the North and in 1811 Luddites started breaking machines in industrial areas, not only in protest against mechanisation but also to resist wage reductions. The breaking of wool and lace machinery became a capital offence in 1812 and the government employed an army against the Luddites as large as that which Wellington led in the Peninsular campaign.

All this unrest came at a time when the penal code had reached unprecedented levels; the number of offences attracting capital punishment, for example, was nearly 200. Accused smugglers might well find sympathy in many local courts but not so thieves and other villains. Sir Samuel Romilly, humanitarian and criminal reformer, succeeded in passing a Bill through the House of Commons in 1810 to abolish the death penalty where anything worth less than five shillings had been stolen from houses or shops, but it was rejected by the House of Lords as a 'dangerous innovation'. Many death sentences were commuted to transportation but even when it was not a capital offence the punishments were harsh beyond modern belief. At the Sussex Assizes of 1811 and 1812 typical sentences of seven years transportation were imposed for each of these offences: stealing a rope and a sail; taking three fowls; taking seven bushels of wheat and for stealing a watch and a basket (total value 6d). In the Sussex County Gaol in 1816 there were 30 felons and 40 debtors but within one year these numbers had risen to 41 and 103. With such deprivation, unemployment and crime in rural areas it was obvious that smuggling would increase when the ex-servicemen started to return home. A Treasury minute dated 2 February 1816 advised that '. . . many daring professional men now discharged . . . will be ready instruments for those desperate persons who have capital and wish to engage in the smuggling trade.'

The government's answer was to introduce three changes to the organisation and management of it's preventive forces, the second and third of which were quite fundamental. First the conditions of recruitment for preventive boatmen were changed so that entrants would be aged between 20 and 35, with at least six years experience at sea. Secondly the Preventive Waterguard was re-organised on naval lines, under one senior naval officer reporting direct to the Treasury and in February 1816 Captain John

Hanchett R.N. was appointed to the post as the first Comptroller General of the Waterguard. Later that same month almost the entire fleet of revenue cutters, or cruisers as they were now known, was transferred to the control of the Admiralty.

The Board of Customs still had to supply and maintain the preventive boats and watch houses but this apart it had, within the space of a few weeks, lost control of its maritime and coastal forces being left with two vessels for quarantine work and the Land Guard of riding officers. The Board of Excise, with a smaller fleet, fared better but even so was left with only four cutters. The Treasury now managed the Preventive Waterguard and some 44 revenue cruisers with their officers and men had joined the Navy.

From his new office Pall Mall Captain Hanchett set out to strengthen his force with ex-naval men. But, as before, there were still insufficient volunteers, now with appropriate sea-service, willing to leave their home areas for the front line in Kent and Sussex. As a result some preventive boats in the South East were still forced to accept local men some of whom had no sea service whatever – all they needed was a local dignitary to act as patron. Inevitably in such small communities some recruits, and patrons, would have been friendly with local smugglers for years – they may even have dabbled in the Trade themselves.

The Preventive Waterguard was now divided nationally into 31 districts, each under an Inspecting Commander, covering a total of 150 stations. The prime task was to prevent smuggling but in the event of a shipwreck the preventive men were also responsible for bringing the cargo under their control to prevent looting and the loss of revenue. They were also required to render assistance to all those in danger on the wreck and for this purpose some stations had Captain Manby's Life Saving Apparatus. This used a short barrelled, heavy mortar to fire a shot, with line attached, out from the shore. More about this apparatus is given in Chapter Seven.

The revenue cruisers transferred to the Admiralty were allocated to naval commands around the coasts of Britain. In the English Channel the eastern and central sectors came under the Commanders-in Chief Medway and Portsmouth respectively. The initial muster at Sheerness in March 1816 showed there were four with the C-in-C Medway: *Griper*, *Swallow*, *Hawk* and *Ranger*. The muster also gave some idea of the size of the largest and smallest of these four: *Swallow*, length 70ft, beam 23ft, depth 9ft had forty five crew, six boats and twelve six pounder cannons. *Hawk*, length 54ft, beam 18ft, depth 8ft had eighteen crew, three boats and four six pounders.

In the summer of 1815, with the onset of peace, the Navy was able to use some ships on preventive patrols around the coasts. There were few French privateers now and the naval patrols could concentrate on trying to prevent smuggling but, once again it seems there was little success. One of the ships deployed in the Channel in the autumn and winter of 1815 was H.M.S. *Ganymede* a 24 gun, sixth rater, captured from the French in 1809. Her commander, Captain J.W. McCulloch, was destined to become the central figure in the early years of the Navy' campaign against smuggling in Kent and Sussex from 1816 until his untimely death in 1825.

H.M.S. Narcissus *a sixth rate frigate slightly larger than H.M.S.* Ganymede.

Born in Scotland in 1782, William McCulloch (his early records showed only the 'W') became a Midshipman in 1798 and served on stations as far apart as the East Indies and the Cape of Good Hope before taking promotion and successive appointments to ships on the Leeward Islands station of the West Indies. He remained there until 1815 serving in one of the major areas of conflict in the Napoleonic wars where Britain lost over 40,000 men, mainly from disease and fever.

As a young Lieutenant in this war zone McCulloch soon caught the selector's eye and in January 1810 was promoted to Commander and given command of the sloop *Asp*. His star continued to ascend and in July 1814 he 'made post' at the age of 32, as Captain on the third rater *Venerable* from where, after a few months, he took command of *Barrosa* a new fifth rater and flagship of the Admiral of that station. Whilst on *Barrosa*, in the last few months of the American war, he captured an American privateer and several merchantmen. Returning from the West Indies in July 1815 McCulloch was appointed to command *Ganymede*, based at Portsmouth, and given the task of patrolling the Channel between the Isle of Wight and Dungeness, essentially to prevent smuggling.

That first winter in the Channel was a cold one by all accounts and must have been arduous for McCulloch after ten years in the warmth of the West Indies. It was even worse for his crew; in a later report he said the ship had patrolled for a whole winter with a crew newly raised who were in the most wretched state for want of clothing, with nearly one third of them laid up with rheumatism and other complaints occasioned by the cold. The ship's surgeon, Charles Miller, had pressed McCulloch verbally at first, then in writing, for the supply of proper clothing both for the sick and to preserve the rest of the crew. The Captain ordered the supply of '. . . such articles as were absolutely necessary from slops taking care each man had sufficient pay to cover . . .' But when the clothing account was closed there was still an outstanding debt of £7-17s7d and, under Navy Board regulations, the Captain was ordered to pay this himself! The report he made later was an appeal against this demand.

These new recruits did not receive free issues of winter clothing (probably due to fraud somewhere in the system of supply) and hence had to buy them from the slop chest, known generally as 'slops', on board ship. The cost was then deducted from the pay due to the man – provided he was in credit. No credit, no slops. Reading between the lines of McCulloch's report it seems when pressed he had enough compassion to allow issues of clothing regardless of the credit arrangements.

The system known as slops, from the old English word 'slop' meaning breeches, was first introduced into the Royal Navy in 1623 and by the nineteenth century slops were sold on board men-of-war by Pursers, under arrangements prescribed by the Navy Board. They were allowed one shilling in the pound commission on sales and this, along with other commissions, provided opportunities for much fraud and abuse. Although only of warrant rank Pursers always seemed to be amongst the most wealthy of those on board!

With the transfer of revenue cruisers to the Navy in February 1816 arrangements had to be made to absorb their commanding officers (Lieutenants) into the pyramid of naval command. As part of these new arrangements *Ganymede* was transferred to C-in-C Medway and stationed in the Downs. By April 1816 the four revenue cruisers at Sheerness had grown to eight and they were also based in the Downs with their commanding officers reporting to Captain McCulloch. These eight: *Rattlesnake*, *Scourge*, *Lively* (Excise), *Lively* (Customs), *Seagull*, *Swallow*, *Nimble* and *Asp* were ordered to patrol on stations that stretched from Beachy Head to the Wash.

The Navy, whether it liked it or not, was now much more involved in the day-by-day fight against smuggling and *Ganymede* became the centre for naval preventive work in the South East with Captain McCulloch as the sector commander; a propitious appointment that would prove to be a fine example of the right man being in the right place at the right time. Other Captains of fifth or sixth raters were given similar responsibilities in other naval sectors around the coast, but there was still considerable distaste for anti-smuggling work amongst some senior officers. McCulloch could have paid superficial attention to the task aboard his own ship and left the work to the revenue cruisers. Provided he ran a well disciplined ship, producing the odd seizure of contraband now and then, he could expect further naval command appointments as he moved up the seniority list.

Captain McCulloch, however, was not one for a superficial approach to any operation; he had been given the brief to prevent smuggling and threw himself wholeheartedly into the task. Throughout the next eight years, as his campaign developed, he produced a steady stream of reports and plans all dedicated to the fight against smuggling. By nature he was a hustler – always polite and often witty – but still a hustler who reacted to rejection or resistance from those on high by pressing even harder for his objective. When he had to accept a refusal, it was only after a long and often wordy struggle. Opposition from those outside the Navy, particularly Customs Collectors and local magistrates, usually brought pithy remarks and the occasional broadside.

A strict disciplinarian, but probably no more so than many of his contemporaries, McCulloch was nevertheless willing to praise those who performed well. After a large scale assault on the 'Blockade Line', as it was known, on Christmas Day 1820 he spent several days there with his men and reported to the Admiral '. . . it was impossible for me to do justice to the Midshipmen here, their very excellent conduct and zeal surpasses anything I have ever witnessed. During the short time I have been here I have been obliged to restrain their exertions in preservation of their health . . .'. Praise indeed from someone so lofty as a Captain!

H.M.S. *Ganymede* was anchored in the Downs, the stretch of water between the Goodwin Sands and the coast around Deal that had provided a sheltered anchorage for shipping for centuries. In the deepest part, which lay between Sandown Castle to the north and Walmer Castle to the south, there could sometimes be as many as 400 sailing ships anchored awaiting good weather or a favourable wind. Deal hovellers in luggers and galleys made a living carrying supplies of fresh provisions, water and stores out to the ships and for many years had also taken Channel pilots out to ships bound for London.

Bad weather sometimes brought welcome work for hovellers although it was too haphazard to provide regular incomes. A strong gale might prevent ships from making the shelter of the Downs; Deal boatmen would go out and offer to put a local pilot on board to guide the ship away from the dreaded Goodwin Sands to the safety of Ramsgate or Margate Roads. If the ship went aground a lugger would offer to help by running the ship's anchor out so that she could haul herself off. If an anchor was lost a lugger could supply another; anchors of all sizes, recovered from wrecks on the Goodwins, were kept in a field near Deal Castle. All these services brought good money at times, perhaps £50 for a few hours, but it was never enough to maintain the levels of prosperity enjoyed by many in Deal. That wealth, despite all the efforts at suppression over the years, still came from smuggling.

A Deal lugger

Throughout the Napoleonic wars the Deal men had fared well, what with golden guineas out and brandy, geneva and fine goods in. There were occasional setbacks when a few cargoes were intercepted at sea but this apart once the goods were landed they could be moved around the area with impunity. Brute force, bribery and the weight of numbers had enabled the locals to dominate the area around Deal for as long as many could remember. To station *Ganymede*, with her dedicated commander, on the doorstep of the town was a sure recipe for a local war.

As well as being a favoured anchorage for shipping the Downs, just 22 miles from the French coast, had been used by the Navy for centuries. In the reign of Charles I a Navy Yard was established at Deal to provide light repairs for warships and to supply the one thousand and one items listed as 'naval stores'; later that century came full victualling facilities. An eighteenth century Naval Hospital was re-built during the Napoleonic wars and opened in 1812 and by the end of the wars there were extensive Army barracks. But for naval operations it was only a forward base, the headquarters for that command remained at Sheerness with full dockyard facilities at Chatham.

In the battle against smuggling the government had three lines of defence – the revenue cruisers at sea, the preventive boats inshore and the riding officers on land. In theory this provided a formidable defence but if a smuggling vessel evaded the cruisers the other forces provided opposition that was at best intermittent, at worst non-existent. Between Dungeness and North Foreland in March 1816, for example, there were ten preventive boats, each with a Chief Officer, a sitter (coxswain) and six or eight boatmen, stationed at Dungeness West, Dungeness East, Brockmans Barn, Sandgate, Folkestone, Eastware, St Margarets, North End Deal, No.2 Battery and Broadstairs. A token watch was kept by day and at night each boat patrolled its stretch of coast; if the weather was too bad the men were supposed to make beach patrols on foot. But the boats were sometimes short of men and even where there was no bribery many of them, like the riding officers, were only too keen to avoid a fight where they would be heavily outnumbered.

Aboard *Ganymede* in the April of 1816 Captain McCulloch manned his three galleys and sent them to patrol the Downs in operations that augmented the work of the preventive boats, although it seems there was no liaison with them. The first noteworthy seizure came on 22 April when the Dutch schooner *Celeritas*, out of Antwerp, anchored in the Downs. In daylight a Midshipman aboard *Ganymede* watched as a Deal lugger quickly went alongside the new arrival with a good deal of bustle from all concerned. Taking some seamen he boarded and searched the schooner which was said by the master to be in ballast (empty of cargo). In one hold they found 48 kegs of gin which the master said was his private stock due to be exchanged in France for brandy! The ship's log showed she had cleared out of Antwerp regularly in ballast and seemed to be making little by way of profit on any voyage. As Captain McCulloch noted dryly '. . . the master would seem too busy making exchanges of spirits, but for English money, not French brandy . . .'.

The *Celeritas* and her cargo were seized and transferred to Customs at Dover; the master and crew, being foreign nationals were allowed to return to Holland. The casual manner in which kegs of spirits were going to be transferred in the Downs in daylight showed not only the ease with which the Deal men could operate but also the incompetence of local preventive boats.

In July 1816 McCulloch started to receive information from some person in Boulogne and, although his name was never mentioned, he served the Captain well for the next few years. The first piece of news was passed quickly to the C-in-C: 'Boat builders have gone over to France from Deal, Dover, Sandgate and Folkestone to run cargoes to this country. Building boats under licence in France on condition that one third of the crew shall be French. At present sixteen are building in Boulogne and six at Dunkirk. The revenue cruiser Cameleon took one yesterday with a crew of nine (three French). She brought six Englishmen to Ganymede this morning.' The smugglers of Kent were certainly planning a return to the Trade of the good old days!

The release of foreign nationals caught smuggling was just one of the legal difficulties encountered by both the Customs and Excise authorities. If they were satisfied the man was an alien then he could not be charged with a smuggling offence. At times this led to Englishmen pretending to be Dutch and it was said that some of their wives even had their babies born in France or Holland to ensure the children had foreign nationality – a fine example of forward planning!

All naval officers engaged in the war against smuggling, whilst not under the control of the Board of Customs, had to act in accordance with Customs laws and accept any legal advice given by the Board's solicitors. All seizures of ships and contraband had to be handed over to the nearest Customs Collector who, after an often lengthy delay, paid the rewards. Delays in payment became a sore issue at times; some six months after the seizure of the *Celeritas* Captain McCulloch was still pressing the Collector, Dover to pay up. In later years the rewards were paid by Customs in London, via the Navy Board, and there were still long delays.

The prosecutions of smugglers caught by the Navy were conducted either by Customs solicitors from London or locally appointed prosecutors, with the naval men called as witnesses. In the early days of this naval campaign it was apparent some naval officers found difficulty in assimilating Customs laws and procedures. They already had volumes of Kings Regulations and Admiralty Instructions from the Admiralty and Navy Board. They already had rules and regulations from the Victualling Board and Board of Ordnance and *now* had to add more material from Customs.

Even Captain McCulloch made mistakes at first in dealing with captured smugglers. Englishmen found smuggling were brought on board *Ganymede*, clapped in irons and examined by the ship's surgeon. Those fit for naval service were despatched straight away to H.M.S. *Bulwark* in the Medway and the remainder were produced to magistrates for prosecution.

This novel approach did not last for long. Someone, probably the local Collector, told the Captain the correct procedure and after that all English smugglers captured by his men were brought before magistrates. But more

"Le Contrebandier". French smugglers look anxiously towards a British revenue cutter.

than a few were not convicted, much to McCulloch's anger, because many Benches were either in sympathy, or in league, with the accused. Where a prosecution did succeed it was for the magistrates to decide the sentence and if that was for, say, five years in the Navy then the impressment order was signed by the Board of Customs.

By July 1816, three months after his arrival in the Downs, Captain McCulloch had reached the conclusion that the local Preventive Waterguard was totally useless in the fight against smuggling. And being McCulloch he decided to act. Using the three galleys of *Ganymede* he landed armed seamen and his few marines every night and stationed them, within hailing distance of each other, along the beaches in and around Deal. This cordon was something new for the local smugglers to contend with, right on their doorstep, and they acted with predictable aggression. On 8 August 1816 McCulloch reported to Sir Charles Rowley, Rear Admiral of the Blue, on board *Bulwark* in the Medway 'a shore party from Ganymede has been attacked and fired on by Deal men. The system of placing men along the shore at night has been so great an annoyance to the smugglers that they are determined if possible to put a stop to it.'

From a naval viewpoint this use of armed shore parties was a new concept and the prudent Rear Admiral ordered they be stopped until he heard from the Admiralty. McCulloch, true to character, was not to be put off so easily and within the week was reporting intelligence from Boulogne that three galleys with tea, two sailboats each with two hundred kegs and the *Salus* and *Nancy* schooners with dry goods were operating '. . . because the Deal men thought the removal of shore parties was permanent.' Rear Admiral Rowley was spared the need for further comment when the following day the Admiralty authorised the resumption of shore parties.

When the Board of Customs lost control over sea-borne preventive work

The revenue cruiser Prince George *overhauling an East Indiaman.* – Alan Hay

in February 1816 it was perhaps understandable that their staff in Kent would resent the arrival of these naval newcomers who knew little about the limitations of Customs laws. Over the years that followed McCulloch had to deal with more than a few derogatory reports from Inspectors of both the Waterguard and the riding officers as he steadily encroached on their districts. These hostile remarks were indignantly dismissed with a pithy comment or two but he did try to maintain, for much of the time, good working relations with the Collectors at Dover and Deal.

They told him that their problems were not confined to straightforward smuggling across the Channel or from homeward bound East India men. The latter, when outward bound, were now said to arrange to meet ships in the Channel and off-load some of the cargo taken aboard in London duty free for export. There was another problem with French fishing boats that were now working off the South Coast. Each crew member was allowed to have up to two gallons of spirits which meant perhaps a total of ten gallons waiting to be landed illegally. McCulloch, with his Boulogne informant supplying valuable despatches, wisely decided to concentrate on the cross Channel smuggling and left the other problems for the Collectors to deal with.

The use of shore parties found favour with Lord Liverpool, the Prime Minister, and in November 1816 Captain McCulloch was called to a meeting at the Admiralty with Lord Melville, John Croker and Sir John Hope, a Lord of the Admiralty. There it was agreed that fifty marines would be sent to Deal where, under the Captain's command, they would be used in the 'Prevention of Smuggling'. Later that month McCulloch sent a list of officers to be deputed by Customs to seize ships and contraband and reported to Mr Croker that accommodation was ready for the marines who would each require a pistol and cutlass.

Pending their arrival McCulloch believed he had already shaken the local smugglers to the extent that they were now operating more to the west and he told the commanders of *Scourge* and *Asp* to concentrate on the area between the South Foreland and Dungeness. But, alas, his complacency was shaken badly on the night of 12 December 1816 when his men on *Ganymede* tried to land the usual shore parties during a strong gale. One galley was lost and although efforts were made to launch a sailboat from the Dockyard the wind was too strong. Revenue cruisers driven off their stations in the Channel were obliged to find shelter in the Downs.

Next morning McCulloch's chagrin can be imagined when he was told 'by a reputable public person in Deal' that during that dreadful night 2000 kegs of spirits and other goods were landed in or near the town from ten boats! Some must have passed close to the sheltering cruisers and one boat landed on the beach opposite the Dockyard! This was indeed convincing evidence of the audacity, courage and seamanship of the Deal men and, from McCulloch's viewpoint, proof of the need for his parties to be based permanently on shore. A few weeks later the Captain mentioned that the 'public person in Deal, who had told of the landings, has been threatened with assassination and will henceforth keep his peace.'

On 22 December 1816 the detachment of 50 marines from Chatham arrived at South Barracks, Deal where they joined another 24 from *Ganymede* to form a unit that included three officers and their servants. Unfortunately the barracks had been broken into a few days before and robbed of military stores so a permanent guard of four marines had to be mounted around the clock.

Within a few days the remaining marines were joining naval officers and seamen from *Ganymede* to provide shore parties at night along the beaches from Sandwich Haven to St. Margarets Bay. But the numbers of marines dropped still further when it was found that one man had arrived from Chatham inflicted with something described as the 'Itch'. Two weeks later McCulloch was complaining that 17 marines had succumbed and it was still spreading '. . . it affects our numbers which are very low indeed.'

Those fit enough to patrol soon found they were in hostile territory. One evening Corporal Hood and four marines were at Kingsdown when a respectable looking man confronted them shouting 'You damned infernal rascals, if it had not been for you I might have been a gentleman.' What lay behind the remark will never be known – perhaps he lost a fortune when his contraband was seized? – but he was no gentleman that night because he promptly struck the Corporal and that give the signal for forty or more men to rush out from cover attacking the marines before they could fire a shot. Three were badly beaten and joined their itching colleagues in the Navy Hospital at Deal.

The bitter reaction to these shore parties showed itself not only on the beaches but also in the town of Deal where officers and men could be under threat at all times, on or off duty. In February 1817 McCulloch reported that someone had recently fired at him on the Walmer Road and he had also received a letter threatening him with death. Of more worry was the discovery that three men had been seen , about 6pm one evening, reconnoitring around the back of the house where Mrs McCulloch and the family were lodging. She was pregnant and the Captain sought urgent approval from the Navy Board to move his family into an empty house in the more secure grounds of the Navy Hospital. Permission was given by Mr Barrow, on behalf of their Lordships '. . . provided the public are not put to any expense . . .' McCulloch quickly made the move and, undaunted by Barrow's provision, applied hopefully for the relief of taxes and rates due on the house but for the time being their Lordships remained adamant.

At this time McCulloch had no accommodation for his men on shore other than South Barracks and with some ten miles of coast to cover he needed a tender to carry men to and from the more distant patrol areas. He applied to the Navy Board and, quite surprisingly bearing in mind the surplus naval craft that must have been around, approval was given to buy the *Flying Fish*, a 62ft schooner, from a private owner at Ramsgate. The first of many naval tenders used in the Coast Blockade she served in that capacity for three years before being transferred to the West Indies.

At that meeting in Whitehall in November 1816 it seems that plans were laid, at least in outline, that went well beyond the initial use of 50 marines on the beaches around Deal. In February 1817 McCulloch was sending small units to notorious landing places west of St. Margarets Bay and Mr Sampson, Collector Dover, was urging they be sent to Eastware Bay.

That same month McCulloch made a report to the Admiralty setting out his condemnation of the Preventive Waterguard and proposing a complete take-over by the Navy on the coast between North Foreland and Dungeness. The criticisms were no doubt exaggerated to support his own ideas but the grains of truth were there:

> 'Nothing can be more inefficient that the preventive system as it now exists. Men are generally natives of the places where they are stationed for the purposes of seizing persons and property of their nearest relations and others they have know since infancy. Move the men elsewhere if need be and man the boats with our own people. They have always been afraid of coming under my comptroll and I am convinced are as anxious to get clear of me as the smugglers are.'

To replace the ten preventive boats between North Foreland and Dungeness McCulloch estimated he would need 400 officers and men, including the 50 marines already on hand. *Ganymede* would be too small to act as the headquarters for the force and he asked for a larger ship. The proposals showed just how costly this operation would be. In place of some 90 Waterguard men McCulloch would be using 400 naval officers and men with elaborate support that included another 200 or more on the depot ship. It was going to be expensive but on this occasion any dissent from the Treasury came second to the government's very real fear of insurrection.

At the time when the Admiralty received these initial proposals a House of Commons Committee reported there was a revolutionary movement in existence amongst the lower classes in Northern England. Anyone over 40 could remember how weakness of central authority in the French

Revolution had brought anarchy. A nervous government, determined to be seen taking strong action to maintain control, suspended the Habeas Corpus Act and introduced measures to tighten controls over public meetings. The unrest in the North was spreading to East Anglia where starving agricultural workers raided food stores and destroyed farm machinery. Another era of anarchy in the South East caused by intensive smuggling had to be stopped at all costs and the arrival of new, albeit expensive, ideas to fight the smuggling with a naval beach cordon was welcomed by Lord Liverpool even though he knew the costs would inevitably escalate. An undoubted factor in McCulloch's favour was the support he received from the Admiralty and in particular from Barrow and Croker. Thanks to their supervision and influence this new naval service would be quickly established and then expanded over the next eight years.

On 9 March 1817, following a request from John Croker, Captain McCulloch set out in more detail his proposals 'For the Suppression of Smuggling between North Foreland and Dungeness.' and sent them to the Admiralty via the Rear Admiral, Sheerness:

1. The whole of the preventive duty to be performed by parties of seamen and marines under the orders of Captain McCulloch.
2. Four hundred officers and men to be provided including twenty five petty officers and one hundred and fifty marines (the Rear Admiral said they should have three subalterns and no captain). One Midshipmen for every twelve men. Shore parties will be ten to twelve men under a Mate, Midshipman or Sergeant. Ten Midshipmen and seventy men would be employed in preventive boats stationed as they are now.
3. Fourteen galleys (in naval terms these were boats with six or eight oars) to be provided.
4. Arrangements to be made for provisions to be conveyed.
5. Parties to be quartered and provisioned in military posts blockhouses or temporary guard houses.
6. Quarters to be furnished with necessary barrack utensils for cooking (the Rear Admiral stipulated – 'only at moderate expense').

The proposal to use the existing preventive boats had to be dropped because the Preventive Waterguard refused to hand them over and McCulloch had to order more galleys. In the years ahead as the Blockade Line extended along the coasts each permanent station would have a galley not only for inshore patrols but to ferry men and supplies to and from the visiting tender when it had to anchor off shore.

As a naval operation this started out as a minor exercise, employing only the same number of men as found on a fourth rate warship. The circumstances were, however, quite unique because for the first time regular units of the Royal Navy (rather than an auxiliary body such as the Coast Guard) would be on shore in England, as a law enforcement service, fighting fellow countrymen.

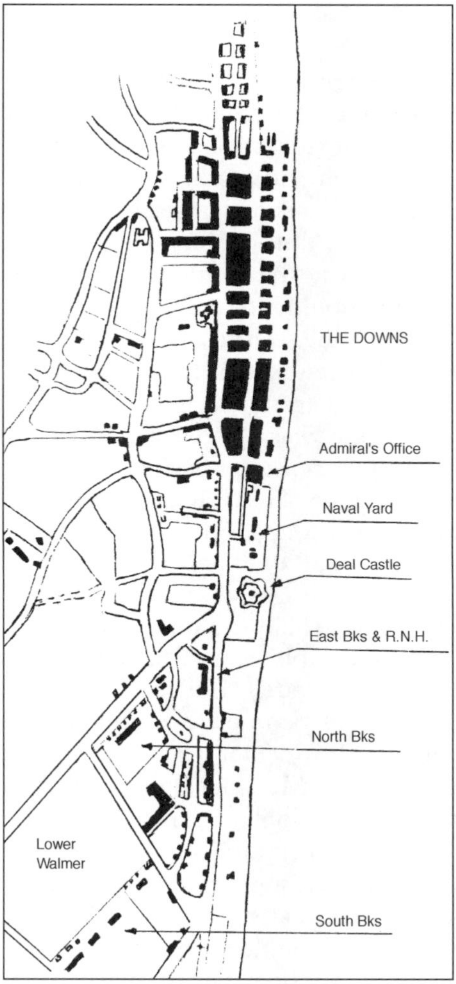

Sketch map of Deal c.*1825*

The first of the new officers arrived on *Ganymede* within two weeks and by the end of April 360 men and petty officers with 36 inferior officers, mostly Midshipmen, were deployed to 20 stations newly set up along the coast from Broadstairs to Dungeness.

According to later comments by Captain McCulloch the first officer sent to the Blockade was Midshipman David Peat who also had the distinction over the next four years, again according to the Captain, of being the most outstanding. There would be other heroes throughout the years of the Blockade with stalwarts such as Sam Hellard, Charles Newton and Joseph Clarke but David Peat epitomised the bold and dashing young naval officer always ready for action whatever the odds. Born in Kirkcaldy in 1795 he served as a Midshipman aboard ships in the West Indies and before his transfer to *Ganymede* had spent two years on *Ajax* (74) in the Mediterranean. During his hectic four years in the Blockade Service Peat would gain three promotions to become a Commander and be praised frequently by McCulloch who on more than one occasion described him as 'the finest officer under my command'.

Within a few days of his arrival David Peat was in action at No.1 Battery near Sandown Castle, north of Deal, when during the night of 25 March he saw a boat attempting to land 180 tubs of spirits on the beach. Calling on a marine to help he drew his pistol and ran over to seize the boat but met threats from ten armed men. Despite this Peat and the marine stood by their capture until help came from other seamen stationed nearby.

Two nights later David Peat and Charles Newton, another Midshipman, kept watch on men working in the sand hills north of No.1 Battery. After the men had left the two Midshipmen and their parties found stow holes built in the sand containing 78 tubs of brandy and 121 of gin. Each hiding place was '. . . about four feet deep and square built of two inch planks with a scuttle on top. A trough filled with shingle was fitted as a cover to prevent discovery by pricking . . .' These places had apparently been in use for some two years and local smugglers were said to be very annoyed over this discovery.

In making those detailed proposals on 9 March Captain McCulloch knew only too well that one of his major problems in the years ahead would be bribery. It had always been a problem amongst riding officers and preventive boatmen and some of his lowly paid seamen and marines would prove just as susceptible. He believed a fairer system of allocating seizure rewards would give his men more money and, hopefully, thus enable them to better resist temptation. On 15 March he wrote again to the Admiralty proposing the quite revolutionary idea that rewards should go only to the Party (Midshipman and, say, twelve men) who made the seizure.

Up to 1819 all naval prize money, including rewards from Customs, was paid on a general scale of shares that extended from the Commander-in-Chief down to the lowest seaman. One example was the reward of £8,579 paid in 1818 for the seizure of a large smuggling cutter and her valuable cargo off Ireland by the revenue cruiser *Vendeleur*. This was divided to give the C-in-C £1,072; the cruiser's commander £2,144; First Mate £1,072; Purser £425; Gunner, Bosun and Carpenter £225 each and the rest of the crew £112 each.

Within the Coast Blockade Service, as it would become known, all officers and men were regarded as part of the complement of the depot ship *Ganymede* and they therefore all shared in the rewards. But the Mates and Midshipmen making the seizures were classed as petty officers and entitled only to the same paltry sums as their seamen. More senior ranks safe in their cabins aboard *Ganymede* would receive far more. McCulloch's proposal, of giving all to the seizing party, meant nothing would be paid to senior officers, including himself. Not surprisingly this proposal found no favour with Rear Admiral Rowley who could see his handsome prospective bonus disappearing. He sent the paper on to the Admiralty with his alternative solution of holding out promotion as a reward coupled with 'rigid observance of discipline'; a totally ineffective answer to the problem. Naval discipline was already rigid and the increase in pay on promotion from, say, seaman to petty officer was trivial compared to one decent reward under McCulloch's proposal.

The Admiralty took it's time – nearly two years – in considering such a fundamental change and, as will be seen in Chapter Four, when a revised scale of revenue rewards was introduced for the Blockade Service it only covered those seizures made on shore. Belatedly it was realised this excluded any made afloat! There was further incompetence in drafting the amending legislation and it was not until 1823 that McCulloch had the reward scale he wanted. Even after that the arrangements seemed to be open to some manipulation and in later years were still not satisfactory for Captain Mingaye in the Sussex Blockade.

In April 1817 *Flying Fish* crept up 30 half ankers of spirits off Sandgate, which showed that McCulloch was making full use of his vessels for preventive work whenever possible. He was still short of galleys and said they were sorely needed in Sandwich Haven: '. . . the men have to march six miles via

R.N. Hospital and East Barracks, Deal, c.1820. – Deal Maritime Museum

a bridge to get to their station and are too exhausted to keep good watch and march back again'. More galleys were required and once again he was able to provide his superiors with some intelligence from Boulogne to prod them into action '. . . the sloop May landed 2,800 pieces bandanas at Sandwich a week ago . . .' (Bandanas were large patterned handkerchiefs).

Urgent permission was obtained for the men to be quartered in Pegwell Battery overlooking Sandwich Haven and seven more galleys, each 32ft long, were ordered from Mr Kidwell, a Deal boat builder. With those details about the *May* came three other letters from Boulogne about landings west of Dungeness and these were passed to Captain Hanchett via the Treasury.

For a short period in May 1817 Captain McCulloch had to leave his preventive operations and revert to normal naval duties to deal with something that stemmed from action taken earlier by the Navy in Algiers. For many years the port had been a base from which pirates, known as Barbary Corsairs, had harried British shipping sometimes taking Christians for slavery or ransom. The Dey of Algiers, Nadshi Ali, was ruler of the Barbary Coast and Britain decided some punitive action was called for to put a stop to this piracy. On 27 August 1816 Royal Navy warships under the command of Lord Exmouth attacked the town and its harbour sinking every vessel they could find.

But within a few months the Dey had restored his fleet and soon two of his corvettes appeared in the North Sea where they captured the *Ocean*. a Hamburg vessel. She was later re-captured by the revenue cruiser *Alert* and returned to her grateful owners but the two pirates were still at large. Whilst they had not attacked British shipping the Royal Navy took the threat seriously and stepped up its off shore patrols. *Ganymede*, accompanied by the revenue cruiser *Eagle*, were ordered out into the eastern part of the Channel. On 20 May the corvettes were sighted sailing west but Captain McCulloch reported that 'having no reason to suppose they had committed acts against British ships I followed them until they were west of Beachy Head'.

Three days later, after returning to the Downs, McCulloch transferred his command to H.M.S. *Severn* (50) a fourth rate frigate built in 1813 that coincidentally had taken part in the attack on Algiers, sustaining some damage. This had been repaired but as a vessel *Severn* was not very seaworthy being one of a number of warships built experimentally of pitch pine instead of traditional oak. That summer she was absent for a few weeks to undergo urgent repairs and McCulloch transferred temporarily to *Orontes* (36), but apart from that brief absence *Severn* was moored off Deal for the next six years as the depot ship for the Coast Blockade.

Rather belatedly a Treasury note of 19 June 1817 announced that the preventive district between North and South Forelands was to be assigned to Captain McCulloch and the crew of *Severn*; men and boats of the Waterguard were to be withdrawn. But by then McCulloch, with Admiralty approval, was already deploying his men along the coast as far as Dungeness. Within a few weeks papers from the Admiralty were referring to the 'Royal Naval Coast Blockade Service for the Prevention of Smuggling' and in their reports the officers were using the words 'Sentinels' or 'Blockade Sentinels' to describe the ratings and marines employed on preventive watch.

Some years later, in July 1825, a Captain Renwick R.N. applied to the Treasury, via the Admiralty, for recognition that it was at his suggestion that the Coast Blockade was established. He enclosed a copy of a long letter, dated 2 March 1815, he had sent from his ship *Mercurius* in the Downs regarding the shortcomings of the revenue services. This ended by suggesting the posting of military units on shore between the Forelands, with two or three naval ships and their boats on patrol off shore. When he made the suggestion, he said, Captain McCulloch had been in the West Indies and the subsequent delay in asking for recognition was because Renwick had been on the Continent for some years.

When the papers reached the Admiralty someone, almost certainly John Croker, made several terse comments in the margins and finally noted 'my Lords command me to add that Captain Renwick's letter had not the slightest effect towards the establishment of the Coast Blockade'. Thereafter Renwick's application, of unsound construction and now badly holed, sank without trace.

The Admiralty acknowledged Captain McCulloch as the creator of this new system to combat smuggling and in many respects the way in which it was introduced shows something of the character of the man. The essential difference between the two Captains in their approach to the problem was that Renwick made suggestions on paper for yet another joint operation, similar to those involving riding officers and dragoons, with all the difficulties of divided command. McCulloch tried out his ideas in action first, before making proposals, and ensured everything was under his command with the ultimate control vested in the Admiralty.

For the next eight years McCulloch waged continuous war against the smugglers by establishing and extending when he described as 'an unbroken Blockade Line of Sentinels'. But, despite his careful planning not even he could foresee just how difficult the logistical tasks would be.

CHAPTER THREE

Creating the Blockade line 1817–1825

The Royal Navy of 1817 was probably no different from many other organisations, then or now, in being something of a rumour factory. The gentlemen's clubs in London and the provinces frequented by senior naval officers on half pay were, no doubt, hot beds of gossip and rumour. Admiralty archives for other years contain a steady trickle of letters from Captains and Commanders on half pay reminding their Lordships at the Admiralty that the writers were available for appointment. In 1817, however, more than a few letters were applications for appointments specifically '. . . to stations on the Coast . . .'. There was obviously some story going around about the creation of this blockade against smuggling and some Captains could envisage themselves in commands in the South, West and East of England. But all applicants were disappointed to find the Admiralty was confining its attention to the coasts of Kent and Sussex.

From 1817 to 1825 Captain McCulloch commanded the Coast Blockade Service in its war against smuggling, a war that is described in Chapter Four. Throughout those same years he was also busy first establishing and then extending the Blockade Line. This was work that brought a wide range of tasks from planning new sites for stations and obtaining buildings to resolving complaints and issues provoked from time to time by local hostility that was there, in some form or other, at virtually every station along the line.

Before he could make a start on this new work McCulloch first had to deal with a naval disciplinary case concerning the revenue cruiser *Badger* which was supposed to patrol off East Anglia. An anonymous letter alleged the commander, Lieutenant Williams, generally slept on shore with his family in Gorleston. Upon investigation it was found that the vessel spent most of her time in Yarmouth Roads and was seldom, if ever, under way at night. Not only that, Williams had ordered the First and Second Officers not to report in their logs the periods when the vessel was under way! There were also instances of bad provisions and irregular issues of food. A court martial was recommended and Lieutenant Williams was subsequently dismissed from the Service.

On 3 July 1817 Captain McCulloch met Captain Hanchett, of the Preventive Waterguard in Deal, to discuss the hand over of preventive stations along the coast to Dungeness. Hanchett said the buildings and fixtures could be transferred as soon as possible but the boats would be taken away leaving the Navy to supply their own craft. McCulloch advised the Navy Board that a further 17 galleys were needed urgently; the Deal boatyards were already working on his first orders, could the Board find other contractors in the area quickly please? They were soon found in Ramsgate and Folkestone.

The building of galleys for the Coast Blockade Service brought a fair amount of work to local yards in East Kent who had, of course, been constructing such craft for many years. Those supplied to the Navy for Coast Blockade work were between 26ft and 38ft long with six or eight oars and clinker (or 'clencher') built with overlapping longitudinal planks nailed through the overlap and clenched (hammered over) on the inside. Usually painted white, these galleys were good, fast, working boats more easy to repair than carvel built craft with their smooth sides. Throughout the 14 years of the Blockade arrangements for the supply and repair of galleys were made through the Navy Yard at Deal with boats being delivered and returned by Blockade tender. During those years the output of galleys for the Navy from Deal and other local boat builders was taken exclusively for Blockade work; none were available to other naval ships or stations.

In the main, any sizeable galley intended for smuggling was built in France, a point that Captain McCulloch knew from his Boulogne informant. Customs laws forbade the construction of any private or commercial rowing boat over 28ft long. Deal boat builders did their best, however, to satisfy local clients wherever possible but there was always the possibility of discovery. In September 1817 a shore party of Coast Blockade marines under Lieutenant Cockell R.M. found a newly built galley hidden close to the beach near Walmer Castle and ready for launching. Being 38ft long the boat was seized and taken into Blockade Service.

Despite the initial approval in April 1817, the barracks at Pegwell and Broadstairs were not ready for occupation by the Blockade Service until September. The purchase of quarters at East Cliff took until December 1818 to resolve, but in Ramsgate itself Messrs. Underdown and Company offered to provide quarters at their own expense subject to negotiations on rent. Elsewhere there were unexpected problems. At Sandown Castle, which was occupied jointly by the Army and the Blockade Service, the Captain of Artillery locked the only gate at night and refused permission for anyone to enter or leave! – an irritation that was smoothed out eventually at senior level.

Despite these difficulties in obtaining suitable accommodation along the coast, McCulloch and his superiors in the Admiralty pressed ahead with the next phase in the Blockade. This was to extend along the north coast of Kent as far as East Swale and west along the coast of Sussex to Cuckmere Haven. On 17 September 1817 the *Times* announced 'the Government would be strengthening the measures already existing for the suppression of smuggling' and on 17 November it reported 'We understand that 1400 seamen, 12 Lieutenants, 12 medical officers and assistants and 114 Midshipmen are to be employed on the coasts of Kent and Sussex to prevent smuggling'. Although these figures were approximate and included the 280 crew of *Severn* and the 400 officers and men brought in during

"The New Taxes paying a Visit to John Bull" A popular view of taxation in 1819.

March and April, it nevertheless marked a massive expansion in this nascent Service. Over 1,200 naval officers and men would now man Blockade Stations along the coast from East Swale to Cuckmere.

The reports prompted a letter to the *Times* and a well informed correspondent from Portsmouth wrote 'I perceive that it is intended to employ a corps of English douaniers to prevent smuggling in Kent and Sussex. A more weak and inefficient invention, I will undertake to predict, was never hit upon. The only remedy is to lower duties by half . . . remove the temptation to purchase spirits . . . all the host of riding officers, revenue cruisers and the new anomalous corps would be saved and the disagreeable service of patrolling troops on the coast become unnecessary'. Some in the government were already inclined towards this need for reduced tariffs. The Board of Trade itself was involved in the policy when William Huskisson became President in 1823, but the aim was not achieved until the 1840s.

The complement for the extended Blockade Line had been approved quite readily by the Prime Minister, Lord Liverpool, but the task of recruitment was to be much more slow and difficult. Impressment was now used only for convicted criminals and ordinary recruits joined as volunteers at 'rendezvous' in large ports or on board H.M.S. *Perseus* and H.M.S *Confiance* moored in the Thames. Captain McCulloch wanted experienced naval petty officers and seamen to re-enlist for Blockade duties but for many recruits he had to be content with raw entrants taken on as Landsmen, the lowest form of life in the Royal Navy.

A near contemporary writer, Captain W.N. Glascock R.N., commented on the Coast Blockade Service in his '*Naval Sketch Book*' published in 1831. He noted that the 'Naval men have a general disinclination to the (Blockade) Service from the apprehension that accepting an appointment in it may be a bar to their future employment afloat. Able seamen and petty officers rarely enter. The roll is filled with waisters from discharged crews or, which is more frequent, by unskilled though hardy Irish Landsmen whose estrangement from the sentiments, habits and religion of those placed under surveillance seems to point them out as peculiarly adapted for a service whose basis consists of an invidious watchfulness over others and a hostile segregation from their fellow men'.

In the hierarchy aboard ship 'waisters' was the nickname given to those at the very bottom. Unskilled and too dim-witted to do anything but the most menial jobs, they lived midships in the waist of a man-of-war. In truth, Captain Glascock had a rather jaundiced view of Blockade men. There was undoubtedly a steady intake of raw recruits, some from Wales and the North of England and many from Ireland, as well as those dubious waisters. But over the years there was also a steady flow of experienced petty officers and able seamen re-enlisting for blockade duties. In mid 1825, for example, in one of the few periods when the Blockade Service (then split into separate commands for Kent and Sussex) was at full strength, there were 346 petty officers all of whom had previous sea-going service mainly as Quartermasters, Bosuns Mates or Captains of the Top.

All men for the Blockade Service were enlisted for three years with standard naval pay. All petty officers and seamen were rated (placed in a post) by Captain McCulloch, those with previous naval service being taken on at their old rate. Petty officers received £1-19s per month, Able and Ordinary Seamen £1-14s and Landsmen £1-3s. They also had free food and lodging both for themselves and any accompanying wives.

In the early days McCulloch sent recruiting officers only to *Perseus* and *Confiance* and arranged for each entrant to have a free issue of jacket, trousers and so-called 'beach shoes' (heavy boots) which were supposed to be more hard wearing than those from slops. But, alas, he soon had reports that some men were joining merely to obtain the free clothing and deserting the next day! William Miller, Master of *Severn* 'employed on raising men in London seized a pair of trousers bearing the King's mark from a shop near Tower Hill'. After that issues of clothing were made only when the man had some pay in credit and were stopped altogether in the spring with, as McCulloch said, 'the approach of fine weather' – he was ever the optimist.

The attitude and distaste of some senior naval officers for preventive work provoked McCulloch to complain to his Rear Admiral, now Sir John Gore, that 'the Captains of Perseus and Confiance were exercising undue influence in order to induce good men to decline entering the Coast Blockade Service. The Purser told one man, John Pike, a Bosuns mate, that it was a shame for a young man like him to lie behind a bush and shoot smugglers. Good men are particularly important when their officers had such frequent occasion for their support'. McCulloch was making a significant point. An incompetent rating could be absorbed more easily in the decks of a fighting ship then in, say, a party of five sentinels positioned along a beach at night.

Some recruits were not exactly in the best of health on arrival in *Severn*. One sent from *Perseus* was invalided within two months with 'progressive infirmity' whilst another 'a very weak, debilitated subject without any specific disease' was sent forthwith to the hospital ship *Argonaut* for survey. Two naval pensioners from Cork had to be sent back. One aged 46 was 'full of age and appears to be a heavy bloated subject without tone or vigour in his system'; the other aged 50, 'represents himself as subject to rheumatic affection upon every slight exposure to cold or damp – he has also been severely wounded in the head'. Henceforth McCulloch decreed, no pensioners over 40 would be accepted and all Irish volunteers must first be medically examined in Cork.

As the complement of the Blockade Service grew so too did the problems of finding enough recruits; the Line was rarely at full strength in those early years. Sometimes batches of petty officers and seamen would be drafted by the Admiralty to a newly commissioned man-of-war that was destined for an overseas station. Some Blockade men deserted whilst others were not re-engaged after the first spell of three years. Tragically others were killed or wounded whilst on Blockade duties, either in action or in one of the many accidents.

In the spring of 1820 *Flying Fish* was replaced as a tender by *Industry* and in May and June she was employed raising volunteers in Hull and other Yorkshire ports on two successful trips. She also made worthwhile voyages to Portsmouth and Plymouth to raise ex-naval ratings. But efforts to recruit more Landsmen were not so successful until McCulloch sent *Industry* to Cork and found plenty of willing raw recruits. The poverty and deprivation in Ireland was even worse than in England. From then on, throughout the years of Blockade, a steady stream of recruits came through Cork and Waterford. The background to their willingness is shown poignantly in a letter to Captain McCulloch sent in August 1824 by Lord Bantry and Mr Baldwin, Magistrates of Cork, thanking him for giving employment to so many poor inhabitants 'as the redundant population were for a considerable time past in a state of starvation through the general want of employment; and we trust that should more men be required . . . you will be pleased to send your tenders to this or the ports adjacent when those wanted will be speedily furnished'.

The recruitment of ex-naval petty officers and seamen was boosted in April 1821 when an Admiralty Order allowed Greenwich Out Pensioners to retain their pensions if they enlisted in the Coast Blockade Service. This was yet another idea from McCulloch whereby he hoped that the increased income for at least some of his men would 'buy their fidelity and thus combat bribery'. As such it was not very successful but it did bring more experienced men into the Blockade Service. Some 200 posters announcing this special provision were printed and sent out to offices, including those of Customs and of Excise, where naval pensions were paid.

Early in 1818, with well over 1,200 officers and men due to come under his control along the coast, Captain McCulloch's role came closer to that of an Army commander and he had to devise an appropriate command structure. At first he divided the coast into nine Districts but changed it later that year for three Divisions: Left, Centre and Right (looking seaward), each covering some 42 miles of coastline. The Divisions were sub-divided into Districts each of which controlled six to eight Blockade Stations. The early formation varied sometimes but a return in July 1820 shows the Districts as:

Left Division	Whitstable, Reculver, Westgate
Centre Division	Broadstairs, Sandown, Deal, Sutherland, Dungeness
Right Division	Rye, Hastings, Eastbourne

A senior Lieutenant was appointed to superintend each Division. In those days it was common naval practice to distinguish between Lieutenants with less or more than eight years seniority; in the twentieth century the distinction created the new rank of Lieutenant Commander. Divisional offices were at Whitstable, Deal and Hastings although again these arrangements changed as the Blockade expanded. Each Division also had a Surgeon, some Assistant Surgeons, a Purser and support staff that included Clerks and Armourers Mates. Districts were supervised by junior Lieutenants with Mates or Midshipmen in charge of stations. The Party at a station varied from 2 petty officers and 7 to 12 men in small units, such as those at Martello Towers, to 4 petty officers and 18 to 20 men in larger quarters.

South Barracks at Deal became the headquarters for the Blockade Service and also, temporarily for its Centre Division until that was transferred to Walmer. At first Captain McCulloch and his headquarters staff took over only part of the barracks but by August 1821 they occupied all the buildings. Later the Captain moved his wife and family from the house in the grounds of the Navy Hospital to quarters within South Barracks. Accommodation was not, however, so readily available to other staff. Purser Philip Thovez, secretary to Captain McCulloch for some years, was living in private lodgings in the town. He asked for rooms in South Barracks because they would be closer to his work – and safer – but had to be content with some across the road in North Barracks which was used, in part, as a military hospital.

At Captain McCulloch's request each Divisional and District Lieutenant was supplied with a horse and he applied successfully for those officers to be given the same relief from the tax on horses as that afforded to riding officers. All officers employed in the Blockade Service were also allowed one servant free of tax.

One interesting sidelight is shown when McCulloch reported to the Navy Board that as he was now obliged to reside permanently on shore he was nolonger entitled to the normal duty free wine allowance, for Captains, of two tuns per year. This was the equivalent of 500 gallons per year or around eight bottles a day! The Navy Board acknowledged the loss of entitlement and gave him an allowance of £80 per year. For the same reason every Lieutenant in the Blockade Service received £20 a year.

The rapid expansion of the Coast Blockade during 1818 and 1819 brought the need for more units of accommodation along the coast and by September 1820 McCulloch had obtained whole or part occupation of virtually every government building along the coast from Whitstable to Eastbourne. The Board of Ordnance alone transferred over 70 buildings to the Navy Board. Some were occupied exclusively by the Coast Blockade Service whilst others such as Forts Twiss, Sutherland and Moncrief – all close to Hythe – were shared with the Army. Some brick buildings along the North Kent coast, at places such as Tankerton Hill, Sea Salter, Navgale and Herne Bay, were of a standard size 48ft by 28ft. On the western end of the Blockade Line the Navy occupied three batteries at Dungeness and 34 Martello Towers between Eastware and Eastbourne.

Where necessary, for example at St. Margaret's Bay, new Blockade stations were built close to the shore. Others were established by using small naval vessels either moored in waterways or drawn up on beaches. H.M.S. *Congo* was manned as a watch vessel and moored at first in East Swale. At Cuckmere McCulloch had already arranged for the Haven to be surveyed before the extension of the Line had been approved. Early in 1818 the commander of the revenue cruiser *Jacobus* reported $8^1/2$ft of water there in the spring but said the channel filled altogether in the winter. Later that year *Congo* was moved to Cuckmere and replaced in the Swale by H.M.S. *Beresford*. At Rye Harbour H.M.S *Enchantress* was drawn up on the shore early in 1819.

Living conditions in some buildings must have been primitive but at least the sleeping arrangements were far better than those experienced on board a man-of-war. There, below decks, hammocks might only be fourteen inches apart in stinking and cramped conditions that can only be imagined, particularly when the ship was battened down and pitching or rolling in heavy seas. In Blockade Station buildings men did have a reasonable space in which to sling their hammocks – and plenty of fresh air. And on a watch vessel there was adequate space with perhaps 25 Blockade men instead of a normal naval crew of 60 or more.

Overland communication between the Admiralty in London and major naval bases had become an important factor during the Napoleonic wars. An efficient shutter telegraph system was installed and that from London to Deal operated from 1796 until it was closed down in 1814. Thomas Goddard, although only a Purser in the Royal Navy, had become an expert on installing telegraph systems and in 1815 he was ordered by John Barrow, Secretary to the Navy Board, to establish an experimental line from London to Chatham. This used a

The Blockade Station at No. 2 Battery, Dungeness. The signal station on the roof was added in 1820 when the new semaphore system was introduced. Taken from a contemporary sketch by Thomas Goddard.

new semaphore system, invented by Rear Admiral Sir Home Riggs Popham, that operated with two 8ft arms, one above the other, on a 30ft hollow mast. The system was a success and Goddard was told to survey a branch extension to Deal, but this was not built and indeed the equipment from London to Chatham was dismantled in 1822 and used on a new line to Portsmouth.

Toward the end of the previous century the Navy had also built signal stations on many parts of the coasts around Britain. These used flags and 'shapes' (black canvas spheres) to pass short messages to men-of-war in the offing but were not intended to relay signals along the coast. Many of these coast signal stations were also closed in the general shut-down in 1814 when the war seemed to be over. The expansion of the Coast Blockade in 1818 persuaded the Navy Board to look again at it's communications in Kent and Sussex and Thomas Goddard was ordered to install the Popham semaphore system from Deal to Beachy Head. It was to be used to relay messages to Blockade Divisions, Districts and Stations and to revenue cruisers patrolling off shore. Fortunately 15 of the 17 semaphore stations built by Goddard (see Appendices C and D) were at old signal stations that had merely been enlarged to become Blockade Stations.

On 10 December 1820 Captain McCulloch notified all officers on the Line that the semaphore stations from Deal to Beachy Head were now in operation and reminded them that requisitions for signal books and spyglasses should have already been placed. At Deal the terminus of the system was described by the Captain as 'the tall building known as Semaphore house at the south end of Beach Street, near the Dock Yard'. Traditionally a naval telegraph or signal station was manned by an elderly Lieutenant or Mate and a petty officer. Blockade complements did not include any additional staff just for signalling duties and McCulloch never referred to anyone specifically for this work. This was probably because as a daylight task it was one that could be carried out by any officer or petty officer at the stations concerned. The two separate signal stations at East Hill (near St. Margarets) and Kewhurst Hill (near Bexhill) were manned by petty officers from nearby Blockade Stations. At Kewhurst there were problems (and probably some mayhem in communications) when two petty officers in succession were charged with drunkenness.

As mentioned in Chapter Two, Martello Towers were built as a coastal defence system between 1805 and 1810. Modelled on a successful coastal fort encountered by the Royal Navy at Mortella Point in Corsica, these circular towers were built of bricks set in a 'hot lime mortar; – a mixture of lime, ash and hot tallow. Capable of withstanding a direct salvo of heavy cannon balls, each tower was around 35ft high and 55ft base diameter. The few still standing, for example at Rye, Dymchurch and Eastbourne, show the only access originally was by outside ladder to a door in the wall at first floor level. From this floor a trapdoor led down to ground level store rooms whilst a staircase, set in walls up to 13ft thick, led up to a solid parapet surrounding the one 24 pounder gun. When occupied by the Blockade Service the first floor in many towers was divided into three areas: for the officer, men's quarters and fresh stores.

Originally built to accommodate one Army officer and 24 men, a typical Blockade party in a Tower was one officer, two petty officers and eight to ten men. In some instances the petty officers and men had their wives with them in the Towers and this caused problems at times. Lieutenant Chappell, Eastbourne District, reported that he had to expel Mrs Oliver from No.67 Tower because she had such a violent temper and browbeat Midshipman Mitchell, the officer in charge. The sympathy of Captain McCulloch for the Lieutenant and poor Mr Mitchell was apparent when he wrote 'the Lieutenant did not exceed the authority necessary to command a proper respect and attention to the Rules of the service from those women who are permitted to remain with their husbands many of whom are individually more than sufficient to throw the Parties into utter confusion'. The problem raised by Mrs Oliver's conduct was obviously not an isolated instance!

Another domestic issue had to be investigated in March 1822 when the Guardians of the Poor at Dover, who were responsible for administering the poor rate, wrote to Captain McCulloch complaining that 'very loose and disorderly women were filling the different buildings occupied by the Blockade some of whom are becoming pregnant continually at great annoyance and enormous expense to the parishes'. The Captain paid visits to each of the three signatories to the letter, Messrs Philpot, Pechell and Fuller but surprisingly, despite the serious accusations, they could provide no specific cases. Mr Philpot of the Parish of St Marys, covering most of Dover Town, had no case in mind. Mr Pechell said there were only two recent instances of bastardy, one was settled by marriage the other by payment (to the

Martello Tower 24 at Dymchurch. The external staircase is modern, access was originally by a removeable ladder.

parish) of the sum demanded. Mr Fuller said little. The complaint fizzled out, dismissed by McCulloch as yet another local attempt to make trouble for the Blockade. His report to the Vice Admiral concluded with 'there are 81 men stationed within these parishes with whom there are 22 women and only one of these not married'.

Later, from the Guardians in the parish of Pett came another complaint that Masters Mate Charles Puckett, in charge at No.31 Tower, was keeping a prostitute in the tower, now with child. In his report to the Navy Board McCulloch exclaimed that 'this was in direct violation of a standing order issued by me to which I have been particular in drawing attention'. He recommended that Puckett be demoted but the Navy Board said 'discharge him'.

The Surgeons in each Division were based in hospitals (perhaps no more than one or two rooms) at Whitstable, Deal and Shorncliff Battery. Assistant Surgeons, three or four per Division, were at sick quarters in various Blockade Stations, including one or two Martello Towers, despite the difficulties this must have caused for access by sick or wounded men. Support staff at these hospitals and sick quarters were drawn from the wives of ratings; it was quite normal in those days for some wives to be on board a man-of-war and help care for the wounded.

Apart from wounds, typical ailments for Blockade men were rheumatism, pneumonia, swollen feet and diarrhoea as well as the traditional naval problems of alcoholism and venereal disease. Through his medical staff Captain McCulloch was always on the watch for men who attempted to obtain a 'smart ticket' by wounding themselves deliberately to gain a permanent pension for the wound. Depending on the nature of the injury some men were re-engaged for active service with the wound pension paid in addition to full pay. Conditions in the Blockade hospitals and sick quarters, and the treatment given, were very primitive indeed by modern standards but even so they were better than anything available to many ordinary folk in Kent and Sussex – they had nothing.

By July 1820 the Blockade Service had a complement of 14 Lieutenants, 25 Mates, 105 Midshipmen, 199 Petty Officers, 12 Armourers mates, 562 Able Seamen, 221 Ordinary Seamen, 96 Landsmen and 39 Boys. In addition to this total of 1273 there were Pursers, Clerks and medical staff. By now Royal Marines had been withdrawn from Blockade Parties although they were deployed sometimes in emergencies. In the main they were used in guard units at South Barracks, Deal and board *Severn*. In later years some marines would be posted to Blockade Divisional offices.

With so many men and Blockade Stations the routine day-to-day administration at the Deal headquarters had become quite onerous and hectic as McCulloch explained – 'the clerks are constantly employed during each whole day and frequently a considerable part of the night. There are voluminous books to be kept, accounts and extensive correspondence with various Public Departments and this line of coast'. The Navy Board granted his request that the clerks be given additional pay to bring them into line with those on guard ships (floating barracks) and flagships.

In keeping with naval practice McCulloch's letters were penned in duplicate by a clerk for the Captain to sign; many routine reports were drafted by his secretary. McCulloch, always in a hurry, always pushing for urgent action, usually made his many journeys along the Line in a private coach accompanied by his secretary and a clerk with letters and reports despatched on the run as it were. One set of letter books in the Public Record Office is devoted to Captain McCulloch's travelling reports.

The Blockade Service, as a Royal Naval force, had to have the obligatory set of Standing Orders. There were additions and cancellations over the years but a basic set issued by Captain McCulloch early in 1819 included:

> Parties are to confine their duty to the seashore and not interfere with anything on the public road or elsewhere unless evidently in the act of smuggling. They are not to trespass on any land, enclosure or private property unless commanded by an officer and he being present.
>
> Passengers Baggage arriving on any part of the coast shall not be opened by any officers or men but must be delivered in charge of an Officer of Customs . . . or accompanied to a Custom House/
>
> Nails are not to be driven into barrack room walls.
>
> If glass is broken and the offender not discovered the whole Party will pay for the replacement.
>
> Watch and Station Bills (rosters) must be prepared so that no man is made acquainted with it previous to being placed on look out.
>
> Serious accidents have occurred through want of care with fire arms. They must be held in a secure place and not issued until going on duty.
>
> Grog is to be issued to Petty Officers and seamen mixed one part rum to two parts water

In his 'Naval Sketch Book' Captain Glascock mentioned later Blockade orders demanding 'When on duty all intercourse or even ordinary communication with either stranger or acquaintance is strictly forbidden. No severity of weather is allowed as a pretext for seeking temporary shelter or retreating from the line of water mark guard'.

For any rating with previous naval experience the order about one-to-two grog was the most difficult to swallow, quite literally. He could put up with paying for broken windows and any other petty rules but one-to-two grog was terrible and its weakness cultivated descriptions that cannot be put into print even in these liberal days. Rum had been supplied to the Royal Navy from the mid-seventeenth century, following the colonisation of the West Indies, and for many years was issued neat in measured tots daily to all men on naval ships, with the inevitable problems of drunkenness. In the 1750s Admiral Vernon tried to alleviate the problem by ordering issues to be diluted one part rum to two parts water. He was known as 'Old Grogam', from the material of his favourite boat-cloak, and his dilution was soon christened 'grog' but the daily issue of two gills (one half pint) of rum was usually diluted one-to-one with water. This was divided and served midday and evening; the midday tot could be saved until evening. In 1825 the evening tot was discontinued throughout the Navy and from then on the issue of grog was only made at midday.

Every station in the Blockade Service had its store of Navy rum with the officer supervising the daily issue. Captain McCulloch was obviously concerned that drunkenness could present real problems in some of these small isolated units if the officer was weak or lazy in his supervision, especially when the sentinels were supposed to be wide-awake on watch at night. McCulloch's solution was to order the one-to-two dilution. But it must have been a contentious matter because Captain Pigot, who succeeded McCulloch in 1825, cancelled the order within a few weeks of his arrival.

In a Blockade Service divided into territorial Divisions and Districts with small, fixed, units of men supervised by officers on horseback some may have been excused at times for thinking they had joined the Army. If so their thoughts came sharply back into focus whenever they saw the Watch Calendar at a station – this was Navy through and through. Issued as a Blockade Regulation, the Watch Calendar set out the methods by which petty officers and sentinels were to be rostered for watches:

> No excuses or errors will be accepted for watches or clocks.
>
> Officers will attend to the Sun's Meridian altitude and make calculations to ensure clear daylight at time of change of watch when Parties can see small objects . . . at a distance of at least 3 miles.
>
> Petty Officers and Sentinels are to change every 20 or 30 minutes during a night watch and once an hour during a day watch.
>
> All destinations and relief arrangements are to be kept secret until men are going out.

The Calendar then gave detailed examples of rosters for winter which commenced on 9 October and summer – which started on 6 March! A typical day watch was from 7am to 5pm in February and 4am to 8pm in July with a night watch covering the remaining hours. A Party was divided into Larboard and Starboard watches each sub-divided into First and Second Parts.

A typical night watch comprised a petty officer and four or five sentinels strung out along a stretch of shore or cliff. Captain McCulloch refrained from laying down a regulatory number of men per mile at night but he probably aimed for around four. The figure had to be variable because stations were not equidistant. There was only a half mile between some Martello Towers but other stations might be four miles apart. In later years the Watch Calendars were changed by the Captains who followed McCulloch and a typical watch then had six hours out, six hours in, twice every 24 hours.

Before being posted to a Blockade Station a raw Landsman had to be given some training on board *Severn* because there was no formal naval training available elsewhere. In the harsh life aboard a man-of-war there was much for a raw recruit to know and he soon 'learnt the ropes' or else he got a rope's end across his back from any nearby Boson's Mate. Life in the Blockade Service was under the same code of naval discipline but all the new Landsman needed to know was how to row a galley and use a cutlass

Walmer Beach with East Barracks (and R.N. Hospital) in the background. c.*1825*
Deal Maritime Museum

and firearms. Training was therefore limited to just two to three weeks on board *Severn* and although this probably included instruction in handling weapons, the only reports sent to the Admiralty were, for example, that '52 Landsmen in the service of the Coast Blockade have been instructed to pull in boats. Some have been rated Ordinary Seamen as they are found deserving.' Amongst the men who achieved this quick promotion to the next rate would have been those who already had experience in boat-handling although only a few may have handled firearms – legally.

The Blockade Service used 'boat service' pistols and the short version of the standard sea service flint lock musket ('Brown Bess') of .75 calibre which was 4ft 8ins long and weighed about 8lbs. Every sentinel carried a cutlass and, in the early years, one pistol but this was later increased to two. Muskets were usually brought out by petty officers and the off duty watch in response to any alarm. With all firearms it was essential to keep the priming powder dry (difficult on a beach on a wet night!) otherwise they 'snapped' – failed to fire. A sentinel would try to keep his firearm dry under his beach jacket but this was cumbersome with the long pistol. It became easier in later years when the short pistol was issued which could be held inside the jacket and under the arm. Traditionally a naval officer on duty only carried his sword but in the Blockade Service he also took one or two pistols when making his nightly rounds and was usually accompanied by his orderly armed with a musket.

Hostility simmered in the neighbourhoods of many Blockade Stations and local folk were quick to exploit any stories about the bumbling incompetence of some recruits. On board ship a gormless Landsman was seen only by his officers and ship-mates; in the Blockade Service every man-jack was in the public eye. At first some locals scathingly dubbed the Blockade men

'Warriors' but this nickname faded after the bitter fights of 1820 and 1821.

Gormless or not, every sentinel was under tension night after night as a lone target on a beach or cliff top in danger of being killed or injured by smugglers. And when there was a fight the naval men would always be heavily outnumbered, often by men who lived locally. In such tense circumstances it is not surprising perhaps to find that when the Blockade men carried out local searches of boats and buildings they were accused of being rough and brutal. It was said they smashed open cottage doors and wrecked furniture and whilst this was certainly true at times many of the accusers were themselves involved in smuggling. Since childhood they had hated all preventives and it was second nature to seek cause to complain.

One instance when there was good cause to complain occurred at Fairlight where Mr Watson, Masters Mate, wanted to make a fence around the station. He asked the landowner, Mr Thorpe, if the men could cut some timber from nearby trees. Mr Thorpe said 'No' but sent over a gift of 50 hop poles. Later he was extremely annoyed to find the Blockade men had still cut down some of his valuable trees. He wrote to the Navy Board threatening to give notice to quit and Captain McCulloch had to pay a diplomatic visit to placate the irate landowner. Another complaint came a few months later when four men at No.3 Tower, Eastware Bay, stole and killed a sheep belonging to Mr Ford, a Folkestone butcher; McCulloch reported to the Navy Board that this was 'the first instance of so disgraceful an act by Parties of the Coast Blockade since first establishment'.

On the credit side Mr Croft, a hitherto belligerent owner of land between Ramsgate and Broadstairs, who had previously warned off Blockade men, now relented and not only charged a trifling five shillings per annum rent for liberty of free passage but even gave a key to the gate at Dompton for exclusive access to the beach. McCulloch noted with pleasure that 'the friendly feelings of Mr Croft towards the Coast Blockade have lately become more general along the coast then it had hitherto been'.

A complaint from George Martin, bootmaker of Winchelsea, about unpaid accounts from three Midshipmen brought Captain McCulloch to investigate this as a general problem but one with which, he admitted, he seldom concerned himself. He found that 'many Midshipmen come to the Coast Blockade Service to get clear of one set of creditors that they might begin accounts here and when they could go on credit no longer they got their friends to apply for (their) removal into ships proceeding to foreign stations'.

Another more important complaint in June 1821 at Rye showed not only that some officers ignored those standing orders about not dealing with passenger's baggage but that it took very little to excite their zeal, an admirable quality in other circumstances. The story commenced at Rye Harbour with the arrival of the packet steamer *Liberty* from Boulogne with 28 passengers including, according to one subsequent letter of complaint, 11 respectable ladies. Five passengers disembarked at the harbour entrance with the remainder staying on board until the packet berthed in Rye Town. Coast Blockade men from *Enchantress* checked the five as they came ashore and, finding one to be carrying some contraband, they promptly took him aboard the watch vessel as a prisoner.

Meanwhile, Mr Mason, Tide Surveyor of Customs, accompanied by a tide waiter arrived at the harbour and, being unaware of the arrest, went on board the packet to clear the other passengers through Customs formalities as she moved up to Rye Town. When the *Liberty* started to move Midshipman Smith and five men ran from the *Enchantress* and launched their galley in hot pursuit. In an effort to make the packet heave-to Mr Smith fired a pistol shot through her rigging but Henry Paine, the master, ignored this because, as he said later in his letter of complaint, he already had Customs men on board and was 'abiding by the demands of the law'.

Halfway up the harbour the Blockade men caught and boarded the *Liberty*. Midshipman Smith ran to the steamer's bridge, drew his pistol, demanded the helm and deliberately ran the ship ashore proclaiming she was seized. Three of those respectable ladies fainted. District Lieutenant Blake then came on board, ordered all members of the crew below and despatched a man back to *Enchantress* to 'work the telegraphs and declare along the coast (presumably to the Divisional Office at Hastings) that the Rye packet had been seized'. Rather belatedly Lieutenant Blake then ordered his men to search the vessel for contraband but nothing was found. All this drama because just one passenger was found to be carrying contraband!

Within a few days letters of complaint were coming from many directions. One of the passengers was a prominent agent for Customs in London and, as the reader might imagine, Mr Mason made a very detailed report to the Commissioners of Customs. After such drama any official remedial action was bound to seem tame. Apologies were made to all and sundry. The two Blockade officers were admonished and Captain McCulloch published a reminder about relevant standing orders. Later, new orders were issued to the effect that in ports where Customs officers were stationed they should be left to deal with all ships, including passenger vessels, arriving from foreign parts. But, as will be seen in later chapters, this demarcation was still ignored from time to time. Some months later Lieutenant Blake asked to be 'superseded' (to return home on half pay) and this was granted, quite readily. The reports do not indicate what happened to that poor, unfortunate, passenger held imprisoned aboard *Enchantress*, but it is safe to assume that the Rye packet suffered a drop in passenger traffic for some time after this episode.

After the first two years of its Coast Blockade the Admiralty wanted to know whether the new Service was effective and in June 1820 Rear Admiral Sir John Gore, C-in-C Medway and Sir John Hope, a Lord of the Admiralty, made an inspection. It seems their report was not published but it must have been favourable because four years later a further expansion would be approved.

Another survey, this time of all the preventive forces in Britain, was made early in 1821 for different reasons. Five years had passed since the transfer of the Preventive Waterguard from the Board of Customs to the direct control of the Treasury and the result was a neglected and inefficient mess.

To extricate itself the Treasury formed a Committee of Inquiry, the members of which were senior Treasury and Customs officials. The report, a whitewash, written essentially by the Treasury and presented grandly to the Prince Regent on 31 July, found:

> the difficulty of protecting the Revenue has been unquestionably very great; the attempts of the smuggler have been carried to a most flagrant degree of audacity and violence . . . they have indeed suffered severe losses in goods, conveyances and men (the capture of the latter being the most effective mode of repressing these practices) but we have found they have succeeded in introducing considerable quantities of spirits and tobacco from the opposite coasts . . . with tea they have not attempted much but prohibited and fine goods such as silks, gloves and laces were brought for the most part clandestinely by individuals arriving in the packets or trading vessels . . .

The Committee expressed grave misgivings at the lack of central control of all preventive services, the most effective of which were the Preventive Waterguard and the Coast Blockade. It recommended transferring the Preventive Waterguard back to the control of the Board of Customs 'attended by a very material reduction in revenue cruisers and riding officers if they were combined in one arrangement and submitted to one authority'. In a more detailed reference to the Coast Blockade Service the report mentioned:

> The peculiar force which is established upon one part of the coast between the Isle of Sheppey and Beachy Head. Upon the whole we are convinced that the Revenue has derived very considerable protection from it and that by the vigilance, activity and resolution of Captain McCulloch and the officers serving under him the smugglers have been greatly baffled in a district peculiarly adapted for their practices and assistance from the inveterate habits of a great part of the population . . . even so the Blockade was not so completely effectual . . . contraband has been successfully landed . . . there have been a very great number of desertions from the force . . . our suspicions are that a great part of them occasioned by corrupt collusion with smugglers. There are no grounds for concluding this naval blockade has been more successful than the Preventive Waterguard might have been but we do not recommend any change'.

The Report also gave some statistics on the preventive forces:

	Men	**Cost £s**
Riding Officers	157	19,507
Preventive Waterguard	1250	92,003
H.M. Ships (on preventive work)	2375	154,399
Revenue Cruisers. Admiralty	1553	158,089
Revenue Cruisers. Revenue Boards	97	7,373
Coast Blockade Service	1276	89,152

This showed that on the coasts there were 1276 Coast Blockade men between Swale and Cuckmere but only 1250 preventive men for the rest of Britain.

The report succeeded in disguising the Treasury's neglect of the Preventive Waterguard which had suffered badly both in the paucity and quality of recruits. Two years later, in 1823, the 17 preventive boats in Sussex west of the Blockade Line were still woefully short of men and further west there was scarcely the equivalent of one man per mile of coast. As far back as 1818 the neglect and inefficiency had become apparent to the Prime Minister and the Admiralty with the result that the latter, with its new Blockade system, had been given responsibility for preventive work eventually on some 126 miles of Kent and Sussex coasts. And in five years it had shown that, despite bribery and desertions, a disciplined and well armed naval force could present real opposition to large scale smuggling. With the Treasury very much on the defensive over its neglect, it is not surprising to find that although the report managed some initial praise for 'this peculiar force' it could not resist that disparaging conclusion – a conclusion the Prime Minister would ignore when he authorised further extensions to the Blockade Line in 1824.

All the recommendations in the report were adopted. Under Treasury orders issued on 15 January 1822 a reduced fleet of revenue cruisers, together with the Preventive Waterguard, was transferred back to the Board of Customs to join the riding officers in one body to be known as the 'Coast Guard' (two separate words in its early years). Captain Hanchett was replaced by Captain William Bowles R.N. who became the first Comptroller General of the Coast Guard. The Board of Customs controlled the new force but it was intended that its officers and men would henceforth be appointed after nomination by the Admiralty. Thus the Navy hoped to exercise some influence over the calibre of this new preventive force. Sadly, as will be seen, these hopes were only partially fulfilled and within a few years Captain Bowles would be complaining that the Customs were taking men with no sea-going experience. Nevertheless, the officers of the Coast Guard were always nominated by the Admiralty from the Navy List thus establishing the long association between the Navy and the Coastguard.

The Coast Blockade Service remained unaltered but one useful change, from Captain McCulloch's viewpoint, was that the total number of riding officers was reduced nationally and, as a consequence, during the latter part of 1822 they were removed from the areas covered by the Blockade Line. The Captain was now in complete command of all preventive operations on the coast from East Swale to Cuckmere.

By 1823 it was apparent that *Severn* was too small (and by now possibly unsound) to act as a depot ship for the enlarged Blockade Service. In June 1823 she was replaced off Deal by *Ramillies* (74) a fine old third rater, built in 1785, that had seen action in Ushant, Copenhagen and New Orleans. The replacement was larger and, even with just its harbour crew, required well over 300 men. She also brought a personal benefit; Captain McCulloch was now in command of a third rate 'ship of the line' and his salary rose from £500 to £598 per year.

He now had a larger depot ship and a Blockade Service almost at full complement – but not for long! In July 1823 200 Seamen and Landsmen

H.M.S. Ramillies
Dover Museum

were drafted, under Admiralty orders, to *Revenge* (74) and another 200 to *Spartiate* (74). McCulloch protested vehemently that in just one week he had dropped to two-thirds of Blockade complement and only had three Landsmen! To replace the shortage he sent his tenders away 'to raise men from as far distant from the Blockade Line as possible'. A new tender *Antelope* made two successful trips to Bristol whilst *Industry* made her regular calls at Cork and Waterford.

As a matter of policy Captain McCulloch always sought 'to keep the men removed from the influence of the inhabitants of the coast' again in an attempt to combat bribery. This extended not only to forbidding any local fraternisation but even to the transport arrangements when someone wanted to re-enlist after the first three years. The discharge and re-joining had to be effected in London; all discharged men and their wives were taken there by tender and those re-joining brought back in the same vessel. Not only did this keep the men from contact with the locals, it was also much cheaper for the Navy Board when wives and accompanying baggage had to be moved.

One of the functions of the Blockade headquarters at Deal was to make arrangements for the supply of fresh food to all stations. The unusual establishment, for the Navy, of small parties of officers and men strung out along the coast brought questions from the Victualling Board regarding the supply of fresh provisions. The Board was told that the Left and Centre Divisions were supplied with fresh beef and bread direct from Deal by Blockade tenders but Right Division obtained it's provisions from local contractors. Fresh meat and bread must have been a welcome bonus for Blockade men, on board ship it would have been salt meat, salt fish and hard tack (ship biscuits). In one interesting note the Navy Board estimated that it cost about £25 per head (officers and men) per year to feed the Blockade Service on fresh provisions and that this was less than the cost afloat for salt provisions. Another sidelight is seen in the requisitions for iron utensils sent in by all stations in the Centre Division. From a list of various cooking pots and pans available a few stations asked for stewpots but everyone, without exception, ordered frying pans.

Obtaining provisions by local contracts could bring opportunities for bribery. Lieutenant Aitchison of the Right Division had problems with vegetable suppliers around Eastbourne who were 'notorious in buying the Sentinels over to connive at Smuggling – tenders for such contracts are often well below normal rates for such supplies simply with a view to corrupting the Parties'. He also had other problems with supplies; Robert Burnham, Landsman, a deserter from Tower 55 hid in Hooe and systematically robbed provisions delivered to Tower 54!

With a Coast Blockade Line of limited length it was inevitable that some smugglers would operate just beyond the extremities. As early as December 1820 Rear Admiral Gore was advising the Admiral of the Nore that 'I have called Captain McCulloch's attention to smuggling via the West Swale not East Swale and hence not within the line of the Coast Blockade'. Galleys and tenders from the flagship in the Medway were deployed but were ineffective in the absence of any co-ordinated command.

From Eastbourne, then the most westerly District, came reports that regular landings were taking place beyond the line at Seaford, Rottingdean and Brighton by gangs who then carried the goods, often 200 to 300 tubs of spirits, in light carts through Sussex behind the Line to Bexhill, Eastbourne and Hastings. The smugglers Beecham and his men from Bexhill were said to be regulars in the trade. The few Preventive Waterguard men who might appear when the tubs were landed would be given five or six to seize. In the summer of 1822 Divisional Lieutenant Edward Chappell discussed the problem with Mr Hamilton, Collector Newhaven, who was very concerned over the constant working to the west of the Line. Later Lieutenant Lory, covering Cuckmere, also met with Customs staff who spoke of £4,000 worth of dry goods being landed at Rottingdean a few weeks back and £18,000 worth at Brighton. Lory suggested extending the Line to Newhaven. Captain McCulloch passed all these reports assiduously to the Admiralty accompanied by his recommendations to extend the Line to Chichester. At one point he offered to operate a task force of an extra 120 officers and men to the west whilst the Prime Minister and Admiralty were considering the matter.

The coast just beyond the other end of the Line was given close attention again in July 1823 when Captain Bowles of the Coast Guard inspected the Medway and reported to the Board of Customs that it was difficult for him to make changes. The Coast Guard could only keep a station watch by day and a force afloat (the preventive boats) at night. The revenue cutter there could only put away one boat at night without overworking the crew and the cutter had problems working in strong winds above the Dockyard. He recommended withdrawing the 41 Coast Guard officers and men from the Isle of Sheppey and extending the Coast Blockade to cover the Island. With the support of the Board of Customs the report went via the Treasury to the Admiralty. By the time it arrived there in November a note had been made in the margin 'Lord Liverpool contemplates a considerable extension of the Coast Blockade'. This would obviously be both in Sheppey and Sussex.

On 12 November 1823 McCulloch was asked how he would extend the Line to the Isle of Sheppey? Being McCulloch he had already made a survey and soon reported back that he would block the east and west entrances of the Swale at Faversham and Queenboro' and extend the Line around the 12½ miles of coast of the island from Shellness to Sheerness and then to Queenboro'. Within a short time three more naval watch vessels

A naval brig used as a training ship in the late nineteenth-century. E.S. Murray

had arrived. *Pioneer* was moored in East Swale about one mile above *Beresford* whilst in the West Swale *Bathurst* was moored off Queenboro' with *Snapper* about one mile further up. All four watch vessels could each send out two galleys every night to patrol the Swale. The vessels had arrived quickly but the provision of adequate buildings for other stations on Sheppey took much longer. For this extension of the Line McCulloch estimated he would need 247 more officers and men at a cost of £7,987 after discounting £3,000 for the departing Coast Guard staff.

A few weeks later he was asked by the Admiralty for estimates to extend the Line westward to Chichester Harbour. McCulloch had already surveyed the coast and on 30 December 1823 provided total estimates for an extra 650 officers and men, including those for Sheppey, at a total cost of £35,000. The Captain's estimates were often strategically on the low side and this was no exception; the actual additional complement would be over 1,000. Nevertheless the Prime Minister had decided and on 2 January 1824 a Treasury minute approved 'the extension of the Royal Naval Coast Blockade Service to the whole of the Isle of Sheppey and west as far as Chichester'.

In the first few months of 1824 Captain McCulloch was busy setting up the extensions, first in Sheppey and then along the coast from Cuckmere to

Chichester. Much of his time must have been taken in travelling to and from his base at Deal although he and his staff would use the Divisional offices occasionally. Numerous meetings were held with Coast Guard officers and the Board of Ordnance to arrange yet more transfers of property. The Royal Engineers were also involved because they supervised the construction of new buildings. All this when McCulloch was also deeply involved in the war against smuggling gangs and at a time when he was probably already suffering from the chronic chest problems that bring about his demise the following year. The list of Coast Guard stations to be transferred covered five in Sheppey and 17 in Sussex. There were detailed inventories of 83 cottages and three unnamed watch vessels two of which, at Elmley Ferry and Minster, had been so neglected that they were promptly condemned by the Navy and removed. The third, moored near the entrance to Chichester Harbour, was taken over but replaced the following year by *Griper* a sloop previously used for Arctic voyages, see Appendix B. At Cuckmere Haven a station was built just above the beach and early in 1825 the redundant *Congo* was moved once more, this time to Rye 'alongside the river bank near the town'.

On 13 April 1824 Captain McCulloch reported 'the Commissioners of Customs have transferred the whole line of coast, which now remains, to be turned over to the Coast Blockade forthwith and I am now prepared to occupy the same'. He was now preventive supremo for almost 200 miles of coast stretching from Sheerness to Chichester Harbour. The extended command required a new structure and so, starting from the east he created six divisions:

First Division	Sheerness to Herne Bay (Shellness)
Second Division	Herne Bay to St Margarets Bay (Walmer)
Third Division	St Margarets Bay to Dungeness (Folkestone)
Fourth Division	Dungeness to Langley (Hastings)
Fifth Division	Langley to Shoreham (Newhaven)
Sixth Division	Shoreham to Chichester (Littlehampton)

As before, each Division would have a Divisional Lieutenant, Surgeon, Assistant Surgeons, Purser, Clerks and other support staff. Divisional offices were located at the places shown in brackets; only Walmer and Hastings were already established and some of the others were in temporary quarters at first. Each Division covered roughly 32 miles of coast and exercised 'superintendance', as the Navy described it, over three to five districts each of which controlled six to eight stations.

During the time the extensions to the Line were being considered the Admiralty, for the reasons given in Chapter Four, made a fundamental change in the Blockade Service by replacing all Midshipmen in charge of stations with Lieutenants. A few stations remained under the command of Mates but by March 1825 there were no Midshipmen in the complements shown at Appendices C and D. By then the total strength of the Service (excluding *Ramillies*) was 2,311 officers and men, an additional 1,038 for the extensions to the Line instead of the 650 estimated by McCulloch. Senior Lieutenants were still in charge of divisions and districts but now the numbers of junior Lieutenants had risen dramatically from 14 in 1820 to 114 in 1825, a move warmly welcomed by Midshipmen and Mates some of whom were promoted if not in situ at least within their divisions.

The further extensions to the Line brought a need for yet more recruits and in January 1824 Captain McCulloch sent four officers from *Ramillies* away to raise men. For Landsmen one went to Cork and another to Hull, whilst for experienced ratings the others went to Portsmouth and Plymouth. It seems they all achieved success because by March McCulloch had too many men aboard *Ramillies* waiting to move into Sheppey where the Coast Guard was taking it's time in leaving. Further drafts were due any day from Cork and Waterford! Last year he had been woefully short of men now he had too many! On 10 March he sent an 'Immediate Note' to Customs (which still had to go via the Navy Board and Treasury) saying he had to place some men on a month's leave – the Coast Guard must vacate forthwith!

Some local folk did not take kindly, to say the least, to the arrival of the Blockade. Those in Whitstable and around the Swale were no exception; the boathouses of both the Coast Blockade and the Customs at Whitstable were burnt down in July 1822. When the three additional watch vessels were moored in the Swale the Oyster Companies of Whitstable and Queenboro' petitioned the Admiralty claiming compensation for disturbance to their oyster beds. The petitions received short shrift from McCulloch 'it is merely a ploy to hinder the extension of the Line. The majority of the oystermen at Whitstable are known smugglers'.

Elsewhere the response, at least on the surface, was more polite. In March 1824 a Sussex newspaper reported 'the Coast Blockade has commenced taking up stations recently occupied by the Coast Guard. A party of the former with an officer marched into the Martello Tower in Seaford Bay on Thursday last. Another party occupied Bletchington Fort on Friday and a party commanded by C.W. Poynter R.N. took possession of Newhaven battery on Saturday. Their flags are now waving on all the stations between Seaford Head and Porto Bello. The Coast Guard parties retire westward as the Coast Blockade parties advance, the exchange being effected with the utmost quietness, regularity and good will'.

By August 1824 problems with the changeover in Sheppey had eased but there was still a lack of progress in providing permanent quarters for officers and men both there and in Sussex west of Brighton. Some stations were in poor temporary buildings, some under canvas. McCulloch's task was indeed difficult; he was seeking to house over 1000 officers and men along the two extensions to the Line where the coast had been covered previously by about 200 of the Coast Guard.

Some eight years had now passed since *Ganymede* had first moored off Deal. It is doubtful if William McCulloch ever found time to sit back and contemplate his achievements, but if he did it would be to remember how the present Blockade force had started with just three galleys from his frigate landing small groups of men at night around Deal. Now in 1824 he commanded over 2,600 officers and men with 300 aboard *Ramillies* and the rest spread over nearly 200 miles of coast in some 130 stations – more than the combined crews of two first rate ships.

As a command the post brought it's own special problems. Setting them out to support yet another plea for better seizure rewards to be distributed to his officers he explained:

> The Force is in every respect similar to that in His Majesty's ships and discipline is the same.
>
> In many other respects the system is materially different. The Force is divided into separate parties . . . acting independent of each other. The superintendance of superior officers is general, personal inspection occasional, whereas on board ships the inferior officers and men are under continued observation and the control of their superiors.
>
> The executive officers of the Blockade, the Lieutenants and Mates, are married men with families, nearly two thirds of them. They are better than the unmarried, less inclined to absent themselves from the Stations and less able to afford the means of procuring entertainment elsewhere. But the married men are often in straitened circumstances, they joined the Coast Blockade because of full pay, free quarters and food. They should be given some pecuniary advantage – an extra allowance from their own seizures. I have never hesitated to recommend the removal of any officer but many . . . are remiss in their attention to their Parties and general performance . . . it is difficult to set up any specific charge, but they too would improve if rewards were given for their own seizures. Extra seizure allowances should be made to seizing officers. The reward already has 5% deducted for the Greenwich Hospital and 5% for Agency. In addition there should be another 10% paid . . . above the present rewards.

The previous year, as explained in Chapter Four, McCulloch had finally achieved his long sought aim of ensuring rewards only went to the seizing party. But that was as far as the Admiralty and Treasury were willing to go and there was no response to this fresh idea of extra rewards for officers.

The Coast Blockade Service with its many small and often remote units of men did present problems for naval discipline when compared to the tight regime on a man-of-war. The Navy placed a rigid code of discipline in the hands of a Captain and gave him complete authority over all ratings. Some minor offences could be punished by junior officers but major crimes such as theft, disobedience, drunkenness and sleeping on duty were dealt with by the Captain. Minor offences in the Blockade Service were dealt with in the same way as on board ship but for any major offence McCulloch invariably ordered a flogging, usually on board the depot ship. Flogging had long been a standard punishment in the Navy although by the end of the Napoleonic wars some officers were questioning its retention. The 'Navy Chronicle' of 1818 carried lengthy articles debating the use of a punishment regarded by one writer as 'inhumane' and by another as 'of little ultimate value'.

In the Blockade Service the punishment took place usually on Mondays on the open deck of the depot ship in the presence of the Captain, officers, marines and both watches of the crew on special muster. The offender, who had been held in irons, would be brought on deck stripped to the waist and

Dover Harbour and Pier c. *1830*

tied to a vertical wooden grating set near the gangway. The Captain would read aloud the offence and punishment and then, at his order, the sinner was lashed with a 'cat-o-nine-tails' at full strength and stretch by a Bosuns Mate who knew he dare not ease up. Typical sentences on board any man-of-war went up to 50 lashes – sometimes more – but much depended on the nature of the offence and the Captain's temper.

Captain McCulloch was certainly a 'flogger', so much so that he became known throughout the Blockade Service as 'Flogging Joey'. Extracts taken from the Captain's Log of *Severn* in 1821 show punishments for: drunkenness 24 lashes; desertion 36; disobedience 12; theft 18; for being bribed 24; for being absent without leave and found in a smugglers house 36 asleep at his post 24; sitting down at his post and neglect of duty 24; corrupt conduct 40.

These were punishments meted out by a man who drove himself and others to create a unique Blockade system in the shortest possible time often using the rawest of recruits in remote stations. For many men the temptations must have been quite novel; how often would a lowly seaman be offered a bribe on board ship? McCulloch was a hard taskmaster for whom harsh discipline would have been an essential feature in his new system. Even so, punishments apart, there were times when he did show compassion and one wonders whether he would have been so harsh if he had continued his career afloat.

The incidence of flogging in the Blockade Service attracted some public attention. A letter to the *Sussex Advertiser* in June 1821 complained 'the men who comprise the great body are driven to their duty with the cat at their backs and for the least deviation from duty are thrown into the hold, ironed and kept there until the pleasure of their Commander be known. Would you believe it? There were no less than twenty six of these poor creatures tied up and flogged yesterday, their cries piercing and reached Rye'. Presumably those floggings took place aboard *Enchantress* in Rye Harbour. In later years, when *Hyperion* was at Newhaven in the Blockade Service under Captain Mingaye, floggings were carried out on board, every Monday, to the disapproving shouts of onlookers on the riverside. Typical sentences then were 36 lashes for disobedience and 12, 24 or 36 for drunkenness. Flogging, more than anything else, showed quite literally and dreadfully that this was a Royal Naval force doing preventive work the Navy way. The punishment was also used extensively in the Army up to 1859 but remained with the Navy until 1871.

Due to violent gales in January 1825 *Ramillies* suffered some damage and had to be taken to Chatham for repairs. As a depot ship she only had a harbour crew of some 300 men and so another 200 were withdrawn from the Line in East Kent for the voyage to and from Chatham.

That same month Captain McCulloch had another complaint to answer but this was somewhat different from the usual hostile reaction. The Reverend Barre-Phipps, Rector of Selsey, who lived in what is now Norton Priory , wrote to the Admiral, Portsmouth, complaining that the local Coast Blockade officers and men never attended church service. The letter came to McCulloch via the Admiralty and in a sharp reply he said the Rector lived very near Blockade Stations ' why not visit them to promote the future welfare of the Parties? His services would be highly valued. Our present weak strength means absence in church provides an opportunity for the smuggler'. After some lengthy comments on the problems of church attendance where some men were Protestants and others Roman Catholic, the Captain could not resist one well-aimed parting shot – 'With this arrangement (of Rector's visits) we shall avoid the evident risk of giving those parishioners any opportunities to land the usual supplies of genuine port wine and other foreign luxuries with which they have hitherto supplied their friends in ample abundance'. The Reverend Barre-Phipps was known to spend some time abroad each year because his wife could not stand the cold and wet winters at Selsey. Some of that time was spent in Spain and Portugal where genuine port wine was plentiful.

Also in January 1825 McCulloch, still beset with the problems of extending the Line, sent a note to the Navy Board with copies to all Divisional Lieutenants and Pursers. Venting his exasperation at the slow progress in setting up the new Divisions and the attitudes of some Pursers he said: 'All Bosuns and Carpenters stores for the service of the Blockade are drawn from the Deal Naval Yard and Gunners stores from the Ordnance Department at Dover . . . Pursers of the old Line performed their various duties without murmur . . . but those of the new Line are disappointed in not finding everything the same complete. The First, Fifth and Sixth Divisions have not yet so much as the Form of a Blockade owing to the delay in certain departments where I could not be expected to have either control or influence . . . it is recommended that responsibility for all the above stores be transferred to Lieutenants superintending Divisions and for these purposes each should have a clerk'. The Navy Board was content to agree to this devolution but the request showed that the extended Line was already proving difficult to supply from just one naval base well to the east.

Early in February 1825 the Captain was in the Worthing – Selsey sector urging those 'certain departments' to complete the necessary quarters for his men. The Parties in the area were still suffering from privation and shortage of men; Kingston only had 11 men instead of 24 and Worthing 12 instead of 24. But, as ever, his report to the Vice Admiral had an optimistic conclusion – 'Notwithstanding these restrictions I am convinced there is not one tenth of the smuggling carried on when the Preventive Waterguard were there'. His optimism was justified to some extent when an anonymous letter from Brighton told local Blockade officers that 'on Thursday last thirteen men from Hastings, Bexhill and Eastbourne being the crew of a lugger commanded by George Harrington and owned by Wisden of Brighton passed behind the Blockade from west to east by coach having landed an immense cargo near Lymington . . . George Harrington the Eastbourne smuggler had never in his life before run westward of Chichester'.

The shock came out of the blue on 27 February 1825 when Captain McCulloch paid a visit to Newhaven and found, to his surprise, that all work on the proposed new building for the Fifth Division's office had been stopped. That day he sent an urgent query to the Navy Board which crossed with an order coming from the Admiralty instructing him to transfer all Blockade officers and men employed in Sussex to the command of the Captain of H.M.S *Hyperion* as soon as she arrived at Newhaven. Captain McCulloch would henceforth confine himself to the Coast Blockade in Kent. The effect of this order was to create two separate naval forces, the Kent Coast Blockade under the C-in-C Medway and the Sussex Coast Blockade under the C-in-C Portsmouth, and thus did they remain until abolished in 1831.

The separation of the forces was achieved with minimum disturbance to the Line by moving the old boundary, between Third and Fourth Divisions at Dungeness, just a few miles west to coincide with the county boundary near Jews (later Jurys) Gap. Each county force had three divisions and each division covered roughly 32 miles of coast.

The Admiralty had decided the extended Blockade system had become too long to be controlled effectively by one commander positioned so far to the east. Despite his debilitating illness McCulloch was still a fully effective commander but he drove himself hard to extend the Line and it is possible that overwork hastened his death which would come before the end of the year.

Captain William James Mingaye was appointed to command *Hyperion* (42) and on 6 March 1825 he reported to Vice Admiral George Martin at Portsmouth that the ship had arrived in Newhaven to take the moorings previously laid down. To the excitement of many inhabitants she was towed into position by *Comet*, one of the Navy's steam vessels. A newspaper correspondent in Lewes reported 'the Hyperion . . . cuts a noble figure in the water and is distinctly to be seen, with the help of a spyglass from the yard of St Anns Church in this town'.

The Commander-in-Chief, Portsmouth was now involved in the Coast Blockade system for the first time and had to be advised by the Navy Board about the peculiar arrangements for matters such as payment of rewards and local contracts for the supply of fresh provisions. The Board also set out the pay and special allowances for certain officers:

	Full Pay	Travelling Expenses	In Lieu of Wine	Other Benefits
Captains	£598	£500	£80	House Free of Rent, Rates and Taxes
Divisional Lieutenants	£119	£150	£20	–
Other Lieutenants	£119	–	£20	–
Surgeons	According to Service		£20	
Pursers	£91	£75	£20	–

There was also a hidden allowance, as it were, for persistence because it was apparent that at sometime in the preceding years Captain McCulloch had finally persuaded the Navy Board to give him exemption from rates and taxes on his naval quarters in Deal!

The original proposals for the 'Suppression of Smuggling between North Foreland and Dungeness' were made by McCulloch in March 1817. This chapter has covered his work over the next eight years to first establish the initial Line then extend it to East Swale and Cuckmere Haven and finally to Sheerness and Chichester Harbour. But that was only part of the story because every week, sometimes for days on end, he was also conducting a war against the smuggling gangs who tried frequently, and sometimes successfully, to fight their way through the Line. The next chapter goes back to 1817 to start an account of that war.

CHAPTER FOUR

McCulloch's War, 1817–25

From the autumn of 1817 the new Blockade Service took over preventive stations and any other buildings made available as the Line extended west to Dungeness, but progress was slow at times; some Parties were still in temporary quarters by 1819. Around Deal smuggling continued unabated at first as local gangs fought to keep their long-held dominance of the beaches. In one favourite ploy women and children on the beach would throw a barrage of stones to try to hold the naval men at bay whilst a run was taking place.

But it was not just a matter of catching smugglers – it was going to be difficult holding them pending prosecution, particularly once Captain McCulloch was told he could not simply press the healthy ones into the Navy without trial. In those early years many magistrates would not agree to prisoners being held in irons aboard *Severn*. In September 1817 McCulloch talked with the local Collector of Customs and found the problem was not new. On 27 June 1816 for example one smuggler, George Gard, escaped from the guard house of the 39th Regiment at North End and on 8 August another named Foreman was snatched from an escort of soldiers and Customs men. In each instance a mob of 300 or more, mainly women and children, had arrived and closed in so quickly that firearms could not be used.

Amidst this atmosphere of tension and intimidation one early psychological success for McCulloch came on 6 July 1817 following the routine seizure by his men of a smuggling galley. The craft was handed over to the Excise and placed in their boathouse but that night the smugglers broke in and took the boat away. They saw it as a fine opportunity to cock a snoot at McCulloch and his men but his reply was swift. Next morning, with the help of both Customs and Excise, he ordered a search of the whole town and had some of his boats patrolling off shore to prevent escape by sea. Even then the missing boat was not found but three others were seized because two had false bottoms and a third concealed dry goods and three kegs of spirits! Their owners were livid with the men who had stirred up the trouble and next morning the missing boat re-appeared, close by the Excise boathouse.

Although Deal was at the centre of the smuggling war in the first few years of the Blockade, the Deal luggers were quite accustomed to operating elsewhere. On 12 August 1817 Midshipman Doulton and his men at the Broadstairs Station saw the *Hope* of Deal attempting to land some tubs and gave chase in their galley. They caught and seized her at Margate, with the cargo of 105 tubs, but the crew of four escaped by running into the crowd of over two hundred that had gathered on the beach.

In October came news from Boulogne that seven galleys were waiting to be towed over by the Deal luggers *Ox*, *Po*, and *Salus* who were regularly working the North Kent coast between Marsh Bay and Reculver. The galleys would be used as 'tub boats' and towed behind a lugger, both craft being loaded with tubs of spirits. Close to the English coast the tub boat would be passed over to the locals to manoeuvre ashore whilst the lugger made a landing elsewhere.

Sometimes the Deal luggers carried gold coin over to France to pay for the large and frequent supplies of contraband. Captain McCulloch had specific information on one occasion that the *Nancy* and *Ox* were taking gold but they sailed in an easterly gale which prevented his galleys from overtaking them. As a longstop he had sent a revenue cruiser to patrol off Calais but it failed to intercept.

Smuggling vessels seized by the Blockade Service had to be handed over to the Customs for disposal; technically they were then the property of the Crown. Galleys over 28ft long were usually burnt and any vessel with extensive secret compartments was cut into three but otherwise the lugger or cutter found just carrying a cargo of contraband was seized and sold to the highest bidder. It was an unwritten rule amongst local boat owners that no one bid for another's boat and so invariably it was sold back to the original owner for a trivial sum! Records show repeated seizures of the same craft. The *Po* for example, already mentioned, was seized off Ramsgate on 20 July 1817 with 14 tubs and off Margate on 3 September with 74 tubs. In later years she still featured in Blockade seizures.

The antagonism against the Blockade Service in and around Deal came not only from smugglers, it was also apparent in the reactions of local magistrates and parish constables. By way of some background explanation Captain McCulloch identified 'an ale house called Good Intent, north of the town near Sandown Castle as a centre for the convenience and accommodation of smugglers, where they can arrange operations and make signals by day and night to boats in the offing. Mr Iggulsden, Magistrate, is also principal brewer in the district and so has a strong interest in keeping Good Intent in trade'.

The last few months of 1817 brought a series of vicious incidents that showed only too well the extent of this local opposition. Mates John Robilliard and David Peat, recently promoted, were in charge of Parties at North End Watch House. On 11 October John Robilliard and his men attempted to search the lugger *Belsey* as she beached but an angry mob gathered and retreated only when he cocked his pistols. On 17 October David Peat and his men went to search another lugger but were blocked by some 80 men. Peat was knocked down when the mob tried to corner his men and turn the boat over on top of them. He struggled to his feet and drawing pistol and cutlass stood back to back with seaman James Cavanagh telling the ringleader to desist otherwise 'I will cut you down'. The mob retreated with threats to murder Peat 'you bloody Scotch robber'.

On Deal beach a galley lies in the centre with a lugger in the background.
Dover Museum

Those threats materialised on 17 November around 9.15pm when Peat was making his rounds to inspect his men in the south end of Deal. Walking alone near the 'Hoop and Griffin' Inn he was suddenly attacked by one man and took a hard blow from a stick that broke across his head. Eight others rushed him but he was able to fire his pistol and they ran off. Two sentinels then arrived as did a parish constable who told Peat that by firing the pistol he had disturbed the peace and would be reported to the Mayor, Mr Iggulsden! Further attempts on Peat's life, at least in Deal, were thwarted when seven days later he was promoted to Lieutenant and left the Blockade Service. However, Captain McCulloch valued this officer too highly to let him disappear into general service and when the opportunity arose, in June 1818, David Peat came back to serve at Dungeness.

John Robilliard did not fare so lightly with the parish constable. On 28 December 1817 he sent a note to McCulloch headed 'From Deal Gaol' explaining that the previous night he and Mate Arguinhau found three men near Deal shore each carrying a tub in a sack. During the fight and chase Robilliard was knocked to the ground three times by a tub-filled sack before he could draw a cutlass and cut his assailant on the shoulder. The smugglers attacked again threatening murder so he fired his pistol, but missed. The attackers ran off and fetched the parish constable who promptly arrested the two Mates on charges of wounding and breach of the peace and marched them off to Deal Gaol! Three days later they appeared before magistrates Iggulsden and Mercer; bail was refused and the two sent back to gaol until bail was obtained eventually in the High Court by the Admiralty. Both men were acquitted of all charges at Maidstone Assizes on 11 January 1818 and , in a gesture that emphasised the Navy's support for their conduct, both were made Lieutenants that April.

When the case was over Robilliard reported that whilst he and Arguinhau were in prison at Deal all doors were locked. But other inmates told him that before his arrival the doors were never locked between 7am and 9pm; prisoners could come and go as they please. After his release the prison returned to its old ways and Robilliard recognised some men, who he knew to be prisoners, spending their evenings drinking gin in the Black Horse, a nearby inn.

Will Worthington, a well known local scoundrel, was one of those who had fought Robilliard and Arguinhau and later gave evidence against them before the magistrates. Looking for some way to vent his frustration at the release of the two Mates Worthington and four others cornered James Taverner, a Blockade petty officer, in a Deal shop and beat him up saying 'if we had your Captain, that bloody Scotch bugger, he would get the same'.

In contrast to the violence around Deal at this time the smugglers in Sussex, just beyond the western end of the Blockade Line found conditions much more peaceful. In September 1817 a correspondent to the *Times* wrote 'it is surprising to what extent smuggling is carried on along the Sussex coast. A few days ago I saw no less that eleven boats employed removing goods in broad daylight near Hastings and not a soul appeared to molest them.. They were all French vessels whose crew I am informed are particularly expert in these fraudulent expeditions'. This part of the coast was supposed to be patrolled by the Preventive Waterguard under direct Treasury management and it was reports such as this that persuaded the Prime Minister, late in 1817, to extend the Navy's Coast Blockade Line, with all possible speed, westward from Dungeness to Cuckmere Haven.

The Blockade Line as far as Dungeness was still creating problems in the summer of 1818 because, despite the agreements with Captain Hanchett, there were delays in taking over some stations. Captain McCulloch received information about a run into Dymchurch on 6 August 1818 and Bosun John Bias took a Blockade galley out on patrol. Soon he spotted a long white galley well laden and heading for shore. As he got near, the preventive boat from Brockman's Barn came out and moved close to the smuggler's galley. The preventive men shouted 'Keep off, its the Severn's boat' whereupon the smugglers landed on the beach and ran away. The next day Captains McCulloch and Hanchett met at Brockman's Barn 'to discuss the incident and make a full investigation'.

Charles Newton now a Masters Mate was given command of *Flying Fish* for a while in 1818 and no doubt welcomed the chance to have a change of action and to get some sea time. He and his crew boarded some French fishing boats off Margate and on one they found an excessive amount of geneva stored in glass jars. He seized eleven gallons but, alas, that was reduced to three when two of the jars broke on board the tender. Undeterred his men boarded another fishing boat and seized an excessive quantity of brandy, also in glass jars. This they handled very carefully because there was no telling what a mixture of gin and brandy would do to the bilges of the tender!

With such tension and violence around Deal it was not surprising that the first murder of a Blockade man occurred there. This came about on 20

October 1818 when local Customs officers obtained warrants in London to arrest two Deal hovellers for smuggling. They were known to be in the King's Arms at Deal and Blockade officers agreed to provide assistance. Six armed naval seamen were quietly posted around the inn but before the Customs officers could enter the wanted duo were tipped off and ran out. One of the seamen, John Nelson, barred their way and was shot dead as the pair came out of a door. They made good their escape by crossing to Calais the next day but then came back to Ramsgate. The murderer was identified by several witnesses as William Dowers, but the Mayor of Deal refused Captain McCulloch's request for a warrant because although he had every desire to do so he was afraid of the wrath of the locals 'several had extolled the murder openly'. McCulloch controlling his rage – at least on paper – arranged for a Bow Street warrant to be issued, but information then reached him that Dowers had probably boarded an American merchantman that had just left Ramsgate.

Further tragedy came in the evening of 26 November 1818 when a Blockade galley with a Midshipman and nine men was lost on patrol in Eastware Bay, between Dover and Folkestone. It was last seen at about 4pm one mile east of Eastware Watch House in little wind and when the wreckage was later recovered and examined there were indications that the galley had been run down by a larger vessel. At Appendix F is an extract from 'A Naval Sketch Book', written by Captain W.N. Glascock R.N. in 1832, which gives a fine, descriptive account of a Blockade galley's patrol that also ended in tragedy.

Throughout 1818 there were incidents around Deal involving attacks on Blockade men as the locals fought in vain to intimidate their naval opponents and restore the good old days of domination and anarchy. Captain McCulloch knew this was one contest, right in the neighbourhood of his headquarters, that he had to win. As he explained 'all the information indicates the locals are determined to resist the system of Blockade'; some accounts say he vowed to make grass grow in the streets of Deal.

There was no particular time at which he claimed to have won because it was a process of attrition but a letter received on 8 August 1819 from the Reverend M. Pennington of Deal gives an insight into the changes that had taken place by then in the town. The letter accompanied a memorial (or petition) from local boat owners and boatmen to the Admiralty asking that the Dover pilot cutters cruising in the Channel be withdrawn in favour of the old practice of using Deal boats to ferry the pilots to and from calling merchantmen. Captain McCulloch forwarded the papers to his Vice Admiral with a covering note 'the system for prevention of smuggling has certainly deprived the greater proportion of the inhabitants of their usual means of subsistence. They supported themselves entirely by that traffic. 300 or more are receiving charitable aid but the greater number are reduced to selling or pledging boats and house furniture. Many who enjoyed comfortable, well furnished houses are now reduced to being unable to pay rent and parish taxes. A great many wish to return to the old ways of carrying pilots out to ships in the Downs but are prevented by the cruising pilot vessels. Local men are not even able to repair their boats but they are invaluable in time of shipwreck when cruising pilot boats are useless'. Captain McCulloch added that he had consulted ship owners and Lloyds agents and all wanted to see the suppression of cruising pilots 'they charge a fare which the Deal boatmen should have. . . I recommend the prayer of these petitioners for favourable consideration'.

It seems neither the Admiralty nor the pilotage authorities took any action over this plea, probably because the Dover pilot cutters provided a better service. Nevertheless McCulloch's comments do show that he still had some concern for the plight of his erstwhile enemies – if they kept within the law. A few months later he supported another petition from the fishermen of Folkestone who complained that during the mackerel and herring seasons upwards of 100 French fishing boats sold their catches at reduced prices just off shore 'by which means your petitioners are very much injured . . . the French invariably refuse to allow English vessels to carry fish into their ports'. A good, early example of the French version of a common market!

Local opposition to McCulloch's men came not only from smugglers and their sympathisers but also occasionally from riding officers. There was some friction at times until the riding officers in areas behind the Line were withdrawn in 1822. At Deal Tom Hampstead, Captain of the Top, seized a smuggler's boat after the three crew had run off. He was on the beach unloading the tubs of spirits when a mounted party of two riding officers and two dragoons arrived. Without making any challenge or shout of enquiry a riding officer named Grasely promptly ordered the party to open fire. Fortunately only one pistol out of four went off and that missed Hampstead who yelled repeatedly that the boat and tubs were seized already. Grasely insisted he was the only one empowered to seize anything. When Midshipman Doveton joined the heated argument Grasely suggested a joint seizure but Doveton, signalling up some sentinels said 'Begone', or naval words to that effect, and the mounted men withdrew to vent their exasperation elsewhere.

As is often the case, these local conflicts between the naval men and riding officers usually arose from a clash of personalities. There was good co-operation at Rye Harbour when George Haffle tried unsuccessfully to

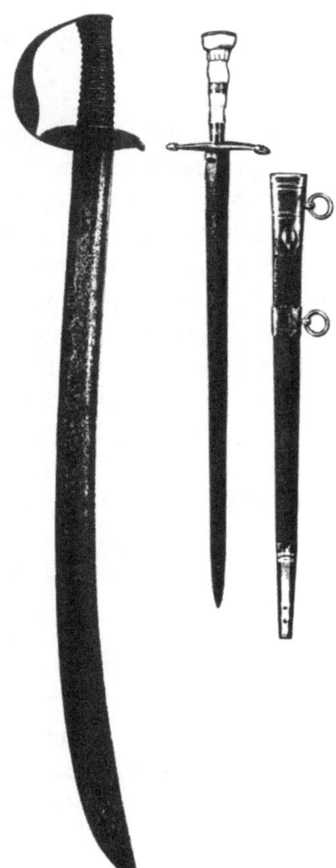

A naval pattern cutlass and a midshipman's dirk.

bribe two sentinels and in the follow-up operation Midshipman Henry Haddy with four of his men worked with Mr Burns, a riding officer and two dragoons. They caught Haffle and John Russell landing contraband in the sandhills east of the Harbour and seized 56 tubs of spirits, 6 packs of tea and a parcel of French paper. At the magistrates court in Winchelsea Russell was fined £100 and Haffle went to prison.

Similar co-operation was well and truly absent a few months later near Bexhill. Mr Bennett, Inspector of riding officers, and two dragoons held off when they saw Midshipmen Fitzgerald and Dyball and a few sentinels being attacked and clubbed by a large body of smugglers. In the flurry of complaints and reports that followed Mr Bennett said the two Midshipmen were drunk and furthermore 'riding officers in Hastings and Bexhill do consider themselves in danger whenever they fall in with a party of the Coast Blockade in making a seizure because they fire away in all directions'. Captain McCulloch, then at Bexhill, noted coldly that not a shot was fired in this action either by the Blockade or the riding officers and their dragoons. In the same report McCulloch also described 'the prevailing practice on the coast of Sussex where gangs who come down to carry off cargo consist of 150 to 200 men who run with 2, 3 and frequently 4 half ankers each. Even when . . . discovered and attacked yet by dispersing and running off in all directions they seldom lose more than 40 or 50 half ankers out of a cargo of perhaps 400. The most effective method is to prevent those men assembling in companies'. One such gang was frustrated near Pevensey Sluice on 5 March 1819 when Lieutenant Collins and five sentinels beat them off to seize a boat and its cargo; the local newspaper reported that John Aston, seaman, had been badly beaten in the attack.

On one occasion a potential conflict ended in pure farce. Without naming the date or locality, probably because he was too embarrassed, a Divisional Lieutenant sought the advice of the Commissioners of Customs about an incident where the smugglers, carrying tubs, were being chased by Blockade men. In imminent danger of capture the smugglers stopped suddenly, turned to their pursuers and said 'these are contraband goods and we claim the reward!' The Blockade men were nonplussed – this was completely new and unexpected – but the Commissioners advised that, if it happened again, the boat and goods were to be detained pending their consideration. Much to the Lieutenant's relief, there was no evidence that this became a popular ploy.

As the violence against Blockade men decreased around Deal so it increased elsewhere on the Line as local gangs fought against the incursion of this new naval force. Lieutenant David Peat at Dungeness was in action frequently during the summer of 1819 and one seizure resulted in four smugglers being convicted by Mr B. Cobb, magistrate at Lydd. In his subsequent letter to the Admiralty, Mr Cobb explained that on 13 August 1819 the four convicted men were to be taken by cart from the Court to Dungeness for examination by a naval surgeon before transfer to H.M.S *Severn*. Fearing trouble he requested an escort and Lieutenant Peat, together with three of his men, walked alongside the cart as it left Lydd. They were soon surrounded by an angry mob and one of the prisoners, George

Walker, jumped down and ran off chased at first by Mr Cobb. David Peat overtook him and reached Walker only to be surrounded and attacked by the mob throwing stones. Mr Cobb cried 'Secure your prisoner' and Peat, with sword drawn, held Walker shouting to the mob 'if you attempt a rescue I'll run him through'. But the mob still surged forward and so he executed his threat. The wounded man died a few hours later and the subsequent coroner's inquest recorded a verdict of 'self defence'. Mr Cobb ended his letter by noting that the dead man had been a sailing captain to the desperate Brooklands gang.

Three days after the incident at Lydd a much more serious happening took place in Manchester that would have wide repercussions in a Britain still racked by disorder and economic distress. Thousands of men, women and children from the cotton working districts had gathered peacefully at St Peters Fields to hear a popular speaker. Local magistrates, alarmed at the size of the crowd, sent mounted yeomanry in to arrest the orator but this proved difficult and the regular cavalry, already held in reserve, were ordered to charge. Eleven people died, including two women, and well over 300 were wounded in a tragedy that quickly became known as the Peterloo massacre. Across the industrial North and Midlands the crisis created by Peterloo brought more tension and unrest as workers sought revenge. In Kent and Sussex the impact was less because many folk were unemployed and destitute; they did not even have the luxury of bad working conditions. Even so the memory of Peterloo would be in the minds of many whenever armed servicemen, including those in the Blockade, were called to deal with a rioting mob.

Around this time the problems of bribery were once again never far from McCulloch's mind. At one point he noted proudly that two sentinels had refused bribes of £2 each to allow 16 tubs to be landed but later was deploring an instance where another had accepted 9s to allow 250 tubs to come ashore. Both the Captain and his superiors at the Admiralty saw the payment of seizure rewards as a good counter to bribery, but one problem was the inordinate delay by Customs in making payments. At one point McCulloch told his Rear Admiral that local arrangements had been made to give instant rewards varying from 3s 8d to 2s 0d per half anker, depending upon the circumstances, but this did not become a permanent plan.

Another problem seems to have been the confusion in Admiralty regulations over just how the rewards were to be apportioned because those rules became so detailed and confused they ended up as the opposite of the original intention! An Order in Council, signed by King George in 1819, gave revised arrangements for rewards paid in the Royal Navy for revenue seizures made afloat and decreed they should be divided three quarters to the person(s) making the arrest and one quarter to the officer present. But those new 'afloat' rules did not apply to the Blockade Service on shore and in March 1820 McCulloch was still protesting about the anomalies of the old rules '. . . the shares of Warrant Officers, Chaplins and subalterns of marines (who take no part whatever in the executive duties of the Blockade) are greater than the Lieutenants superintending Divisions. Midshipmen are classed as petty officers. Certain Midshipmen should be classed as Mates to give them better seizure rates and a command structure more in line with H.M. Ships'. Twelve days later, no doubt in response to a prompt from John Croker, Captain McCulloch submitted a list of 24 Midshipmen recommended for promotion to Mates.

The Admiralty also paid heed to McCulloch's request for revised arrangements on seizure rewards in the Blockade Service, but it was not until 5 May 1821 that His Majesty signed another Order in Council designed to cater specifically '. . . as an encouragement to the Parties of the Coast Blockade who are stationed on shore in giving the whole of the Reward for the arrest of smugglers to the individuals actually present and engaged therein . . .'.

Alas! – the confusion continued because the legal draftsmen had now created a situation where if a Blockade man made a seizure *afloat* '. . . perhaps in a Boat lying close to the shore . . .' (and many were taken that way) he only received a nominal sum for his exertions! '. . . it appears from the manner in which it is expressed to have an operation at variance with its intention . . .'. Oh dear! There were many red faces at the Admiralty and whilst there were no official comments on record from McCulloch his private feelings may be judged with some accuracy! Once again the remedy would take some time to accomplish and it was not until 31 January 1823 'At the Court at Brighton' that His Majesty signed yet another Order in Council for 'rewards for all arrests and seizures . . . whether the same shall be made on land or on the water . . .'.

Almost every year there was some accidental loss of life in the Blockade Service. On 21 January 1819 Midshipman Edward Lampen was drowned in Folkestone Harbour and on 3 April 1820 a Blockade galley on passage from Hastings to Dungeness overturned off Rye drowning the occupants, four Blockade men and a wife; their bodies were interred at Winchelsea.

The circumstances leading to the death of Sentinel Sam Atwell on 9 March 1820 near Cock Point at Folkestone were more dubious. Midshipman Lundy Dickenson saw six men armed with clubs in the vicinity of Bakers Gap but they ran away as he approached. Nearby he found three tubs and then came across the dead body of Atwell, at the foot of the cliff, still warm with a badly fractured skull. Atwell might have fallen 40 feet onto the beach, but Dickenson had his doubts.

By 1820 the Blockade had become consolidated along the coast from East Swale and Cuckmere Haven but the strength of the Line waxed and waned at times. Men would be drafted away to H.M. ships leaving stations undermanned whilst fresh intakes were recruited. Successes against smuggling varied, some attempts were beaten off completely, some resulted in seizures with, typically, the capture of 20 to 50 tubs and three to six men. Now and then a large gang, well protected by flanks of batmen, would make a determined landing. Captain McCulloch was at Rye in November 1819 when, after one such brutal fight, his men captured a large number of bludgeons, as he called them. Next morning he had three bludgeons packaged and despatched by coach to the Lords of the Admiralty with a covering note to say '. . . their Lordships would wish to see what our Parties have to contend with when gangs of 100 to 200 are so armed'.

Having caught the smugglers it was proving even more difficult to hold them in gaols at various points along the Line. On 11 May 1820 the Captain wrote 'As I expected the escape of smugglers from prisons belonging to the several corporations along the coast has absolutely become a matter of course and the more aggravated their offences may be the evasion of the penalties is more certain'. Four had overpowered the jailer at Rye Prison and two had simply walked out of Lydd Gaol. But the worst escape came some days later at Dover on 26 May 1820.

A galley from the revenue cruiser *Lively*, still under the command of Lieutenant 'Hellfire Bill' Lilburn, had caught eleven Folkestone men trying to land goods in Eastware Bay and ten were sentenced at Dover on 24 May to five years in the Navy. They were in Dover Gaol for two nights under an armed guard provided by Lilburn and 18 of his men pending transfer by Blockade tender to Chatham. Next day the jailer heard an escape was planned and told Lieutenant Philip Graham. He offered to augment the guard but the Mayor, Sir Thomas Mantell, declined saying such precaution was unwise and unnecessary.

At 11am on 26 May Lieutenant Graham arrived with two other officers and 20 armed seamen to join Lilburn's unit and form a strong escort for the prisoners down to the harbour. Guarding the main doors of the gaol were a sergeant and 30 privates of the 84th Regiment.

An angry crowd of around 1,000 had gathered near the prison entrance and all nearby shops were closed. As the gaol doors opened the appearance of the party of prisoners and Lilburn's escort immediately brought shouts of 'Liberty for ever' and a furious barrage of stones from mob. The party, and the soldiers, ran back into the gaol and closed the doors leaving Graham and his men isolated outside. He shouted to the mayor, who was inside, to read the Riot Act but was told this was unnecessary.

Dover Town Gaol c. *1822*. – Dover Museum

When some of the mob started to attack the fabric of the prison wall his worship was persuaded to send for a copy of the Act – but it could not be found! He appeared at a window and read something from a book but some in the crowd yelled 'thats not the Riot Act – we want the Riot Act'. By now a large hole had been made in the wall and ten smugglers, plus a few other prisoners, all in leg-irons, shuffled through with the help of their friends in the waiting crowd. Both Blockade parties, inside and outside, advanced with muskets at the ready but the mayor, remembering Peterloo, shouted to them not to open fire.

All the prisoners made good their escape and were taken to blacksmiths to have the leg-irons removed before disappearing into hideaways and safe houses. The *Times* report on the riot said the mob included the smugglers ten wives and forty children. One of the leaders of the riot was caught almost immediately and handcuffed to two parish constables but they in turn were held by the mob until someone fetched a hammer and chisel to effect separation and another escape.

The escape and the attendant publicity was a spectacular success for the smugglers but along the coast there were signs here and there that after three years the Naval Blockade, as an ever present barrier, was having some effect on the Trade. As an alternative to open runs and violent fights some smugglers were now hiding their goods on board vessels, something that would grow steadily in popularity over the next ten years. This Blockade report was a typical example: 'Deal, 22 May 1820. Lugger *Active* came on shore at night, was searched but nothing found. A sentry was placed on board and in daylight another search revealed the hollow masts to conceal 20 pieces bandanas and 655 French silk'. Next day, also at Deal the *Snipe* and the *Fly* each had 48 bandanas similarly concealed. Over at Folkestone Midshipman Lundy Dickenson and his men found the lugger *Friends Society* to have a false forecastle and a double deck aft carrying 126 packs of playing cards, 576 lbs tobacco and 14 tin boxes of tea.

By 1820 the mayor, magistrates and parish constables at Folkestone were proving just as hostile to the Blockade as their fellows at Deal. Sentinel James Caverner, stationed at Shorncliff, saw two boats land opposite the National School at Sandgate and bales were passed to some men who ran off. He fired a warning shot without hitting anyone but later one of the men, Edward Hopper of Deal, having delivered his bales returned with a constable to accuse Caverner of shooting with intent to kill. He was arrested and committed for trial to Maidstone Assizes where he was subsequently acquitted, Captain McCulloch noting that 'the magistrates at Folkestone acted with their usual attention to the feelings and wishes of the smuggler'.

On another occasion, after Lieutenant Graham had encountered outright hostility in the Folkestone Court whilst giving evidence, McCulloch complained to the Admiralty of the magistrates '. . . open hostility to the officers and men under my command . . . using insulting language . . .acting as advocates for the smugglers . . .'. As often he could not resist a parting shot '. . . the Mayor of Folkestone, James Major, has two sons-in-law in smuggling cutters that run between Flushing and the coast of Scotland'.

On the same theme of magistrates and their attitude to the many statutes on smuggling, McCulloch drew attention to two apparent ridiculous inconsistencies in Customs law. One Act gave a reward for finding casks of spirits and taking them to the nearest Custom House, whilst another imposed heavy penalties on anyone who conveyed spirits that were to be 'laid on land'. Thus it appeared anyone finding a cask of spirits could either be paid a reward by Customs or prosecuted and fined by a magistrate! As the Captain said 'Any magistrate who is inclined to favour the smuggler, as many are, had an ideal opportunity to do so. One Isle of Thanet magistrate has said he will convict anyone in possession of spirits and asks anyone who finds spirits to leave them there and inform the authorities'.

Although the attention of contemporary newspapers was drawn inevitably to violent fights, there was also a routine and mundane side to Blockade work in the form of small seizures usually of tubs found on the shore or in the water. They were listed in periodic reports to the Admiralty and one taken at random shows: '20 half ankers made fast to Dover Pier; 6 floating in Sandwich Creek; 2 off Dungeness; 12 crept up in Eastware Bay; 4 at Folkestone on rocks under seaweed; 3 found by Rye inhabitant at low water and 1 in possession of Tom Storey, shrimpman'.

During the summer of 1820 McCulloch received disturbing news that servicemen discharged from the Army and Navy were training smugglers into armed parties. No names were forthcoming but in fact two such gangs were formed that year in Kent and both would give vicious accounts of themselves over the next few years. The first to appear was the North Kent Gang with men from Wingham, Ickham and Canterbury which started operating in March 1820, quietly at first around Sheppey and so beyond the Blockade Line. Later that year came the Aldington Gang which drew men from the marshes inland of Dymchurch. In the early years of the Blockade Service officers seldom gave titles to gangs merely referring to, say, 'the men who last attacked the Line on 6 June'. Between 1819 and 1824 Blockade records do not mention the Aldington Gang but there are occasional references to the 'Brooklands Gang' and seeing the villages are only a few miles apart across the marshes it is possible this was the same gang. Whatever name was used this gang quickly made it's mark with a successful landing through the Line near Sandgate on 8 November 1820.

That night Lieutenant David Peat, now in charge of Folkestone District, was making his rounds just west of Sandgate with his orderly, John Green. They saw a flash and ran to the beach to find some 200 men unloading a large boat under the protection of 50 or so armed guards. Peat immediately charged them firing a blunderbuss but was hit by five shots in his thigh. Whilst he was re-loading the nearest Blockade Party, headed by Midshipman James Burton, arrived and together they attacked the armed guards who acted with some semblance of discipline – halting, grouping, and firing in volleys – until the contraband had been unloaded and carried away. David Peat was helped to safety by two riding officers who had just arrived on the scene; two Sentinels, Daniel Sheehan and James Walker, were also wounded. The boat was seized but only five tubs of spirits were found.

The Aldington men made another armed assault on the Line at Romney Warren early on the morning of Christmas Day. Midshipman Tudor was severely wounded and as a result Captain McCulloch went to Romney that day. He stayed until the 29 December and wrote to the Rear Admiral 'it is impossible for me to do justice to the midshipmen here. The very excellent conduct and zeal surpasses anything I have ever witnessed. During the short time I have been here I have been obliged to restrain their exertions in the preservation of their health'. This action heralded the start of what would prove to be the six worst months during McCulloch's time with the Coast Blockade Service.

The next large scale attack on the Blockade Line, probably by a local gang, was at Langley Point near Eastbourne on 8 February 1821 but this was beaten off by three Parties led by Lieutenants Chappell and Sweny and nothing was landed. Records show Sentinel James Leith died in action on this day and although the place is not given it is possible that he was killed in this fight.

Three days later came another attack by the Aldington Gang, in what became known later as the Battle of Brookland. This time the gang arranged a landing just east of Camber again assembling a working party of some 200 tub carriers protected by about 50 armed men. The alarm was given when a sentinel saw them gathering and his pistol shot brought out the watches from nearby stations led by Mates Newton and McKenzie and Midshipmen Digby and Jones. The revenue cruiser *Rose* had been in the offing and she also sent some men to assist. Once again the gang held off the Blockade men until the cargo was landed but this time there were more naval officers and men.

The armed guards fought fiercely and with some discipline to cover the rear of the gang as it dispersed with loaded horses and carts across the flats and through the ditches of a wintry Walland Marsh. With muskets, pistols and swords the four officers led their men in repeated attacks as the fight rolled inland towards the village of Brookland. James McKenzie, bleeding from gunshot wounds, wandered off in a daze until he dropped dead some hours later about one mile from Brookland. The other three officers were all wounded as were three of their men and three from the *Rose*, including a deputed mariner. Four smugglers were killed, sixteen carried off wounded and two captured in what had been the bloodiest fight in the short history of the Blockade Service. Blockade men and smugglers were treated alike by Dr Ralph Papworth Hougham, the surgeon of Brookland, who lived in Pear Tree House.

In the midst of the fight, Cephas Quested, the leader of the Aldington men mistook Charles Newton for one of the gang and passed him a musket urging 'take this and blow some bloody officer's brains out'. Quested and Richard Wraight, said by Captain McCulloch to be 'principals in several attacks on our parties on 8 November and 25 December', were captured and taken for trial in London. Wraight swore he was out shooting rooks at the time and had lost his way before wandering innocently into the battle. It was a feeble defence but the London jury was persuaded and he was

Revenue cutter Vigilant *towing her prize into port* – Alan Hay

acquitted. Cephas Quested was convicted and hanged on 4 July 1821 having been caught red-handed and , as McCulloch noted, 'from his own stupidity, something I am reliably informed will not happen again with those men'. His report concluded 'The gallantry and address displayed by officers on this occasion against a force in all respects superior . . . so far surpasses anything of the kind I have met with on this Service'.

All three surviving Blockade officers were promoted after distinguishing themselves in the Brookland fight. Charles Newton, who had spent three hectic years in the Blockade Service since those early days and nights around Deal, was promoted to Lieutenant and transferred to sea duties. Midshipmen Digby and Jones became Masters Mates and stayed with the Blockade Service for several more years.

A few weeks after the Brookland episode Captain McCulloch had to switch his attention to a flare-up at Hastings where sentinels were often trying to check perhaps 50 or 60 fishing boats as they returned to the beach. The fishermen wanted any searches to be done whilst the vessels were still off the shore waiting to be hauled up but it was a slow process going from boat to boat and the Blockade men preferred to go on board once the vessels were drawn up on the beach.

On the morning of 15 March Sentinel George England wanted to search a boat whilst it was being hauled up but the owner, Joseph Swaine, who was busy keeping her upright during the winching told England to wait until she was stopped and properly secured. When the sentinel ignored the request and climbed aboard there was a scuffle during which his cutlass was knocked out of his hand. The fight then moved on to the beach where England drew a pistol that was grabbed by Swaine and in the continuing struggle a shot was fired killing him instantly. A furious crowd of fishermen promptly cornered England intent upon murdering him but he held them off until a strong force of Blockade men and some cavalry came to his rescue.

George England was arrested and tried for murder at Horsham Assizes on 28 March 1821. The prosecution alleged cold blooded, wilful murder and produced nine Hastings fishermen as witnesses. The defence said it was an accident and there were five Blockade men to testify that the pistol went off accidentally when Swaine suddenly released his hold on it. The judge summed up in England's favour but the jury found him guilty. As the judge duly passed the sentence of death a distraught England protested over and over again that it was an accident. He was due to be hanged the following week but to the fury of many in Hastings and Horsham the execution was stayed pending an appeal for a Royal Pardon. On 8 April Captain McCulloch wrote to the Keeper of Horsham Gaol advising him that 'George England has been recommended to his Majesty for a free pardon. On release he is to be ordered to go directly to the Admiralty in London and not return to Hastings'. England was discharged from the Navy and presumably kept well clear of Hastings for the rest of his life.

The day Swaine was killed Lieutenant Mark Sweny, then in charge of Right Division and based at Hastings, reported the incident to Captain McCulloch and ended with an urgent plea '. . . the inhabitants threaten us with vengeance and I much fear that without the most active interference by the magistrates many lives will be lost . . . so circumstanced I feel how much I stand in need of your instructions and, if your multifarious duties and health would admit, your presence'. The Captain paid an immediate visit and made several more over the next few weeks during which time the local fishermen wrote to Lord Liverpool, Prime Minister, complaining about the intensive searches of their boats.

Politically the Swaine incident served to turn a spotlight on to the continuing fights and antagonism between the Blockade Service and the people along the coast. Mr Curteis, a Sussex M.P. put down a motion in the House of Commons asking that a return be made 'of all inquests which have been taken on the bodies of all persons who have lost their lives since the institution of the Coast Blockade and Preventive Boat system, by reason of any circumstances arising from or connected with smuggling, or the Protection of the Public Revenue'. The motion also called for a list of the men wounded or killed in the course of their duties with the Coast Blockade. The government did not supply these statistics and although several M.Ps pressed again for a drastic reduction in duties as the solution to this mayhem the matter petered out in Parliament after a few weeks. After McCulloch met Mr Milward, Mayor of Hastings and several deputation's of fishermen the heated atmosphere in the town cooled gradually although there was some underlying tension in the area for many months.

In his urgent note to McCulloch Lieutenant Sweny had mentioned '. . . if your . . . health would admit . . .' and this seems to indicate that the Captain's chest illness was already causing him trouble some four years before his death.

There was an armed fight, without casualties, at Tower 18 near Hythe on 21 April 1821 between Blockade men and about 100 smugglers when a boat and 48 tubs were taken. Apart from this, the action in April was mainly on the north coast of Kent when instead of direct confrontation the North Kent Gang tried a new ploy to overcome a sentinel before he could raise the alarm. On 16 April one of the gang, dressed as a Blockade man, strode boldly up to a sentinel at White Posts near St Nicholas with a letter which he said was for immediate service to Lieutenant Tilley in the next Blockade Station at Reculver. As the sentinel walked over to deliver the letter he was seized, disarmed and bound by a large group of men who had hidden behind a bank. Fortunately the assault was seen by two men of the St Nicholas Party who fired their pistols as alarms to bring out their own men and the Reculver Party. The frustrated smugglers made off across the marshes firing long duck guns; some split off and ran quickly over to the Reculver Watch House hoping to ambush Lieutenant Tilley and his men as they came out. If they had succeeded there would have been some deaths that night for sure, but fortunately the gang were too late and found 'only the women belonging to the Party in their quarters'.

The night of 24 April 1821 was full of tragedy for the Blockade Service. At Hythe a Party under Lieutenant Turner became involved in a running fight with armed smugglers which led eventually to a bout of intensive firing by a bridge over the Military Canal. Turner was hit in the leg, chest and head and James Bond, seaman, in the chin, leg and thigh before Quartermaster Alexander Steward arrived with more men and drove the smugglers off. As Captain McCulloch reported later to his Rear Admiral 'I was on the point of leaving Deal early that morning to see Lieutenant Turner and his men at Hythe when I received the report of the dreadful injuries to Midshipman Snow at Herne Bay'.

At about 2.30 that same morning Midshipman Sydenham Snow of the Herne Bay Station had seen a boat standing towards Bishopton. He went to fetch Quartermaster David North and some Blockade men in Herne Bay village but before he reached there some 30 armed smugglers from the North Kent Gang ambushed him and brought him down with a musket ball in his left thigh. The shot brought out David North and his men but they were on the opposite flank of the gang and unable to reach the wounded 'Midi'. Limping badly and losing blood rapidly Snow drew his pistols to fire but they both snapped. Tossing them aside he drew his sword and dirk and charged his attackers only to be hit again, this time in the left shoulder. The gang made off but Sentinel Jeremiah Crawley of the Bishopton Party, hearing the noise, came running over and fired at four of them wounding one.

Within twenty minutes of the attack on Snow there were 60 officers and men hunting for the gang, but no one was found. Snow was carried to the nearby Ship public house where, in great agony, he was attended by a Blockade Surgeon day and night until his death came at 8.30am on 27 April. That day, reporting the sad loss to the Admiralty, Captain McCulloch said 'we have lost an officer who was in every respect an ornament to his profession'. A spirited and courageous young officer, Sydenham Snow died in this 24th year and lies buried in Herne churchyard.

Before he died Snow made a statement to the magistrates and this gave enough evidence for the arrest of five men. Written statements also came from David North and his men and from three smugglers who turned King's evidence. When the trial was held at the Old Bailey on 9 June despite the seemingly weighty evidence against them all five smugglers were acquitted. A Blockade officer who attended the trial reported '. . . owing to the great levity of the judge the men were acquitted upon the ground of some slight deficiency of evidence . . .'. Normally the eternal optimist, the verdict brought McCulloch down to a rare moment of despair when, as he told the Rear Admiral, '. . . this will be acclaimed amongst all the communities . . . where men carry out these activities . . . whenever they determine to disregard the laws and cease to dread the verdict of a jury we have no force to withstand them . . .'.

The despair soon passed because the Captain was already attending to reports and papers about another vicious attack that had occurred two days before the trial. May had been a quiet month for smuggling; too quiet for McCulloch. Looking at his tide tables the wily Captain made a few calculations and came up with an accurate forecast, the outcome of which is detailed in his report to Rear Admiral Sir John Gore from Folkestone on 7 June 1821:

> The smugglers having desisted from any attempt at landing on this coast for some time I believe it probable they would make a push to bring goods during the first quarter of the Moon when tides would best suit their purpose. I sent reinforcements of 10 men to Folkestone and 15 marines to Hythe on Saturday. I thought west of Dungeness would be the probable spot because of previous attacks . . . and the wind was favourable. I went to Rye at 7 that night and remained on the beach between the harbour and Dungeness until 8am. knowing that zealous and excellent officer Lieutenant Peat would keep vigilant lookout further east.

The Captain did not say why it was necessary for him to be there – perhaps he was temporarily short of officers. More likely it was simply that as a commander he wanted to be where he thought there would be an important fight because this was where the Battle of Brookland had started just four months before and there was the strong possibility he would be fighting the same gang. His report continued:

> At 8am I received a telegraphic message that Lieutenant Peat and his men had been attacked by a large party of armed men at Eastware . . . near Martello 2 Peat and his men found a large body of smugglers assembling. He went close but found they had nothing. They called out keep off and a volley of muskets killed Richard Woolridge, Quartermaster. Peat was wounded, got up but fell again when struck by further shots. Robert Hunter and John Walker, seamen, were also wounded before Midshipman Lascelles and his party arrived from Martello 1 to rescue to four men. Lieutenant Peat was riddled from head to foot with twenty wounds from musket balls, pistols balls and shot. Eight balls have already been extracted. The Surgeon does not at present apprehend danger. This is the second time that Lieutenant Peat has been severely wounded in the gallant support of his duty, he is my chief support in all cases where courage and steady conduct were particularly necessary. I am now deprived of his services on which I could at all times rely and I trust . . . my Lords . . . may consider him deserving of their favour and support. The boat which the smugglers expected did not arrive but . . . will probably make an attempt in the same place tonight and I shall be on the spot myself.

Alas, the gallant McCulloch was deprived of the chance for action on that or any subsequent night because it was quiet for some time after. The Lords of the Admiralty did indeed consider David Peat, then almost 26 years old deserving of their favour and, for his conduct on 7 June 1821, he was advanced to Commander by a commission bearing that date. On 29 July 1822 he was awarded a permanent pension, for his wounds, of £91-5s per year.

It seems highly likely that Peat was recognised by the gang and so the second salvo of shots was intended to finish him. After a period of recovery it no doubt gave him great satisfaction to appear in his Commander's uniform in and around Folkestone so that some of his enemies could see he was again fit and ready for active service. David Peat entered the Blockade Service as a 'Midi' in 1817 and left a Commander in 1821. He remained on sea duties until 1836 when he returned to the coast as an Inspecting Commander in the Coast Guard. Promoted to Captain on 1 January 1847 he achieved flag rank as Rear Admiral on 13 April 1865 at the age of 69.

Late in August 1821 Captain McCulloch was anticipating assaults on the Line at Eastware and Romney and sent out a unit of 60 marines under a Captain R.M. to augment Station Parties. However, the news of the deployment got around and there were only minor skirmishes that month. The next real armed attack came at Marsh Bay on 2 September when about 60 men of the North Kent Gang, gathering for a landing, fought with Midshipman Washington Carr and four sentinels. Carr wounded two men but was cut around the head from his own sword after it was wrenched out of his hand. Tom Cook, seaman, was shot through the thigh and later had to have the ball removed from the lower part of his spine. During the fight a Blockade man recognised one of the gang as James Taylor and called out his name; at this the whole gang took fright and fled.

Fortunately for Captain McCulloch the magistrate's clerk at Margate at the time was John Boys a solicitor who had no sympathy whatever for smugglers. Using the recognition as evidence he arranged for Taylor to be arrested and this led four members of the gang to turn King's evidence. With much help from McCulloch John Boys steadily built up the case against the gang and, as a result a further 17 were arrested and subsequently tried, with Taylor, at Maidstone Assizes in March 1822. All were found guilty and condemned to death but for 14 that was later commuted to transportation for life. The remaining four, Edward Rolfe, John Wilsden, Daniel Tagg and John Meredith were executed at Penenden Heath near Maidstone in the presence of some 40,000 people.

The diligence and zeal of Mr Boys brought praise from Captain McCulloch and the Crown Solicitor – 'his conduct is entirely the reverse of that of many of the professional gentlemen on the coast . . . he has undertaken difficult tasks in dangerous circumstances . . . and was the object of general hatred in the town . . . assaulted and his windows smashed. The successful result is attributable to Mr Boys'. A total of some £500 was distributed as rewards to those informers, officers, constables and Blockade men who took part in the capture of the North Kent Gang.

Stephen Lawrence, described by McCulloch as one of the principals involved in the attack at Marsh Bay, was not taken with the rest and proved to be a very slippery villain. On 10 October 1822 Blockade men at Broadstairs caught two smugglers both of whom were recognised as having taken part in the fight at Marsh Bay. They were tried at Maidstone in December 1822 and sentenced to five years impressment. One was an ex-petty officer from the Blockade Service named Sandland, the other called himself Tom Brown but was identified by the authorities as Stephen Lawrence. In March 1823 Lawrence managed to escape from his ship at Plymouth but on 24 April was re-captured by Lieutenant Bardon and Blockade men at Ramsgate 'after two hours exertion in a very severe struggle'.

Around this period it seems the relationships between the Captain and some Collectors were not at their best. What seemed to be a routine seizure suddenly brought matters to the boil and started one night in September 1823 when the small Dutchman *Friendschap* anchored off Dungeness. She was boarded by Midshipman McTavish and some of his men who first found that, according to the ship's log, she was at that time well out in the Channel! They found 4 tubs of spirits and a further search next morning produced 18lbs of tobacco; the master also admitted he had another six tubs under the cargo of olive oil. McTavish seized the ship and arranged for her to be taken to the Downs where, after quarantine clearance, she was handed over to the Collector of Customs at Dover as a seizure. But he refused to accept the seizure of the vessel because the quantities were trivial! Furthermore, he had the temerity to write '. . . we only have the statements of the seizing officers who, of course, make the most of their story . . . the subject may admit of explanation'.

With an indignant broadside Captain McCulloch fired back – 'the seizing officers in this instance are Mr McTavish and myself! I repel the insinuation! It has given great offence to me and my executive officers! . . . I am obliged to observe that on this and all other occasions these gentlemen consider the officers of this Service as their inferiors and shew every inclination to treat them in all respects as their own subordinate officers'. A raw nerve had obviously been pressed but the autumnal chill in official relations worsened still further when a letter from the Dutch consul was passed from the Collector to McCulloch. This claimed, on behalf of the master of the *Friendschap*, £200 damages for loss of trade and the Captain had no choice but to submit it to the Admiralty seeking 'the protection of their Lordships'.

When the next armed attack came, on 10 November 1821, it was probably made by the Aldington Gang but this time it seems there was a distinct lack of leadership. About 250 of them, again with 50 or so armed guards on the flanks, were unloading tubs from a boat just west of Sandgate Castle when they were attacked by Mate William Lory and his Party. After some intensive fire the smugglers, according to Lory, 'behaved with unusual slackness, many deserting the gang when attacked, running to houses in the town and begging to be taken in'. He believed two were killed and eight wounded. The boat and 34 tubs were seized and a riding officer and some dragoons seized another 170 tubs 'being the remainder of the cargo, some distance inland'.

The now shallow river entrance (above) at Cuckmere Haven (below) where H.M.S. Congo *was moored from 1819 to 1825.*

During the fight Lory was hit by a pistol ball in the stomach and a musket ball through his arm; two of his men, Thomas Clack, Quartermaster, and Robert Bains, seaman, were also wounded. Captain McCulloch commended Lory to their Lordships for his bravery and he was promoted to Lieutenant with a commission dated from that day of action. He had been a Mate in the Blockade Service for three years and a Midshipman for the previous thirteen. Lieutenant Lory took charge of *Congo* and the Cuckmere Station for a year or so but for domestic reasons then asked to be superseded so that he could return to his home in Cornwall. His request was submitted to the Admiralty and granted, but McCulloch was sorry to see him go.

Another tragic and accidental loss of life came on the morning of 3 December 1821 when eight Blockade men landing from *Industry* were drowned after their boat overturned in the heavy surf off Hastings beach.

The Aldington Gang, still rather disorganised, attempted another landing, this time of about 500 tubs, near Romney on 22 December 1821. Midshipmen William Dunnett and William Higginson had seen a vessel hovering off shore; when she made a run on to the beach they ran over and reached her well before the usual reception gang and their armed guards who were slow off the mark. Cutlass in hand Dunnett jumped on board but was wounded twice in fighting the crew and thrown overboard. A wall piece was fired from the bow of the vessel and wounded him again as he waded ashore but, from the beach, Higginson took careful aim and shot dead the bow gunner.

As was usual in such landings, the boat on it's run-in had dropped an anchor secured to a line from the stern so that if danger loomed she could be hauled off by the crew and this they now did – frantically. Grabbing another cutlass Dunnett struggled again through the icy surf attempting to cut the line but was knocked back into the water with a long boathook. Four Blockade Parties led by Midshipmen Cobb, Sheriff, Broman and Miller had arrived just after the main body of smugglers and there was a brief fight before the gang made off. The vessel and it's cargo also got away but, as McCulloch noted proudly, 'Not an article was landed or moved from the boat'. William Dunnett, who had been a Midshipman for 13 years, was commended for his courage and determination and promoted to Mate from the date of this action.

After this attack the Line was quiet for some weeks except for the usual crop of small seizures such as '27 tubs buried in sand at Sandwich; 5 on a raft off Tower 10 and 5 tied to an iron bar at low water off Sandgate'.

There were two substantial attacks in February 1822, one on the 11th and another on the 23rd, both it seems by local men using only bats and no firearms. On the 23rd the assault came early in the morning at Pevensey between Towers 52 and 53 when six men tried to overpower William Tucker before he could give the alarm. They hit him across the face and head but he managed to draw his pistol and shoot one of his attackers dead. Sentinel James Meads ran to Tucker's assistance but he too was badly beaten with bludgeons. Some 250 men had gathered but they made off when Lieutenant Clark and two Parties arrived from the Towers. Captain McCulloch reported that the coroner's inquest on the dead smuggler '. . . justifiable homicide, is welcome and gratifying, this is the second attempt to import a large cargo in this neighbourhood. On the 11inst. about 250 men seized a petty officer and one seaman at Crowlink but when the alarm was raised by another Sentinel the smugglers and their ship made off". Crowlink, one of the more remote dips in the Seven Sisters cliffs between Birling Gap and Cuckmere Haven, had for long been a favourite spot for running contraband. So notorious did it become that some shops in London sold gin labelled 'Genuine Crowlink Hollands' – presumably to provide a degree of authenticity!

The lack of security at Dover Gaol featured again in March 1822. The hole in the wall had been repaired but general security was still a problem. At Deal the three crew of the *Hero* were each sentenced to five years impressment when she was found to have 15 tin cases in her hollow keel each holding a quart of spirits. Pending arrival of the impressment order from the Board of Customs the local magistrates ordered that the men be taken to Dover Gaol but Captain McCulloch explained there had been several escapes from there – could they be held by the Navy in South Barracks at Deal? Courts elsewhere were usually willing to grant such requests but the Deal Bench refused saying it was beyond its jurisdiction.

Being singularly unhelpful the magistrates clerk said if the prisoners escaped from the gaol the government would see the need for a more secure prison! McCulloch then offered to provide a guard of Blockade men inside the gaol and the gaoler agreed but insisted they must not arrive until after dusk. At 2pm that day the three prisoners, under heavy escort, arrived at the gaol but by 3.30pm one of them, Will Goodchild, had assaulted the gaoler and escaped! Thereafter, the turnkey was happy to accept a naval guard around the clock whenever smugglers were held in his gaol although, as the 1820 escape had shown this could not provide complete security.

At the end of each calendar quarter the Vice Admiral, Chatham, sent the Admiralty a return of seizures made under his command which covered revenue cruisers and the Blockade Service as well as men-of-war. That for the Blockade Service in the first quarter of 1822 was typical with 149 separate seizures of mostly small numbers of tubs of spirits, up to 25 at a time, plus 2,625 yards of cambric and 180 of silk. Seventeen vessels were seized in sizes varying from the *Mary* (1/2 ton) to the *Madeline* (30 tons). Thirteen smugglers were ordered to be impressed into the Navy but two escaped before they could be transferred, one from Dover Gaol, the other into a crowd on Dover Pier. The return made no mention of the convicted men not impressed – were they all deemed fit for naval service?

Later that year the Navy Board announced that the Blockade Service had captured more smugglers in 1821 than either the revenue cruisers or other H.M. ships. To mark this success the Board paid special grants totalling £700 for distribution to the 'Commander, officers and men of Severn', probably as a device to help McCulloch in his fight against bribery. He accepted gladly with just one query – 'should the Admiral have a share?' to which the Navy Board replied 'no'.

Apart from bribery there was one other issue that brought constant frustration for Captain McCulloch time and time again up to 1825. At first it was an irritation but later came real trouble. This stemmed from the basic need for all Blockade officers to have powers, under Customs law, to search vessels and to seize both them and any contraband they carried. Commissioned naval officers (Lieutenants and above) engaged on preventive work had full powers under Customs law, but those below this level had to be authorised, or 'deputed', by the Board of Customs. To the intense annoyance of McCulloch and the Admiralty the deputation's given to inferior officers (Mates and Midshipmen) were strictly limited to the power to seize and did not give them the authority to search anything, but goods must be found before they can be seized! All Blockade Stations were commanded by Mates and Midshipmen and as McCulloch protested '. . . the deputed officers cannot seize goods on a ship until they have been discovered! In many cases this may be prevented by resistance!'.

Petty officers and lower ratings only had the power to arrest persons and could neither seize nor search anything unless ordered to do so by a superior who did have the power. All these legal limitations, however, were ignored by pragmatic officers and men during the daily routine of checks and searches. Midshipman McTavish, for example, had no powers to search the *Friendschap* or to so order his men. On another occasion a Quartermaster and 'some rough rude men' searched Lord Darnley's yacht in Dover. When he demanded to know by what right they searched the Quartermaster drew his pistol and said 'Here's my authority'. His Lordship complained to Captain McCulloch and a few weeks later out came the inevitable Blockade Order: 'When asked by what authority they act, petty officers and seamen are not to produce their pistols as their authority'.

The lack of adequate legal powers, particularly for Mates and Midshipmen, made it extremely difficult for the Navy to maintain, within the law, an effective Blockade. Legally any vessel could only be searched on the orders of a Lieutenant and those officers were spread thinly along the coast in charge of Divisions and Districts. There was no indication as to why full powers were denied Mates and Midshipmen. The Board of Customs lacked the legal authority to depute such powers but this could have been easily rectified by a change in Customs law sometime after 1817. Captain McCulloch supported by the Admiralty, repeatedly sought this in the early years of the Blockade, without success. In all probability there was still resentment and hostility in the Treasury and the revenue departments at the manner in which this 'peculiar force' was moving steadily into their domains. Whatever the reason it would have been reasonable to expect the Prime Minister to step in , knock a few administrative heads together and demand corrective action; but it did not happen.

For the first five years of the Blockade there were no problems because ordinary folk were in ignorance and the lack of authority to search could be forgotten once goods were found. But the situation changed in late 1822 when solicitors acting for some Hastings smugglers found this legal weakness in the Navy's control. In the aftermath of the Swaine affair the local fishermen were only too ready to do all they could to make difficulties and with taunts and jeers blocked any attempt to search a boat until a Lieutenant arrived. This at a time when there were just two in the area, one covering the District, the other the Division. During 1823 the matter became even more serious elsewhere along the Line as more and more smugglers took to hiding goods on board their vessels.

With the extensions of the Line in 1824 and the consequent increase to some 128 stations it was obvious the problems over lack of adequate powers to search would rapidly escalate. By now the Admiralty also had seven years experience of exercising naval discipline in this unique campaign with its small and often isolated units of Midshipmen and men. With these two factors very much in mind the bold decision was taken to remove all Midshipmen from stations and replace them with Lieutenants. Previously there were a few Mates and many Midshipmen, now there would be many Lieutenants (14 increased to 114) and a few Mates. It was an expensive decision but once again the Admiralty (essentially Lord Melville, John Croker and John Barrow) had shown it was wholly committed to the Blockade. Following this decision Captain McCulloch produced lists recommending many of his Midshipmen for promotion to Mates; Lundy Dickenson at Folkestone was particularly commended for frequent acts of bravery. Some became Mates in the Blockade Service whilst others went to sea duties. As Appendix C shows, by 1825 Mates were either second in command at large Blockade Stations or in charge of small ones close to Lieutenant posts – but there were no Midshipmen.

Up to January 1822 the revenue cruisers operating in the eastern sector of the English Channel were under the command of Captain McCulloch and he ensured they kept well off the coast so as not to interfere with Blockade work. Any combined operations were co-ordinated by the Blockade's Divisional Lieutenants. But this co-ordination vanished when the control of revenue cruisers was handed back to Customs in February 1822. Their commanders exercised their restored freedom by running close to the coast at night and sending out their boats to intercept smugglers, much to the annoyance of the Blockade men. Two particular culprits were *Cameleon* and *Asp* who even sent their boats occasionally on to the beach causing even more confusion and frustration.

A gang from Hastings took advantage of this discord after one of their number was killed in an abortive landing near Haddocks on 21 December 1822. The following night Sentinel Thomas Williams was near Haddocks Watch House when he saw a white boat approaching the shore. The men on board called out they were from *Cameleon* but in fact they were smugglers who jumped out and seized Williams saying 'you were one of the damned rascals who shot our man. We'll pay you off now but if you don't make a noise you can have part of our landing – make your choice!' Williams swore he would fire a shot even if they then killed him – and he did. The alarm brought Lieutenant Francillon and the rest of the Party to the rescue and the smugglers ran off, but not before they had slashed Williams with eight sword cuts to the head and arms.

Captain McCulloch had already complained of the interference from revenue cruisers and this incident caused him to raise it again. Two cruiser commanders took exception to some of the Captain's pithy comments and in no time an acrimonious exchange of accusations and insults was flying between the two sides each accusing the other of carrying men who colluded regularly with smugglers. All reports and comments passed laboriously through John Croker and a Commissioner for Customs and were still going strong in February 1823.

In the midst of this acrimony one encounter in the Channel served to revive the close co-operation between the revenue cruisers and the Blockade

Smuggling gear that includes a keg, stone weights for sinking, two types of grapnels or creepers and a shuttered lantern.

Service albeit only temporarily. On 14 January 1823 Captain McCulloch reported the arrival in Dover of the revenue cruiser *Badger*, commanded by Lieutenant Henry Nazer, which had captured the armed lugger *Four Brothers* the previous day. The chase and running fight had started some ten miles off Etaples around 7.30am and lasted until 11.30am when the lugger was rammed. Her crew then asked for quarter but no sooner did *Badger* cease firing than the lugger opened up again killing William Cullum, a deputed mariner. On board *Badger* there were also five wounded including Henry Nazer; the lugger had two dead and seven wounded out of a crew of twenty five.

The two vessels had been evenly matched. The *Four Brothers*, 120 tons with ten guns, had been built in Flushing by James Lowes, a native of Kent. The *Badger*, 121 tons with twelve guns, was an Excise cutter from the boatyard of Ransome and Ridley at Hastings and carried a crew of two mates, three deputed mariners, twenty five seamen and four boys.

In view of the insecurity of Dover Gaol twenty two of the lugger's crew were taken on board *Severn* and held in irons pending trial. When the case was heard at the Old Bailey on 25 April the defence claimed that not only was the vessel Dutch but so too were over half of her crew, thus placing her beyond the jurisdiction of British revenue laws. After a lengthy trial this argument was accepted by the jury and both the crew and the vessel were released. Some reports of the case suggest that most of the crew were actually from Folkestone and whilst this was quite likely it was not mentioned in Blockade papers. A few days later, back in Dover, Lieutenant Henry Nazer on *Badger* had the humiliating task of escorting the *Four Brothers* out of Dover Harbour to freedom, still laden with her cargo of 856 bales of tobacco each 60lbs, 50 tubs of spirits, 13 chests of tea and two casks of sugar.

When those twenty two prisoners had first arrived on board *Severn* Captain McCulloch ordered Captain Theophilus Patterson and Lieutenant Burton, Royal Marines, to 'repair on board and remain forthwith in command of the Royal Marine guard'. In his subsequent report McCulloch noted 'these two marine officers had always lived on shore although their party was on ship. The only duty performed in nearly 12 months was occasional visits to their men in moderate weather'. After the twenty two accused were released McCulloch heard a story that the two Marine officers had applied direct to the Board of Customs for special allowances for guarding smugglers taken prisoner. No such applications had passed through his hands and at first McCulloch dismissed the tale -'I gave it no credit' – but then found the officers had indeed been paid £10 and £6! Controlling his wrath, just, he wrote to their Lordships at the Admiralty 'these officers . . . did nothing more than their common duty – responsibility for the custody of the smugglers was with the Commanding Officer of Severn . . .'. Their Lordships were also annoyed at this conduct. Captain Patterson, who had made the application to Customs, was arrested and held pending court martial but he wrote a passionate letter of contrition and was subsequently offered the option of transfer to the reserve on half pay, which he accepted. Lieutenant Burton was reprimanded and despatched to other duties. Months later Patterson wrote another eloquent letter asking to be restored to full pay but the Admiralty pointed out he was on half pay from his own choice and at their indulgence, – and there he remained.

A fascinating insight into the degree of organisation that could be achieved in the smuggling trade is shown in a report made by Lieutenant Beer, Whitstable District in January 1823. There he listed eleven fast sailing cutters each between 25 and 40 tons owned in shares from £25 upwards by tradesmen in Whitstable and Sea Salter. 'Each vessel has a master and 5 to 17 crew each paid £14 per run plus 2 or 3 tubs and as much dry goods as they can carry. The master is always part owner. If any cargo is lost a proportion is deducted from crew's pay. During the last week in December the crews struck for an increase to £18 per run which most got. They work the Medway, Thames and Essex coasts with tubs already roped, if chased they are dropped overboard with anchors. At all times there are look outs on shore to give timely notice if revenue vessels are about . . .'. This enterprise had all the elements of a sound commercial shipping operation doing very good business, mostly beyond the Blockade Line, which even had the industrial problems of employees striking for a Christmas bonus!

The high degree of commercial sophistication also extended to the goods smuggled. A return of Blockade seizures for the quarter ending 30 June 1823 shows 160 seizures and 15 vessels arrested. One boat the *Victory*, 17 tons, was caught in Dover on 12 June with these 'fine goods' concealed on board : 16 steel chains, 12 gold rings, 36 bead purses, 80 dozen strings of beads, 1 lace dress, 106 prints of material, 5 cotton dresses, 20 pairs silk shoes, 63 pairs leather gloves, 11 yards crepe, 87 yards silk and 110 yards silk gauze. As often in cases such as this the crew soon realised the game was up and escaped whilst the Blockade men were busy searching.

Skirmishes continued at various points along the Line in the summer of 1823. Lieutenant Westbrook of East Swale District returning to *Beresford* from a galley patrol caught three men running a cargo on to the mudflats and seized the boat, 129 tubs and one roll of French paper. The three men, Richard Hunt, Chas Snowey and Will Harman were held aboard *Beresford* to await prosecution but Harman managed to escape and swam ashore. At Deal, Lieutenant Jay and Sentinel George Williams were ambushed and badly beaten by three smugglers wielding sticks reputedly six to seven feet long.

Further west Lieutenant Wheeler at Crowlink reported with some relish how the few Preventive Waterguard men around Newhaven had been duped. A punt carrying 20 tubs was seen to land at Tide Mills, between Seaford and Newhaven, and the two crew ran off. It took a while for the preventive men to get there and bring the tubs ashore, only to find they contained salt water! Meanwhile some 300 tubs of spirits were being unloaded from a boat at a more convenient spot ' . . .near the Buckle . . .'.

Will Palmer was equally well organised for smuggling on the *Stephen and Mary*, but it really was his most unlucky day when he was caught by a Blockade galley off Reculver. Following a search of his vessel, which revealed a creeper and line and seven sinkers for sowing tubs, Palmer was arrested and taken to the Reculver Watch House. There to his dismay, he was recognised by two old naval shipmates, now in the Blockade Service, as a convicted smuggler who had been serving five years impressment on *Vengeur* before deserting in Rio de Janeiro!

Yachting had increased in popularity after the Napoleonic wars and many owners berthed their craft in harbours patrolled by Blockade men whose rough, rude, attitudes no doubt upset the likes of Lord Darnley. In general, written complaints were few except those from the Earl of Harborough who protested so vehemently that he became something of a thorn in the side for McCulloch. 'He has for the last 2 or 3 years offered every kind of obstruction in the character and dress of a smuggler on different parts of the Line and is now troublesome in Isle of Thanet and Sandwich'. The Earl owned several yachts and it seems every time they were searched there was trouble which resulted in letters of complaint to the Admiralty from his solicitors. On 19 October 1823 matters came to a head when the Earl took out a summons against Lieutenant Philip Graham charging that he had not only challenged the Earl to a duel but used insulting language in an attempt to provoke a duel. Regretfully neither the background to the case nor the outcome are recorded but thereafter it seems there were no more protests from the Earl.

Dymchurch saw several fights in the summer of 1823. On 20 May Sentinel John Welch was attacked by 30 men who grabbed his pistol but he managed to give the alarm by firing a musket. Mate John Jackson and four sentinels ran over to find Welch staggering around with three wounds to the head. In the short sharp fight that followed one smuggler was hit with gunshot and later died of his wounds but the boat escaped and the only result that night was the seizure of four tubs.

At the same village on 12 June Midshipman Thomas Hamilton and his orderly Sam Everett from Tower 22 surprised a band of 40 or more men and fired a pistol as an alarm. Hamilton attacked and was quickly joined by Midshipmen Bambridge and Gilson and their men. Five prisoners and some goods were taken but in the running fight around the back of the village a smuggler, Jas Cunley, was shot accidentally by one of his own men. Hamilton was close by and arranged for Cunley to be carried to a nearby cottage where, after a short while, he died. Thomas Hamilton was promptly arrested for the murder of Cunley and held in leg irons in a tiny cell at Dymchurch Lock-Up until he was transferred to Maidstone Gaol. After a further five weeks in prison he was acquitted at the next Assize and then complimented by the judge for his bravery on 12 June.

On Captain McCulloch's recommendation Thomas Hamilton was advanced to Mate and took up a post at Warden Point on the Isle of Sheppey. Misfortune still dogged him and on 10 February 1825 he was again in a vicious fight with smugglers suffering a broken arm and jaw and deep sabre cuts to the head and neck. His attackers left him for dead but happily he survived and, after a long period of recovery, was promoted to Lieutenant with effect from the date of the fight. Hamilton moved to relatively peaceful duties at sea for a while but later returned to join the Coast Guard.

Sadly that year there was another accidental death when Sentinel George Gifford was swept off the beach at Dungeness and drowned trying to recover a tub of spirits.

Smuggling was rampant in 1823 between Seaford and Bognor, west beyond the Line, where the preventive men were weak both in numbers and resolve. When the news came in February 1824 that the Blockade Line would extend west as far as Chichester some gangs obviously wanted a few good runs on that part of the coast before the Navy arrived. On 13 February Lieutenant Chappell of Right Division was told the Brooklands Company had landed 600 tubs right in Newhaven Harbour and carried them in 16 carts behind the Line as far as Winchelsea and Rye.

Slowly the pattern of smuggling was changing from open warfare to shipboard concealment. There were still many fights to come over the next twenty years but in 1823 it was evident that more and more smugglers were hiding their goods on board vessels working into busy ports such as Rye. In November Lieutenant Dicken on *Enchantress* was told by the local Collector that a fishing boat berthed in the Harbour near Southerns public house was believed to have false sides in her hull. The Collector apparently was not going to take any action but Dicken lost no time in finding a carpenter to bore holes in the vessel's sides. Sure enough this soon revealed hidden compartments holding 60 flat casks of spirits, 457 packs of tobacco, 111 packs of choice tea and 17 rolls of chocolate. Everything was seized, including the boat, and passed to the Collector by Dicken who probably wished that all future seizures would be that easy.

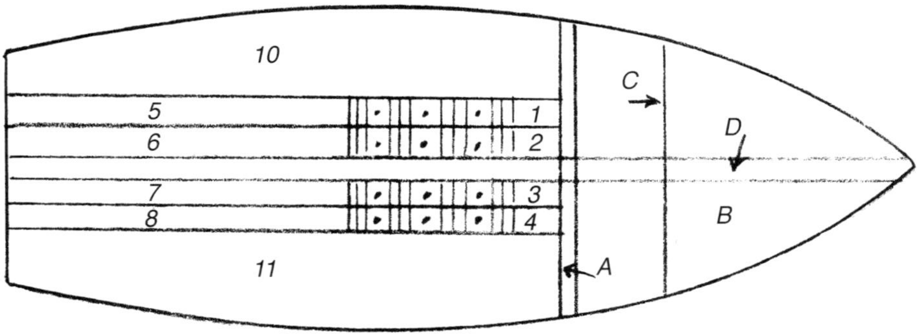

1–4 "Boxes made to fit into trunks 5–8 and so placed as to be easily lifted out to remove the tubs. These boxes were filled with shingle so that you may bore into them though the bulkhead 'A', their after side cased with iron."
B The forepeak
C Cabin bulkhead
D Keelson.
10 and 11 Wing ballast
"A strong platform of inch wood covered the trunks and came close forward to the bulkhead 'A'. On this platform the ballast was stored which was covered by a platform strongly battened down."

Taken from a diagram, in Blockade Service papers, showing the concealment found by Lieutenant Dicken in 1825 when the vessel was at Rye.

It was apparent that some boatyards in Rye were specialising in providing concealed spaces on fishing boats and the like. A punt in the harbour was found to have a complete double skin, in effect a boat within a boat, and the three inch space so created carried 400 pieces of cambric (fine cotton or linen). On 19 November 1824, roughly twelve months after that first seizure, Lieutenant Dicken was boring holes again this time aboard the fishing smack *Diamond*, 25 tons. 'I bored with a gimlet through the bulk head which secures the ballast forward and bored into something which clearly was not shingle'. He had found a clever concealment under the iron and shingle ballast and beneath a specially made wooden platform. Four 12ft long narrow spaces had been created each just wide enough to take a line of tubs roped together end-to-end with the access openings plugged with fitted boxes carrying shingle to fool anyone drilling in from that end.

Lieutenant Dicken seized the boat and the 33 tubs found concealed but the three crew ran off into the darkness when they realised the game was up. Five days later however two of them, Jerry Sowden and Will Collins, sought revenge. They waylaid Dicken and his orderly in Rye and tried to murder the Lieutenant with blows from heavy clubs. Some people approached and the two assailants made off but were later caught and eventually brought to trial. Dicken suffered a badly broken arm and three months later a medical report said that the fracture was still causing problems. The same report also mentioned that, following an unspecified fight, a Lieutenant Lewes had to have an arm amputated.

The sophisticated assortment of goods smuggled – beads, shoes, purses and so on – has already been mentioned but in some instances the Trade really was becoming quite selective and specialised. A veritable mercer's warehouse came to light after the Party at No.1 Battery, Dungeness saw five men run away from the water's edge leaving a bale of cloth on the spot. The Blockade officer obtained a search warrant for a house close by , occupied by William Manser and James Polhill, where a search revealed a total of 47 bales containing: 18,000 cambric handkerchiefs; 693 yards tiffany; 250 pieces cambric; 72 yards silk velvet; 9 piece tulle; 1 silk dress; 36 silk scarves; 173 silk handkerchiefs; 22 yards crepe and 220lbs green tea. All, no doubt, awaiting transport to fashionable quarters of Brighton, Tunbridge Wells and, of course, London.

Although there were few assaults by armed gangs in 1824 there was still some ugly fights with the ubiquitous batmen. At Cuckmere Sentinel William Williamson saw men unloading tubs from a boat about 2am on 1 August. He managed to grab one man but was set upon by three others wielding bats and knives. During the fight Williamson was stabbed in the neck and head before three of his Party arrived to fight off the attack and seize the boat *Ann of Ninfield* with its remaining 19 tubs. One smuggler was recognised as 'Deaf Tom' a shrimpman from Seaford.

On 22 September a gang attempted a run near Tower 50 at Bexhill and Lieutenant William Brand with five sentinels ran to the spot as the tubs were being unloaded. The seven men aboard the smuggling boat quickly pushed her off but not before Sentinel William Welch had leapt onboard. The fight on the beach resulted in another seven men and over 100 tubs being taken but as the craft disappeared into the darkness cries were heard and the next morning Welch's body was washed ashore. At the inquest Issac Dias, Assistant Surgeon in the Blockade Service, said he had examined the body and it appeared the man had been stunned and then drowned. The coroner said this warranted a verdict of murder but the jury disagreed and decided it was 'found drowned'.

The toll of accidental deaths continued but not all were shown in official records; some appeared only in local newspapers. In a thick fog during April 1824 a Midshipman was killed falling off the cliff by the Wish Tower at Eastbourne and Sentinel Thomas Wadham died in similar circumstances. Later, on a dark night Sentinel William Harford stationed at Saltdean fell to his death near Porto Bello Gap. Some idea of the hazards encountered by these men is given in a letter sent to a local newspaper after a sentinel named Sullivan fell from the cliff top near Beachy Head:

> . . .this is not, by a great number, the first death that has occurred in the same way. It is surely a wanton exposure of the lives of these poor men, to compel them to walk the hills on such nights as that. It was utterly impossible for a smuggler to have landed on that night, and it must therefore have been quite unnecessary to have sent out the men to parade to and from upon the downs, at the very edge of the cliff, where to save themselves from the danger of falling over, even on ordinary nights, they were obliged to trust to the guidance of large chalk stones, which are laid thickly along upon the dark turf, from one point of

their station to another. On the night in question the accident most probably happened from the snow, which prevented the poor fellow from seeing the chalk that was intended to be his guide.

The dips in the cliffs of the Seven Sisters, west of Beachy Head, particularly at Birling Gap and Crowlink, provided good landing spots for the smuggler. Sentinels patrolled the cliff tops when the tide was high but as it ebbed they made their way down to the shore with perhaps a walk of several miles in some places. The smugglers could take advantage of this temporary absence and, when the night tide was right, arrange for a cargo to be landed at the foot of the cliffs and hoisted up quickly whilst the sentinels were away scrambling down to the shore. Local farmers used portable wooden derricks to hoist anything worth salvaging that came ashore from shipwrecks, but the same machinery was also used to hoist tubs quickly, with the inevitable accidents. On one occasion the load dislodged large stones from the cliff that dropped on the men below sending one of them screaming into the sea. His cries in the night were heard by a patrolling Blockade galley that came in and seized the boat and the remaining 50 tubs.

In any fight with smugglers the general policy stressed by the Admiralty and Customs was first to capture the men, then think about the boat and the contraband. In 1824 the Navy Board asked for an account of those captured by the Blockade Service, and convicted, from 1 October 1821 to October 1823 and was told that 76 had been taken at sea by galleys and tenders and 46 on shore. A few months later John Barrow announced new rewards (nicknamed 'head money') for the capture and conviction of smugglers: £20 if the man was impressed or £15 if he went to prison. This being in addition to rewards for seizing goods and vessels.

The Severn Sisters looking east to Birling Gap.

The new rewards were introduced partly as further incentives to combat bribery and partly because the Navy and Customs were still finding it difficult to obtain convictions in some magistrates courts. The total of 122 in two years probably represented a minor portion of those actually caught by the Blockade Service. Some magistrates were still ignoring damning evidence on smuggling and releasing the culprits. With the new rewards the Navy Board sought to step up the pressure on these courts by producing more and more offenders.

Amidst such local bias it was obvious that any lesser charge connected with smuggling would get nowhere. A smuggling vessel running into a landing spot would be either guided in or warned off by those waiting on shore with flashes from an adapted lantern or a 'flink' pistol primed to flash rather than fire. Flashing, or any form of signalling to ships off shore, was an offence under Customs law (and still is incidentally!) and whilst Captain McCulloch urged his men to arrest any offender it usually proved impossible to obtain a conviction. Some magistrates not only dismissed the charge but allowed a counter charge of assault against the Blockade man if there had been a scuffle. When the Line extended west past Worthing the local Bench proved no exception. Sentinel James Kenny caught Henry Blann making flashes to a boat off Worthing beach and there was a chase that ended in some fisticuffs. In court the charge of flashing was dismissed but Kenny was found guilty of assault.

A report in the *Times* annoyed Lieutenant Tompson of Lancing Station so much that he felt obliged to reply. The newspaper said the revenue cruiser *Hawke* had chased a smuggling lugger in heavy weather but failed to catch her and prevent the landing of 700 kegs of spirits. The Lieutenant wrote forcefully to the paper insisting the report was absolutely untrue. To this the *Times* thundered that it was true and proceeded to really rub it in: 'There is nothing more ridiculous, in the eyes of those who live upon our sea coasts, than to witness the tender sensibilities of officers employed on the coast blockade whenever a statement is made that a smuggler has succeeded in landing his cargo; as though they formed a part of the most perfect system that can be established for the suppression of smuggling. Now it be known to all England that this is a gross attempt at humbug. Notwithstanding all the unceasing vigilance of the officers and men employed, smuggling is carried on all along the coast from Deal to Cornwall, to as great a degree as the public require. Any attempt to smuggle this FACT may answer the purpose of a party, or a particular system, but it will never obtain belief'. Then came the parting shot, which seem to be quite the fashion in those days: 'It was only a few days since that a party of coast blockade men (we believe belonging to Tower No.61) made common cause with the smugglers, and they walked off together!' Wisely the normally eloquent Captain McCulloch kept out of this controversy. No one knew better than him that his Blockade Line was far from being a perfect system. But even so, at this time it was the most effective force against organised smuggling and still had the full support of the government.

In February 1825, under the arrangements mentioned in Chapter Three,

Captain McCulloch was ordered to hand over the Blockade Line in Sussex to another commander and his command was reduced to the Kent Coast Blockade. By then he must have been quite debilitated at times with chest and breathing problems aggravated, no doubt, by long journeys on dusty roads and tracks. Up to this point in time he had never mentioned his disability in official papers and it would have been typical of the man if, ever the optimist, he had reasoned that now he could devote even more time to actively participating in his war against smuggling. Regrettably the time available to him was going to be all too brief.

CHAPTER FIVE

Kent Coast Blockade, 1825–30

During 1824 the steady trickle of intelligence from the unnamed Boulogne informant eased off until there were only occasional snippets. One such item in February 1825 told McCulloch that one of his old enemies 'Harry Stokes, the well known smuggler of Deal, who had been living near Boulogne, has retired to Brighton' but the Captain doubted if old smugglers ever retired '. . . the habit runs so deep'.

Information from another source in Boulogne brought forth a stinging response from the Captain. The English Consul there sent a note to the Admiralty saying that the amount of smuggling capital circulating in the town was on the increase. Some of this extra contraband could, admittedly, have been destined for parts of the English coast beyond the Line but when the note was passed to McCulloch for comment he took it to heart as a direct criticism of the Blockade. With wild exaggeration, prompted no doubt by the distress of his increasing debility, he retorted '. . . prior to the establishment of the Coast Blockade the whole force employed on this coast was in effect at the entire disposal of the smugglers. No revenue officer ever went on duty without information which the smugglers took care to supply and to satisfy the officer at the same time that he was particularly active and wonderfully fortunate'.

With more justification the Captain was equally sharp a few weeks later when Customs staff in Dover gave some information to Blockade officers that led to seizures of contraband and then tried to claim a third of the reward. McCulloch pointed out that the reverse situation would never occur! To support their claim the Customs at Dover quoted an old order of 1721 but when the case was passed to the Commissioners of Customs for a ruling they found in favour of the Blockade officers.

The next month, on 10 April at Margate, three Blockade men were the victims of some more sharp practice by local Customs staff. Around midnight Sentinel Thomas Butler saw a group of men landing tubs on Margate jetty from a galley. When he fired his pistol as an alarm the men made off in the boat leaving 19 tubs behind. Tom Butler was quickly joined not only by his colleagues, Petty Officer Welsh and Sentinel Sam Edwards, but also by Henry Casswell, Customs boatman, who must have been lurking nearby and who nipped in smartly to say he was seizing the tubs! None of the Blockade ratings had the legal power to seize the goods and although their Lieutenant McLeod arrived within six minutes of the alarm Casswell insisted it was too late, the deed was done, the seizure was his – and the air was, no doubt, navy blue! In his covering note to the seizure report Captain McCulloch complained bitterly of this poaching saying it was the second occasion it had happened in recent times. Happily the Commissioners of Customs once again ruled in favour of the Blockade men and reminded Customs staff that orders forbidding such interference with Blockade seizures had been issued in August 1823; this particular piece of sharp practice obviously had a history.

Following the partition of the Blockade Service into two counties in February 1825, Captain McCulloch made a detailed report of the First, Second and Third Divisions that now comprised his command as the Kent Coast Blockade Force. In a despatch on 27 March to Sir George Cockburn, Vice Admiral, Sheerness, the full complement (not including *Ramillies*) was shown as 57 Lieutenants, 3 Surgeons, 3 Pursers, 18 Mates, 10 Assistant Surgeons, 8 Clerks, 130 Quartermasters, 102 Captains of the Top, 24 Armourers mates, Carpenters mates and stewards and 1,110 Able Seamen, Ordinary Seamen and Landsmen. Out of this total of 1,465 there were 348 vacant posts at that particular date, all for ratings. A list of Kent Blockade Stations at this time, with manning complements, is given at Appendix C.

The lack of Blockade accommodation in the Isle of Sheppey was still causing problems in April 1825 well over twelve months after the extension of the Line around the island. As usual, progress was far too slow for an impatient McCulloch who made repeated visits that month '. . . except for a watch house foundation on Sheerness Point nothing has been erected as quarters . . . in the last 8 months despite repeated representations . . . there are never more than 4 bricklayers there, sometimes only one . . . it should be under the personal control of the Captain of Royal Engineers but he lacks any sense of priority!'.

Captain McCulloch endured more frustration in May when, with some embarrassment, he reported to the Admiralty that Lieutenant Philip Graham, superintending Officer of Second Division would be absent in civilian custody for four months. All absences by officers on leave were reported to the Admiralty and McCulloch asked how should the absence be recorded; back came the advice 'in custody under civil powers'. No details were given as to the reason for Graham's detention and so it was presumably a private or domestic matter. But whatever the background, Philip Graham was promoted to Commander with effect from 29 July 1825, probably as soon as he left prison, and thereafter does not seem to have been employed again on naval duties. After joining the Navy in 1803, Philip Graham had seen action at Quebec and Copenhagen and against slavers off West Africa. It seems probable that in 1825, after five good years as a Divisional Lieutenant in the Blockade, he had become the source of some embarrassment to the Navy and was, in effect, promoted into early retirement on half pay.

Lieutenant Robert Williams took over the superintendency of Second Division, his colleagues in the other two Divisions being Lieutenants James Tilley (First) and Sam Hellard (Third). The latter had taken over the Third Division from David Peat and, although a very different and more mature character than his predecessor, he was destined to achieve just as much personal success against the smuggling gangs in Kent. Sam Hellard, some ten years older than Peat, had joined the Royal Navy in September 1798 as a Volunteer on *Director* (64) under Captain William Bligh and saw action as a Midshipman in the West Indies, South America and the Baltic. As a Masters Mate on *Castor* (32) in 1809 he took part in the capture of the *D'Haupolt* a French 74 and was First Lieutenant on *Podargus* when she sank after action against a Danish squadron off Norway. Sam Hellard 'an officer given to occasional bouts of strong language' was appointed as a senior Lieutenant to *Severn* on 31 October 1820. His name does not feature in the records of early Coast Blockade actions and it is possible that his duties were at first confined to the ship as First Lieutenant. Even when he came ashore to take charge of Third Division he still resided 'in Folkestone and aboard ship'. From then on it seems the Divisional Lieutenants for Second and Third Divisions took it in turns to also double as the First Lieutenant on the depot ship.

The incident off Dover on 15 May 1825 involving Lieutenant Knowles brought an unexpected counter from those under attack. About 11pm he was on patrol with four men in a Blockade galley when they saw the Dover lugger *Nancy* almost becalmed. Knowles ran his galley alongside and two Blockade men jumped on board. But immediately three smugglers from the lugger jumped into the galley and tried to throw Knowles and his two remaining men overboard! The Lieutenant fired his pistol and two of the assailants dived into the sea. They tried to swim for shore and tragically one was drowned but the other was rescued later, in a sorry state. Meanwhile the third assailant had clambered back on board the *Nancy* but he and the other six in the lugger's crew had had enough by now and she was captured intact with her cargo of 6,003lbs of tobacco and 290lbs of tea.

Around this time the quarterly returns sent to the Admiralty showed an average of two to three seizures per day. As before these were usually of small numbers of tubs, up to 20, but occasionally there were seizures of 60 or 70 at one time. Fifteen boats were seized between January and March 1825 and one, the *Fly* of Deal, carried 1249 yards of silk, 2845 yards ribbon and 461 silk handkerchiefs. Silks and satins from France and the Far East were very popular in those Regency days.

Up to this point in time McCulloch's reports had never referred to his poor state of health. The first mention came following the arrival in the Downs of the frigate *Brazen* (24) on 10 May. Her commander, Captain Willes, was senior to McCulloch and naval etiquette required the junior commander to attend and pay his respects. But, as McCulloch explained in his report to the Vice Admiral, he was unable to go afloat that day 'because I was gradually though slowly recovering from a very serious attack of spasmodic and inflammatory affection of the lungs'. To support this he included notes from Mr Williams, Blockade Divisional Surgeon and Dr McArthur of Walmer, both of whom confirmed they had been treating Captain McCulloch for spasmodic asthma.

Captain McCulloch had sent Mr Williams, his First Lieutenant out to

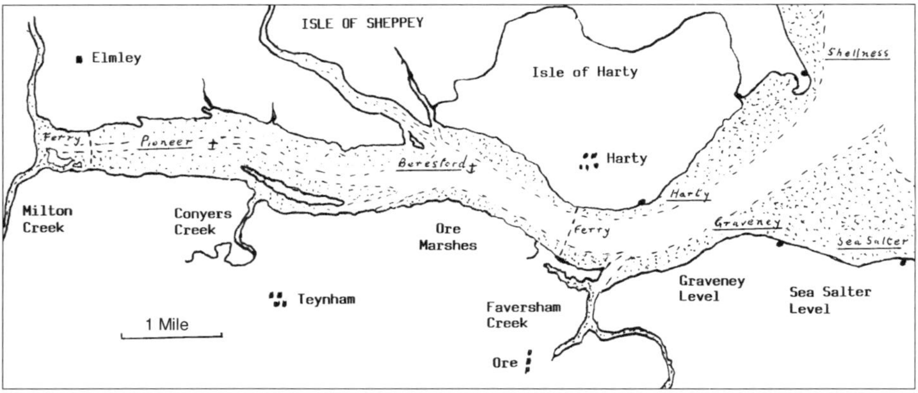

Sketch map of East Swale c. *1825 showing (underlined) the location of six Blockade Stations including two watch vessels.*

Brazen, when she arrived in the Downs but Willes was very annoyed at this lack of respect. When the Lieutenant returned to *Brazen* the next day with a further report on his Captain's health he was cross-examined by the still irate Willes. Although *Brazen* was engaged on preventive patrols in the Channel it seems there was considerable friction between her crew and the Coast Blockade. Chapter Six mentions an incident that had occurred two months before, in March 1825 near Selsey, where an officer from *Brazen* threatened to shoot a Sussex Blockade Sentinel in a dispute over a seized boat. Captain Willes came ashore after that second visit by Lieutenant Williams but did not visit McCulloch even though he was close by the landing place at Deal in his office on the beach.

During the summer of 1825 there were few assaults on the Blockade Line by large gangs; the smugglers that were caught were often in twos and threes as the crews of small luggers. However, an organised landing by a large gang was made near Fort Twiss, close to Folkestone, around 9pm on 9 September when Lieutenant Fabian and his orderly Michael Devine saw smugglers operating near Tower 14. The two ran to the bridge by Waggon Train barracks to cut off the smugglers retreat, but 20 of them had already crossed before Fabian arrived. Devine grabbed the next man trying to come across and was aided by a soldier who had just come out of the barracks. The noise and shouts also brought out an unarmed Army officer; he attempted to help but was promptly knocked unconscious. Fabian and Devine tried to capture more smugglers but were badly beaten and managed to seize only 20 tubs. Lieutenant Fabian was later examined by the Divisional Surgeon at Shorncliff and found to have seven severe wounds to the head. By February 1826 he was reported to be totally unfit for any naval duties: both his eyesight and his memory had deteriorated badly. With admirable optimism he asked the Admiralty to either promote him to Commander or retire him with a wound pension; not surprisingly their Lordships opted for the latter.

During that August and September the inhabitants of Lydd had two more opportunities to vent their feelings against the hated Blockade Service. On 11 August, during a fight between Blockade men and a gang attempting a run at Dungeness one smuggler was shot and killed by Lieutenant Millet. The officer said it was an accident and at the subsequent inquest in Lydd the coroner accepted this, but the jury decided it was wilful murder.

The next month there was yet another incident involving the transfer of convicted smugglers out of Lydd. This time Sam Hellard was in charge of the escort aided by Lieutenant Short and ten men. The prisoners, William Greenstreet and Will Miller, were being taken from the Guildhall for impressment in the Navy when the escort came under attack in the market place by a mob of men and women wielding clubs and throwing stones. The escort survived the assault and managed to hold on to their prisoners but Sam Hellard received two nasty blows to the head. He identified the attacker as John Pain and a local magistrate, David Denne, issued an arrest warrant but Pain had vanished.

Captain McCulloch's health deteriorated rapidly in mid October. He signed a routine report to John Croker on 8 October and three days later sent a request to John Barrow for the continuation of secure stabling arrangements for officer's horses at Shorncliffe 'to frustrate vindictive smugglers . . .'. On 13 October he signed a report to the Vice Admiral, Sheerness, concerning the death of John Houlihan, Ordinary Seaman, murdered by smugglers off Dymchurch. This was the last official paper signed by McCulloch and the next day he was reported by his deputy, Lieutenant Williams, as being 'on Admiralty leave, sick in Deal'.

John Houlihan died during a combined operation by several groups of smugglers to run three large galleys simultaneously into the coast around Dymchurch on the night of 9 October. Lieutenant William Cole of Tower 27 was on patrol in his galley that night when he encountered the *Venus*, a large galley, dropping goods off shore. She was seized without a struggle and John Houlihan, a well armed and experienced Blockade man was placed on board. Cole then used the Blockade galley to creep in the areas near the captured boat in order to recover goods 'sown' but had to stop when his men on shore fired an alarm. Two more smuggling boats had appeared at points well apart on the beach and two parties of smugglers armed with bats and stones were fighting the sentinels. The Lieutenant landed his galley and the combined Blockade Parties chased the smugglers into the marsh behind Dymchurch. It was extremely dark that night and eventually the smugglers were able to slip away but not before they had wounded two Blockade men. Returning to the beach Cole launched his galley again but, although he and his men searched through the night the *Venus* had disappeared. Next morning the body of John Houlihan, cruelly murdered, was washed ashore not far from the spot where 34 tubs, 'sown' from the *Venus*, were found on the sand at low water. The coroner's verdict was 'wilful murder' but the killers were never brought to justice.

Captain Joseph William McCulloch died in Deal at 6.30pm on 25 October 1825. Four days later Lieutenant Williams reported to John Croker that 'Captain McCulloch's body was interred in the burial ground of the parish church at Deal today'. There would have been a ceremonial naval burial party to escort the cortege to St Leonards Church, Upper Deal and the log of *Ramillies* records that Lieutenants Williams and Searle were in attendance. The commemoration tablet still set in the churchyard wall states simply: 'Sacred to the memory of Captain William McCulloch R.N. of Barholm, Scotland, who departed this life on 25 October 1824. Age 45 years'. This apart, his passing attracted little publicity. In and around Deal smuggling may have been subdued but memories were long; the local paper devoted only a few brief lines to the death. The Captain left a widow, Jane, and a large family. He married in the West Indies in 1810 and a daughter Anna had been born at Barholm in Scotland in 1812. The parish registers of Deal and Walmer show the baptisms of eight children, including Anna, between 1815 and 1825.

The *Times*, which occasionally carried reports of large smuggling runs as well as letters on the government's futile efforts to combat the evil trade, made no reference to McCulloch's death. In a perverse way this lack of recognition only serves to underline the man's achievements. With minimal support (and sometimes downright hindrance) from the revenue authorities and against aggression from many local communities that flared at times into open warfare he founded and commanded an unprecedented preventive campaign along 200 miles of coast. William McCulloch commanded the Royal Naval Coast Blockade Service for only eight of the fourteen years it existed and that existence itself occupies only a tiny forgotten part of the annals of the Royal Navy. But at a time when a desperate government wanted action he showed what could be done by a naval commander endowed with imagination, enthusiasm and persistence.

Despite the frequent need for recruits, the ease of desertion and the unparalleled levels (for the Navy) of bribery, Captain McCulloch showed that a co-ordinated and disciplined armed force, split between off shore and on shore, could curb organised smuggling. Dismissed by some as nothing more than a flogging tyrant he deserves better and was undoubtedly the most singly effective opponent to smuggling ever seen in the two counties that formed England's contraband corner.

The vacant command post had to be filled quickly and on 9 November 1825 Captain Hugh Pigot reported to John Croker '. . . I arrived in Deal last evening and this morning took command of H.M.S. Ramillies pursuant to my commission dated 3rd instant'. Hugh Pigot, some four years older than McCulloch had 'made post' much quicker. Entering the Navy in 1788 he served as a Lieutenant in various parts of the globe before attaining the rank of Commander in 1802 and post Captain in 1804. From this he saw action mostly in the West Indies where his tally of captured warships included two French privateers and, in 1812, the American man-of-war *Frolic*. He was commended, first for taking possession of the French island of Mariegalanti to enforce the blockade of Guadaloupe, and later for his part in capturing the French 74 *D'Haupolt*.

Whilst it is difficult to really assess Captain Pigot's character simply from his official papers, it is possible to see some differences between him and his predecessor. Whereas McCulloch was the ideas man ever willing to set out the problem and its solution in full reports with a flow of information, Pigot confined his comments, when he made them, to the bare essentials. The war against smuggling became a vocation for the fiery McCulloch but for Pigot it seems it was just another naval appointment. One could not imagine him sending a bundle of bludgeons to Whitehall for their Lordships at the Admiralty to inspect!

For some years before his death McCulloch had occupied the Port Admiral's office in Deal which also accommodated his secretary and some clerks. The office was old, cold and exposed because it jutted out on to the beach. '. . . the floor cloths had worn out and been removed to the Dockyard a long time . . .' and McCulloch's staff had obviously tried unsuccessfully to get him to ask for replacements. Thankfully the new Captain was more amenable and within a few days of his arrival was asking John Barrow for '30 yards of druggett to cover this place'.

Remembering the early response of Captain McCulloch who, steeped in years of naval discipline, initially sent smugglers direct into the Navy without waiting for a magistrates' hearing, it is perhaps no surprise to find that Captain Pigot wanted at first to do the same. Any post Captain was held in awe by his officers and presumably no one in Pigot's command dared to correct him. When a smuggling galley with 11 men aboard was caught off Dover Castle on 18 December 1825 he declared 10 were British and would be sent for immediate impressment. But Customs at Dover advised him it was for them to decide how the men should be dealt with and on this occasion they would not be prosecuted; obviously the Customs were satisfied the smugglers were all foreign nationals. Much to Pigot's annoyance all 11 prisoners were released after some ten days in irons aboard *Ramillies*.

The quantities and variety of goods carried in that galley were truly remarkable and worth noting. Perhaps there was a clerical error somewhere but this is the cargo listed in Admiralty papers as seized from that boat: '10,240 yards silk; 354 silk handkerchiefs; 21 silk shawls; 11 parcels tulle; 4,980 pairs leather gloves; 314 yards silk gauze; 76 yards silk embroidered; 24 silk scarves; 8 silk dresses; 28 silk handkerchiefs; 1 piece furniture silk; 131 yards tiffany; 29 crepe scarves; 1,365 yards silk ribbon; 153 pieces bandanas; 413 yards crepe; 594 yards silk taffeta; 169 demi pieces cambric; 400 cambric handkerchiefs; 3,480 French handkerchiefs and 2 parcels of cards'. All this in a large rowing boat, with a low freeboard and 11 men on board, crossing the Channel on a December night!

The first few months of 1826 were fairly quiet on the smuggling front and Captain Pigot spent much of his time visiting Blockade Stations. He also decided to change the titles of his three Divisions back to their original designations and so First, Second and Third became Left, Centre and Right respectively, looking seaward.

An incident at Dungeness on 8 February highlighted some of the problems faced by a Blockade commander when there was a weak officer in the Line. Lieutenant Woodham, in charge at Grand Redoubt Station,

Preventivemen creeping up a line of tubs 'sown' just off the coast.

Dungeness, had recently transferred from the Sussex Coast Blockade on a 'smart ticket' granted because he had suffered a severe rupture. No details were given as to why on earth this officer was still employed on active duties but he was at his station on the night of 8 February when a French tub boat ran 200 tubs successfully through the Line. She was seen by a sentinel who claimed he fired his pistol as an alarm but the Lieutenant vowed no such shot was made. Sam Hellard investigated and satisfied himself that the sentinel was telling the truth. Poor old Woodham and his orderly had heard the alarm and walked slowly to the scene of action; by the time they arrived all the smugglers and their tubs were gone. The Admiralty ordered that Woodham be superseded immediately, without waiting for a replacement and Lieutenant George Dyer was sent over from Fort Twiss to take charge temporarily.

Some weeks later George Dyer returned to Fort Twiss and on the night of 5 April was visiting his men, accompanied by Petty Officer George Lewis and orderly Michael Devine, now recovered from the wounds he had suffered the previous September. As Lieutenant Dyer walked along the beach someone shouted to him 'there's a flash to the east sir, – smugglers!' Immediately one of the nearby sentinels, James Leman, fired wildly in that direction and his shot accidentally struck the Lieutenant, some fifty yards away, killing him instantly. Leman was subsequently court-martialled but the tragedy illustrated only too well the tension felt by some Blockade men on duty at night, tension that could even bring them to forget or ignore the Blockade's strict general order that 'No one shall fire without violence being first offered'.

Further to the east, at Eastware Bay, the problem with the Blockade men was more concerned with corruption rather than tension. The watch house was at Hougham but the men's accommodation was some distance away and as they walked to and fro they came into contact, as Sam Hellard put it, 'with notorious smugglers in the neighbourhood who set out to corrupt them'. This must have been a serious problem because to counter it the gun brig *Pelter* was beached permanently at Eastware in May 1826 to become the new Blockade Station housing a Lieutenant and 20 ratings.

In this instance it seems the Navy Board acted too quickly without first establishing whether the Navy had right of access over the land above the high water mark, or perhaps Sam Hellard persuaded the Board to act first and pay later. Whatever the background the matter culminated some months later in an irate letter from Mr John Finnes, then Mayor of Dover, to Hugh Pigot asking that '. . . the Pelter be removed from my property or an adequate yearly rent be paid . . .' Needless to say *Pelter* remained there at least until 1831 and so the rent presumably proved adequate.

Two ominous notes from Lieutenant Sam Hellard were passed on to John Croker at the Admiralty on 14 March 1826 with no covering comments from Hugh Pigot. They advised that 'armed parties of smugglers are again appearing on the coast within the Line of the Blockade . . . believed to be robbers that belong to the parish of Aldington and headed by George Ransley . . .' This was the armed gang that fought so fiercely at Brookland in February 1821 when the then leader Cephas Quested was caught and later hanged. For a while after this battle the gang lacked organisation but smuggling success returned when George Ransley became the new leader. Initially a farm hand at Aldington, George had married into the Baileys, a smuggling family, and soon realised he was well suited for the Trade. Tall and well built he proved to be a born leader and ruthless fighter. Ostensibly the keeper of a beer house in Aldington called the 'Bourne Tap' he was by 1826, at the age of 44, the leader of the most successful gang in Kent and Sussex. Known by now as the Aldington Gang some of them apparently wore blue canvas smocks when working on a run and so were also known as the 'Blues', although this name never appeared in Blockade reports.

The use of firearms by smugglers along the coast had diminished after the armed fights in 1821 and the successful pursuit of the North Kent Gang that September. Blockade officers gave no opinions as to why the guns came back into use in 1826 but it was at a time when the Line was close to full strength and so the gangs were meeting maximum opposition from the Navy. Whatever the reason, the first report of renewed armed attacks by the Aldington men came at Dymchurch on 11 May 1826. A local newspaper reported that as the boat laden with tubs approached the shore near Herring Hang on Dymchurch Wall '. . . the smugglers instantly commenced cheering and rushed upon the coast threatening defiance to the sentinels of the Blockade . . . who perceiving such an overwhelming force gave the alarm, when a party of marines coming to their assistance a general firing took place . . .' As they retreated across the marsh one of the gang, Charles Giles was wounded in the neck but managed to avoid capture. Nothing was landed this time because the smuggler's boat was frightened off when Lieutenants Westbrook, Mudge and McLeod arrived off shore in their galleys.

Perhaps the Aldington Gang were so frustrated by this failure that they were determined nothing would stop them next time. Or perhaps the landing at Dover was, to them , just another routine run. Whatever the reason, Quartermaster Richard Morgan was the next to suffer. Around 1am on Sunday 30 July he was returning to the Casemates at Dover from delivering mail to Townshend Battery when, near the bathing machines, he saw a boat coming into land through the surf. Drawing his pistol he and Sentinel Richard Pickett ran towards the craft and finding a group of men waiting on the beach, shouted to them to surrender. As a reply Morgan received three shots, all close to the heart, from men firing long duck guns. He died instantly and as Pickett tried to help he was clubbed down with the butts of those same guns. The shots brought out more Blockade men but valuable time was lost before they arrived and the Blues managed to get clear away with most of the cargo leaving only 33 tubs to be seized.

The Blockade men were late in responding because their station, in the Casemates below Dover Castle, was too far up the cliff to enable the 'watch in' to get down quickly to the beach to assist the 'watch out'. Richard Morgan's death had been instantaneous and the slow response was not a factor in the murder but it did bring the Navy Board to obtain a more suitable Station building at the foot of the Casemates.

Some months later Morgan's widow applied to the Navy Board, in some distress, for help and charity. Her plea was supported strongly by Captain Pigot who described Morgan as '. . . a man respected by every officer for his courage, activity and attention. He always exercised steady and correct conduct over his parties . . .'. But the Navy Board replied, rather bluntly, that nothing could be done for the widow.

Deal galleys, descendants of ancient Norse ships, were used both for smuggling and to ferry pilots and stores to merchantmen sheltering in the Downs

Just at this time, in the days before and after Morgan's death, Captain Pigot and his officers aboard *Ramillies* were helping to organise the first Deal and Downs Regatta. The growing popularity of resorts such as Brighton and Bognor had persuaded the townsfolk of Deal to set up their own tourist attraction. They chose something for which many in Deal were eminently suited – in more ways than one – galley and lugger races just off shore! As a willing supporter Captain Pigot obtained permission from the Admiralty for the signal guns for the eight races to be fired from *Ramillies* on Regatta day ,10 August, and on that day, no doubt, local dignitaries were entertained on board with traditional naval courtesy.

Not to be outdone, Dover Town followed suit with a Regatta three weeks later and each of these events was brought to a close, in those Regency days, with the obligatory Regatta Ball. That for Deal was advertised in the *Kentish Gazette* of 8 August 1826 – '. . . Tickets, Ladies 4s, Gentlemen 5s. Dancing to commence at Nine . . . ' – immediately above a notice from the Board of Customs offering £500 reward for information on the murderers of Richard Morgan. Next year the same social arrangements were made for a Deal and Downs Regatta on 29/30 August. At all these events the rowing contestants were in either four or six oar galleys from towns such as Deal, Dover or Folkestone. The records do not show whether boats from *Ramillies* took part, but if they did it might have been a good preview of some future race between the same opponents except that it would be at night with the smugglers in much longer galleys under the handicap of a heavy cargo!

It seems Lieutenant Sam Hellard had little interest or involvement in the 1826 regatta. During the first week in August his attention was fully occupied with bringing the killers of Richard Morgan to trial and the day after the murder he asked that Bow Street officers be brought down from London to make covert enquiries. But even whilst these arrangements were being made the Aldington Gang struck again.

Flushed with the success of their run at Dover the gang made another landing the following Sunday, 6 August, this time close to Fort Moncrief near Hythe. About 1am Lieutenant Johnson, from Tower 22, was walking along the shore when he saw two flashes up ahead and heard a pistol shot. It was obviously a warning shot from a sentinel and gathering two more men Johnson ran over to find a party of tub carriers already bringing their cargo ashore under the protection of some 30 armed guards. The Lieutenant ordered his men to open fire and straight away they brought down three smugglers. The naval men closed in for a hand-to-hand fight but were soon in danger of being overwhelmed; George Ransley, the gang leader, was heard to yell '. . . kill the bastards . . .' Luckily, that was the moment when Lieutenant Westbrook arrived with another ten men and the gang made off into the marshes. As before they made a semi-disciplined retreat, turning as a rank at times to fire and hold the naval men at bay. Only 14 tubs and three muskets were seized that night and all but one of the smugglers got away; he was caught and held after being shot in the leg. The only Blockade casualty was Sentinel William Spillane who was badly wounded in the chest and arm.

The captured man, who said he was James Bushell, had to have a leg amputated before being taken to *Ramillies* for questioning by Sam Hellard. There was no question of allowing the prisoner a period of recovery but, although he must have been in great pain, a lengthy interrogation failed to produce any real information, merely that the gang were possibly from Alkham. At this point Hellard had no firm indication this was the Aldington Gang but much more accurate information would come to light during the next few weeks, information that would lead eventually to the downfall of Ransley and his men.

The covert enquiries made by two Bow Street officers soon brought results and within two days they were able to identify the captured man as James Quested '. . . who had a brother . . . hung at Newgate some time since . . . we have no doubt he was with them that shot Morgan at Dover'. This was the brother of Cephas Quested, the one time leader of the Aldington gang. But the Bow Street officers also had a more valuable piece of news to the effect that one of the gang, William Marsh, was willing to turn King's evidence.

A few weeks later the Blockade had a further stroke of luck following yet another run by the Aldington Gang on 1 September, this time near Walmer. On this occasion two of the gang, John Edward Horne and the real James Bushell, were caught and both subsequently offered to turn King's evidence. The three informers soon produced enough evidence to place before the Crown Solicitor and shortly afterwards a batch of arrest warrants arrived on Sam Hellard's desk. He knew he had to bide his time and make careful plans to capture the villains living as they did around Aldington in what the Crown Solicitor described as 'a wild part of Kent twixt Ashford and Folkestone'. Hellard remembered that a previous attempt to capture Ransley five years before had failed 'when his village was occupied at midnight by over 200 (of his) men'. Thereafter George Ransley had vowed he would never be taken alive.

At 11pm on 16 October Sam Hellard set out from Fort Moncreif for Aldington with a party of Blockade men and two Bow Street officers, Smith and Bishop. His report, made the next day, described how 'Having marched in the direction of Aldington reached that place about 3am this morning . . . every house in which I expected to arrest a man was surrounded by sentinels nearly at the same moment. I then instantly advanced to the dwelling of George Ransley the leader of this ruffian band and was fortunate enough to get so close to his house before his dogs were disturbed that he had not time to leave his bed; the dogs were cut down and his door forced; when I rushed in, I had the satisfaction to seize the man in his bedroom. Having handcuffed him to one of the stoutest men in the party, I proceeded to the other houses and was equally successful in arresting seven others of the gang, whose names I subjoin. On my return to Fort Moncrief at 8am, I immediately embarked the prisoners on board the *Industry* for a passage to *Ramillies* where I presume they will arrive as soon as this reaches Deal. Before I conclude this report, I consider it a most particular part of my duty to inform you that the conduct of the officers and men under my direction on this service was most exemplary throughout the night and during a most fatiguing march of nearly thirty miles . .'

By any measure this had been a very successful operation to take eight core members of the gang; George Ransley (44 years old), Sam Bailey (36), Charles Giles (28), Tom Denard (20), Rob Bailey (30), Tom Gillian (24), William Wire (17) and Richard Wire (19). But Sam Hellard soon found that he had not captured all the wanted men in and around Aldington that night. There was nothing for it – another visit had to be arranged! Without doubt some covert intelligence was soon forthcoming because, as before, Hellard bided his time and set out again for the district around Aldington on the night of 14 November. Once more he had a party of Blockade men but his time just one Bow Street officer, Mr J. J. Smith '. . . acting as before under my orders . . .'

Unfortunately this time Sam Hellard had chosen a night of really atrocious weather as he explained in the report he made next day '. . . due to the most tempestuous weather . . . the land in places being inundated and the Coast Blockade Parties being obliged to ford and in some places swim . . .(we) arrived at the first house in Aldington at 11.30pm and captured Edward Panting. Forcing the front door of another house Paul Pierce was found hiding in the oven . . .Some roads were nearly 3 feet deep in mud and the police officer said he must give up . . . he could not proceed any further'. But Sam Hellard and his men pressed on through that dreadful night and reached the next house about 3am. There they took Richard Higgins (alias Ford) and later about 4.30am, they captured John Bailey. Tired but satisfied, Sam Hellard concluded his report '. . . Thus the Party marched back to the coast with four more of George Ransley's men and arrived back at Fort Moncreif at 10.15 am after a march of 12 hours over 30 miles of the most difficult country to be found in Kent'.

Lieutenant Sam Hellard's leadership and exploits on those two expeditions certainly warranted all possible praise and even Captain Pigot was moved to write to their Lordships of '. . . the energy, zeal, address and

George Ransley's house at Aldington Frith

indefatigable exertion which characterised this officer's conduct upon the present and upon all occasions'. He recommended Lieutenant Hellard in the strongest manner to the notice of their Lordships, but despite this Sam had to wait another four years before advancing to the rank of Commander.

During that same month Blockade men captured four more members of the gang: Thomas Wheeler (32 years old), James Hogben (43), James Wilson (32) and James Smeed (23). In his papers the Crown Solicitor made some notes on the gang: Sam Bailey was a naval deserter and, as Ransley's lieutenant, regularly armed and trained about 30 scouts for each night's work paying them £1 per night; he also transported the fire-arms in a cart to the night's spot; the rest of the gang, some 60-80 men, were directly at the leader's call; Hogben (from Hawkinge) organised the tubmen paying them 8s a night.

Twenty men – all core members of the gang who were there at Dover when Morgan was killed – had now been caught. Of these Marsh, Bushell, Horne and Panting volunteered to give Crown evidence and so were not prosecuted. The remaining 16 were taken in parties by *Industry* to Deptford and thence under strong escort to the Bow Street Magistrates. Richard Wire was charged with the murder of Richard Morgan and all the others with being accessories to the crime. All were remanded to Newgate Prison pending the trial which was held before Mr Justice Park at Maidstone Assizes in 12 January 1827. There, all the defendants pleaded 'not guilty' but after plea bargaining between counsels the charges were reduced to that of smuggling and shooting at revenue officers, the latter still being a capital offence. To this 14 of the accused pleaded 'guilty'. No further charges were preferred against the remaining two, Rob Bailey and Thomas Wheeler, and they were released.

In due course all 14 accused were sentenced to be hanged on 5 February but this was later commuted to transportation for life and they were subsequently taken to Portsmouth for passage to Australasia. George Ransley was eventually joined by his wife and settled in Van Diemen's Land (now Tasmania) where he became a respected employer and pillar of the community before his death in 1860.

The Board of Customs paid over £500 in rewards to those who took part in the capture of the gang. As informers James Bushell and John Horne were paid £100 each; William Marsh received £125 as did James Spratford, although no details were given on his contribution to the capture. Two Blockade Officers collected 'head money' of £20 each for taking Bushell and Horne. Other sums were, no doubt, paid (to Edward Panting for example) but not listed. No details were given of any money paid to Sam Hellard and the men who made those two marches, each of 30 miles, into the wilds of Kent to bring back 12 prisoners but they certainly deserved a major share of the reward.

When the North Kent Gang was defeated in 1821 there was a lull of some five years before smugglers started to use fire-arms again in any organised manner. The departure of the Aldington Gang also brought a lull, but it was shorter than before. Unnamed gangs would use fire-arms against Blockade men in the Battles of Bexhill and Eastbourne (see Chapter Six) and in 1829 and 1830 around Margate and Walmer.

The publicity given to the capture of George Ransley and his men did nothing to deter other smugglers who were willing to take their chances with the Blockade, albeit without fire-arms. For some it was probably nothing more than the welcome removal of a major competitor in the Trade. On 18 December 1826 Lieutenant Earle from Kingsdown, near Dover, was afloat in his galley and after a short chase captured a large ten oar galley off the Casemates. During the chase the smugglers threw their cargo of 27 bales of silk overboard and these drifted ashore later at Cornhill and St Margarets. The Lieutenant placed a man on board the smuggler's galley and took it in tow, but with no cargo the crew now had room to move around. They tried to take the Blockade man as hostage and threw everything they could find at the Blockade galley. As Lieutenant Earle said '. . . there were 11 of them and 6 of us. I said I would open fire but they persisted with the attack and so I ordered two volleys into the open boat, but all pistols were without balls. After this the smugglers gave in'. This particular boat load of smugglers comprised ten Englishmen and one Frenchman, the latter as usual being released without charge and returned to France.

In March 1827, some ten years after she had first featured in Blockade records that bad old smuggling lugger the *Po* of Deal was still at it. This time she was caught with 24 bales of tea (probably from an East Indiaman in the Channel) after she came into Deal beach. Lieutenant Marshall had arranged a joint operation between Blockade men and some local Customs officers. They lay in wait until the lugger was being drawn up the beach with all her crew manning the beach capstan. Then the Customs were supposed to grab the crew but, according to the Lieutenant, '. . . there was some neglect . . .' and the smugglers escaped. Later, without doubt, the owner of *Po* bought her back from Customs at a ridiculously low price and she was soon once again on a run.

On the occasion of this seizure it seems there were a few Customs officers and a large number of Blockade men. A few months later the Board of Customs granted a reward of £300 for the seizure of the *Po* and her cargo 'to be equally divided between officers and men of the Coast Blockade and officers of the Revenue'. But how was this to be interpreted? Captain Pigot assumed it gave equal shares to all who took part in the seizure but John Ward, Collector of Customs at Dover, thought otherwise. It became a contentious issue and on 11 June, because it was still in dispute, an irate John Ward wrote to Pigot declaring that the phase 'being equally divided' meant £300 split into £150 for each force! Eventually the Board of Customs confirmed that Captain Pigot's assumption was the correct one. One feature brought to light in this episode was that, some ten years after the establishment of the Blockade, papers from Blockade commanders to the Board of Customs, and vice versa, still had to pass through the Navy Board and the Treasury. A fact of every-day life for the bureaucrat, but a frustrating burden for the commanders.

One preventive measure introduced by the Board of Customs during the 1820s was to require all sailing vessels working out of ports between the

Custom-House, London,

10th November, 1825.

Notice is hereby Given,

THAT from and after the 5th day of January, 1826, all Vessels not square rigged, and all Boats except Whale Boats, Boats employed in the Fisheries, Boats belonging to square rigged Vessels in the Merchants' Service, Tow Boats used in towing Vessels belonging to licenced Pilots, and Boats used solely in Rivers and Inland Navigation, will in pursuance of the Act of the 6th Geo. IV. ch. 108, be subject to seizure and forfeiture, unless the Owners thereof shall have obtained a Licence for navigating the same, from the Commissioners of His Majesty's Customs.

This Notice is therefore given by the said Commissioners, in order that the Owners of all Vessels and Boats, requiring Licences under the above Act, may forthwith make application to the proper Officers of the Customs at the Port to which such Vessels and Boats belong, and take the necessary measures for procuring Licences for the same, prior to the 5th January, 1826.

By Order of the Commissioners,

T. WHITMORE,

Secretary.

Teape, Printer, Tower-hill, London

Licences were introduced restricting the movements of many vessels as yet another measure to combat smuggling.

Thames and Dungeness to be licensed to operate only within a certain distance, usually 12 miles, of the coast. The boat owner also had to take out a bond set at treble the value of the boat and then if the craft was seen outside the licensed area she could be seized and the bond forfeited. Packet boats and ships engaged in legitimate cross Channel trade were exempt but they had to use ports where they and their cargo could be brought under Customs control immediately on arrival.

Blockade tenders frequently patrolled the Channel and would occasionally seize a sailing boat for being beyond the limits of its licence. On 5 April 1827 Lieutenant Sam Hellard was on such a patrol in *Grinder* when he boarded the Dover lugger *Scorpion.* At first he was merely going to seize her for being in unlicensed waters but he knew she had left Sandgate on 22 March with six crew and stood across for Boulogne. A closer examination was required but let Sam continue in his own words:

> She had not been seen since at or near Sandgate, her usual place of hauling up. I saw her steering for Sandgate, boarded her and a few minutes later saw pieces floating stern that I took for cork buoys but sent a boat out and found them to be pieces of French bread thrown from Scorpion. I anchored her and observing mate William Hoad to be anxious I directed him to be searched. He was found to have an invoice for his cargo dated 24 March and sundry bills for himself and crew for food and meals in Boulogne. Dinners at 5s, suppers 4s, beds 2s-6d – from 23 March right up to 3 April. Also written directions for goods to be landed on west side Dungeness between the two watch houses. Various conditions and charges were there :- Freight £14, use of punt £2, loss of punt £14. Two sinkings were to be made on Sunday and Tuesday nights at two rendezvous. The condi-

tions ended "if you see a steady light come on in, if flashing go to sea" The cargo invoice shows 65 tubs brandy at 17s (one for the Captain), 35 tubs gin at 16s. Discount of £8-6s. 10lbs Pedro tea at 3s-6d. 4lbs Imperial tea at 5s-6d.'

Rarely was a smuggling run so well documented! The papers do not show what happened to William Hoad and his crew this time but if there were any subsequent runs he undoubtedly kept his business records well and truly hidden.

Shortly after this seizure *Grinder* was in action again, now under the command of Lieutenant Howes. Off Boulogne the yawl *Brothers*, out of Rye, was sighted and followed. She drew ahead of *Grinder*, making for Rye, but Howes was able to keep close enough for a good view through his telescope. Some six miles off the English coast the *Brothers* suddenly lowered her sails; Howes believed this was to hide the activities of the crew as they jettisoned the cargo. When he went on board the master, J Wheeler, told a likely tale that his vessel had met with an accident '. . . but was now secure . . .' Howes and his men found nothing on board except that many pages had been torn out of the ship's account book. This master was obviously more experienced in the Trade than William Hoad. But Howes did find one discarded receipt for £37 signed William Phillips; Phillips and Co were boat builders based in Boulogne and well known for repairing and 'adapting' smugglers' boats. Finally the Lieutenant noted that Master Wheeler had been imprisoned in Dover Gaol and 'was one of those involved in that escape 6 or 7 years ago'. Master Wheeler certainly had experience in the Trade.

It seems the French coast was a popular hunting ground for Blockade tenders at this time. On 18 November 1827 Lieutenant W. Marshall in *Antelope* encountered the large Deal galley *Norfolk* some four miles off Calais. The galley, fitted with two sails, was caught after a chase but not before, as Marshall believed, she had dropped her cargo overboard as darkness intervened. She was boarded without resistance from the crew because with an empty ship they had nothing to fear (except the wrath of those in Deal who had financed the run!) but the *Norfolk* was seized for being beyond the limits of her licence and handed over to the Customs at Deal.

Sadly, accidents and resultant deaths still continued to feature in the everyday work of the Blockade. Around 9.15am on 29 September a Blockade boat from Townsend Battery capsized on the bar of Dover Harbour in a raging gale. Two Dover fishing boats the *Graball* and the *Swift* crewed by Richard Griffen and nine others went to the rescue of a petty officer and four seamen, but one was drowned.

This was an era when, as shown in Chapter Seven, more attention was being given to saving lives from shipwrecks with the increasing use, along the coast, of lifeboats and life saving apparatus. The Navy too was exploring ways to save the lives of seamen who fell overboard from a man-of-war when, say, she was ploughing through an Atlantic swell. To this end Lieutenant Jackson R.N. had invented what he called a 'life preserver'. The records do not show whether he was a Blockade officer but it is quite probable because the Admiralty gave permission for him to test it off

Ramillies and asked Captain Pigot to report its suitability. It seems to have been a small collapsible dinghy, probably made of canvas, with oars, sail, compass and 'buoyants'. Intended to be dropped to a man overboard when it was impossible to launch a boat, it met with some favour from the Captain but he had his doubts about using it in heavy seas and strong winds.

Back on dry land, the Blockade officers were finding that, whilst some magistrates were now more willing to convict smugglers, it was still quite a problem holding on to them once they were convicted. Lieutenant Webb caught five men near Fort Moncrief and they were duly brought before magistrates William Deedes and James Brackman in the Hythe Court which sat in a room at the local inn, a common arrangement in many towns. When the accused, all local men, were found guilty and given five years impressment there was pandemonium in the inn. In full view of the magistrates one prisoner, William Cocks, was rescued by friends and spirited away. The remaining four were held with difficulty.

Lieutenant Sam Hellard had warned the magistrates of trouble and of a possible escape and asked them to hold the court in Fort Moncrief, but they refused. Sam may have been 'given to the occasional use of strong language with his men' but on paper he was a diplomat – in contrast to McCulloch! – and acknowledged that the magistrates were nevertheless '. . . men for whom I have great respect'. A few days later Lieutenant Charles Johnson caught another six local men and this time strong Blockade escorts were provided to bring the accused from Fort Sutherland and to line the Court Room. Each of the six received five years impressment and they were marched straight to Hythe beach to embark on a Blockade tender.

Towards the end of 1827 it was decided that an additional Blockade Station was needed between Whitstable and Sea Salter. The Fish House at Sea Salter Cliff was reported to be for sale and the owner, Mr Jarrett, was apparently willing to include two acres of land in the asking price of £250. Mr Gunnell, Purser of Left Division was ordered to make discreet enquiries 'to prevent any supposition that the government wished to become the owner because the price would surely rise'. The war against smuggling was indeed a complex affair! Enquiries were so discreet that the purchase took some time but the Navy Board bought the property eventually on 13 November 1828. Further west along that coast an unnamed lighter, fitted out at Chatham, was beached at Milton on 20 May 1828 to provide an additional Blockade Station in East Swale.

Lieutenant Charles Johnson was in action again on 18 August 1828 when, about 5pm, he sighted the French lugger *Le Jeune Rose* towing two tub boats. He launched his galley and tried to board the vessel 'but the Frenchmen cut the painter as often as I made fast. I fired a musket at the foresail and rigging and brought them down. The crew tried to drop 30lb sinkers into my galley but we fired frequently and wounded the helmsman'. The Lieutenant and his four men captured the lugger and her 12 crew together with the two tub boats and 142 tubs and he certainly deserved the commendation he later received for this action.

The first question mark over the future of the Royal Naval Coast

Blockade Service came in 1828. Viscount Melville had been First Lord of the Admiralty up to 1827 but he was then replaced for a short while by Prince William, Duke of Clarence who would later reign, from 1830 until his death in 1837, as William IV 'the Sailor King'. The blunt speaking Prince William, who took the rank of Lord High Admiral, was eased out of harm's way in September 1828, but during his time in office he attempted to reduce costs in the Admiralty and even tried – heresy of heresies! – to reduce the number of senior naval appointments. This brief economy drive may explain why on 31 March 1828 a report was sent from the Board of Customs to the Admiralty headed 'Rough Estimate of probable Coast Guard force on the coast between Sheerness and Chichester to replace the Coast Blockade'. This said that 728 officers and men would be needed plus 8 cruisers with 228 men at a total coast of £63,000.

In passing this to the Lord High Admiral, John Barrow at the Navy Board, was scathing in his covering note 'In 1821 the total number of cruisers (excluding revenue cruisers) between Portsmouth and Sheerness was 22 at the expense of £92,000 and yet smuggling was carried on to a enormous extent. I do not see how 8 can prevent it . . . cruisers are of little or no use in the narrow part of the Channel where smuggling is carried on in boats and by night and generally by concerted signals just after bad weather when the cruisers are in port. Nor do I see how 700 men can effectively resist the shoals of smugglers on shore when 1400 find great difficulty in doing so'. Actually the total complement of the Blockade Service in Kent and Sussex at this time was just over 2800. But whatever the figures, John Barrow's comments evidently scuppered this particular economy measure and it was pigeon-holed for the time being.

The toll of accidental deaths rose again in February 1829 when a Blockade galley from *Pelter* at Eastware was sent out to creep for tubs. Off Copt Point she overturned after striking a submerged rock and all five men on board drowned. It was off Eastware that ten men had lost their lives in 1818 when their galley was believed to have been run down by a larger vessel.

In March 1829 Captain Pigot received two petitions from local fishermen because those French boats were at it again; this time shooting their nets within a few yards of Deal beach. The Deal men complained '. . . our fishermen are not permitted to fish within six miles of the French coast and there are four armed French cutters to prevent this'. Seeking to enlist the Navy's sympathy the second petition, signed by 116 Deal fishermen, mentioned the risk to the security of local boats '. . . in case of sudden rupture with France these (French) fishermen becoming masters and pilots of privateers would be able in the right time to cut out our vessels from their anchorage'. Rich words indeed from local men some of whom had working friends and even relatives on the other side of the Channel! Some took their smuggling luggers regularly into French ports and, during the last 'rupture', had been running gold out weekly to pay Napoleon's army! Wisely Captain Pigot and all Blockade Parties were told by the Admiralty to just report the names and descriptions of offending French fishing boats and take no other action.

H.M.S. Trafalgar *a fine third rater similar to* Ramillies *and* Talavera.

When a warship had to be commissioned urgently, perhaps for some overseas trouble spot, men from the Blockade Service were allowed to volunteer for transfer. In 1828 and 1829 the demand for ships crews was so high that the number of men transferring out greatly exceeded those arriving as recruits and some parts of the Line in Kent (and Sussex) were consequently well below strength at times. In June 1829 for example when 114 men were sent to ships in the Mediterranean the overall deficit on the Kent Line and *Ramillies* was 557 out of a complement of 1,767.

Up to 1828 the First Lieutenants on Blockade depot ships had been senior Lieutenants but the Admiralty changed this in January 1828 by appointing Commander W.J. Hood as First Lieutenant on *Hyperion* at Newhaven and, in June 1829, Commander Vincent Newton took up the same post on *Ramillies*. Also in the summer of 1829 the Navy Board decided to replace *Ramillies*, the grand old veteran now 44 years old, with *Talavera* (74) as the depot ship for the Kent Coast Blockade. H.M.S. *Talavera*, named after the battle of 1809, was similar to *Ramillies* but only 13 years old.

Captain Pigot was appointed to command *Talavera* on 16 September 1829 when she was still in Chatham and he sent Commander Newton with five officers and some seamen to supervise the fitting out. The work took some time and although more crew men were sent in November and December it was not until 12 February 1830 that *Talavera* was brought, under tow by two steam vessels, to her moorings off Deal.

Provisions for issue to Blockade Stations were normally held in bulk on board the depot ship but during the changeover arrangements had to be made for temporary storage in Deal Navy Yard. The records of this storage give an insight into the routine supplies for about 800 officers and men in

Centre and Right Divisions for four months: 2,100 galls rum; 200 galls wine; 3,200 1lbs tobacco; 6,300 lbs sugar; 4,200 lbs cocoa; 1,050 lbs tea; 500 galls vinegar; 60 bushels oatmeals and 3,200 lbs soap. The rum, wine and tobacco were duty free stocks held, in accordance with Customs laws, on board all naval ships in commission. Rum was issued to all officers and ratings in the depot ship and in Blockade Stations, but the wine was only for commissioned officers stationed on board the ship – those ashore received a cash allowance in lieu. Tobacco was also available only to officers and men stationed on the ship where they could buy up to two lbs a month, duty free, from the purser. Traditionally the tobacco was moistened with molasses and bound with cord and canvas into a small elongated parcel known as a 'perique', perhaps ten inches long, that could later be cut into flakes by the pipe smoker.

All officers and men, afloat or ashore, were allowed 1lb fresh bread, 1lb fresh meat and 1/2lb vegetables per day – all supplied by local contractors – as well as 1oz cocoa, 1 1/2oz sugar and 1/4oz tea. Each week they could also have 1/2 pint oatmeal and 1/2 pint vinegar.

Hot cocoa (or 'kye' as it was nicknamed) must have been a welcome drink for sentinels after a spell on watch during a long winter's night. Some idea of the rigours they experienced was given when Lieutenant Sam Hellard was asked to comment on an anonymous letter sent to the Navy Board from an inhabitant of Dover (probably a Blockade man or his wife) about '. . . the dreadful conditions under which Coast Blockade Sentinels operate at night'. Hellard reported that, whenever possible, the men were put into three watches at night and all were issued with Government Beach Clothing. As he pointed out, the winter had already been really severe '. . . so intense was the cold on the night of 1 December 1829 that when a smuggling boat landed near Hythe one of the tub carriers was left drowned on the beach *with* his two tubs . . .' The weather must indeed have been dreadful to sacrifice not only one of the gang but two precious tubs as well!

The same papers were then passed to Captain Mingaye of the Sussex Coast Blockade for his comments. He said his men were divided into two watches causing them to be out six hours each watch during the night. He went on to explain '. . . for clothing they have worsted stockings, stout shoes that cover the ankle, flannel drawers, thick blue trousers made on purpose and supplied gratuitously to the men, flannel waistcoat next the skin, over their shirts a stout woollen Guernsey jacket, a common blue jacket and over that (supplied as the trousers are) a stout blue Pea jacket reaching below the knee, and worsted gloves. Any man found in a turpor from cold is removed to the watch house to find every requisite comfort to hand. In the day the men are not out more than 3 hours and retire to bed at 3pm'.

Captain Pigot, unlike his predecessor, sent few routine reports to his Admiral about fights along the Kent Line. Similarly, whereas McCulloch had always taken the lead in planning strategy and preventive measures, Pigot was content to leave it to his Divisional Lieutenants: George White (Left), William Johnson (Centre) and Sam Hellard (Right).

In the winter of 1829 the shortage of men on the Kent Line was serious

Maidstone Gaol 1828. – E.S. Murray

enough for the Collector, Dover, to send a minute to the Navy Board, via Pigot, noting with concern '. . . the very great increase in smuggling between South Foreland and Dungeness arising we believe to the very slender and defective state of the Coast Blockade in comparison to what it used to be . . . there is a want of some inland force to intercept goods after being run through the Beach Cordon of Coast Blockade Sentinels'. It was evident from the Collector's minute that unnamed gangs were still very active; one report described how 80 men with 12 loaded carts rode through Lydd to the cheers of many of the townsfolk. But Pigot passed the Collector's paper on to the Navy Board without a comment. One can only imagine what McCulloch would have said!

It was left to Sam Hellard to defend his men's work when necessary. On 18 March 1830 he reported that Customs believed several runs had been made east of Rye. Diplomatically as ever, he went on ' . . . I have ever found the Collector and Comptroller particularly attentive to all requests which I have ever had occasion to lay before them . . . the reports originated from Excise officer Hawke . . . Believing as I do that scarcely a single tub of spirits has been landed within the limits of this division since 30 November last. Customs have suggested an inland force of dragoons but this would, in the true meaning of the word, be a useless expense. The Coast Blockade can do the work well if on full strength. At the present spirits are rather scarce in Sandgate, people have to send some distance in the county for supplies'.

By April the Collector was still concerned enough to write again because there had been some reports of arms being used again by smugglers. Captain Pigot was moved this time to add some comments acknowledging

Two Hundred Pounds Reward.

WHITEHALL, 6TH APRIL, 1830.

WHEREAS it has been humbly represented to the King, that about two o'clock in the morning of Wednesday, the 31st ultimo, a large party of armed Smugglers feloniously assembled on the Sea Shore, near Dymchurch, in the county of Kent, and were aiding and assisting in the illegal landing, running, and carrying away of uncustomed Goods; and that in opposing this felonious act, and in seizing part of the said Goods, Lieutenant Gustavus Spicker Baker, and Martin Donovan, seamen, both of his Majesty's ship "Talavera", were attacked, violently beaten with clubs, and severly bruised.

His Majesty, for the better discovering the persons who have been guilty of this felony, is hereby pleased to promise his most gracious Pardon to any one or more of the persons so assembled (except those who actually committed violence on the said Lieutenant and Seaman on this occasion) who shall discover his accomplices, so that they may be apprehended and brought to justice.

ROBERT PEEL.

And the Lords Commissioners of the Admiralty hereby offer a Reward of Two Hundred Pounds, to be paid to, or distributed amongst, any person or persons (except as aforesaid) who shall give information to Captain Pigot, of the "Talavera", or to any of the Officers of the said ship, as shall lead to the discovery, apprehension, and conviction of the said offenders: such Reward to be payable by Mr. CHARLES JONES, the Solicitor of the Admiralty and Navy, on the conviction of the said offenders, or any of them.

J. W. CROKER.

Public notice issued jointly by the Home Office and Admirality

'armed gangs have been met most recently near Margate and Walmer'. With rather rash logic he went on 'if the line of coast covered by the Coast Guard was so thickly manned as that of the Coast Blockade then armed gangs would be everywhere . . .' More sensibly he added '. . . dragoons would be useless guarding bridges over the (Royal Military) canal because smugglers would cross by boat elsewhere'.

That same month Captain Pigot did refer to 'a recent smuggling transaction in which Lieutenant Baker was badly beaten near Dymchurch'. This occurred on 31 March when Lieutenant Gustavus Baker and Sentinel Martin Donovan from Towers 23 and 24 were both severely wounded in the head and legs by batmen in a fight with smugglers on Dymchurch Wall. The Blockade men seized 22 tubs but at least 200 were carted away. The savage attack prompted the government to offer informers a pardon and a reward of £200. The notice making the offer was signed by Robert Peel, Home Secretary and John Croker on 6 April 1830 but it seems no informant was willing to come forward.

The main purpose of Pigot's report about the attack on Lieutenant Baker was to ask for a new item of equipment '. . .men had to repeatedly fire off pistols as alarms and this leaves them almost defenceless. I would request an order of Portfires, one for each officer and man . . . this will also prevent accidents whereby in the confusion the men in the rear fire upon those in front (who made the alarm) mistaking them for smugglers'. Portfires – hand-held blue flares – had only recently been introduced and sadly they came almost at the end of the Blockade's existence. They enabled a sentinel to give the alarm and still have a loaded pistol ready for defence. It was a pity these flares had not been there in earlier years when they would have saved some injuries and even deaths amongst Blockade men.

The shortage of personnel in the Kent Line in 1830 also extended to officers. In an effort to persuade their Lordships to provide more Lieutenants Pigot offered some arithmetic: 'Full pay for Lieutenants = £119-18s, half pay =£91-5s, difference = £28-13s. Pay for First Class Quartermasters = £29-19s'. The Blockade at this time had enough Quartermasters and other senior petty officers and the arithmetic seemed to show it would be cheaper to employ Lieutenants. It was a good try but their Lordships were not swayed by these sums possibly because they conveniently ignored the officer's wine allowance of £20.

Breaches of discipline continued as ever; cases of bribery, desertion and neglect of duty were commonplace. At Conyer Station, Lieutenant William Pinkhorn was inspected by Divisional Lieutenant George White and found to be four gallons and two pints short in the rum store. Pinkhorn admitted he had been indulging at the rate of six to eight gills a time over his allowance! He had already been moved from another station. The Admiralty said he must be superseded at once, without waiting for a relief.

The problem with two Blockade men at Lydd Station was on a much lower scale. Parish constables John and William Smith were given certificates of appreciation for apprehending Charles Bill, Landsman, and Thomas Crawford, Ordinary Seaman, who had 'straggled' from their station. Straggling (absent during the daytime perhaps?) was a minor naval offence and each man duly received 15 lashes. Crawford had joined the Blockade Service after being discharged from the 15th Hussars in 1826 with a pension of one shilling a day.

The moral question of flogging as a punishment was obviously still the subject of some debate in the Navy in 1830 and their Lordships at the Admiralty were willing to try other ideas for physical punishment. At the end of April Captain Pigot reported quite favourably to the Admiralty after a three month trial of experimental equipment. This used collars made of oak that were available in three sizes : 30lbs, 25lbs and 18lbs. Each also had fastenings to attach another two 18lb shots 'in extreme cases'. The Captain gave his general approval and concluded '. . . it lies flat on the shoulders and is secured around the neck with a padlock. Men have more dread of this than being flogged'. Despite this endorsement there were no reports in Blockade records of 1830 that these collars were in regular use but flogging remained as a punishment in the Navy for another 40 years.

The summer of 1830 saw the departure of Sam Hellard when he was promoted to Commander on 22 July. After almost ten years in the Blockade Service he was the longest serving Lieutenant in Kent and those were years he could look back over with pride and satisfaction; his dedication and perseverance had brought some outstanding results. As it happened Sam was not away from the smuggling scene for long because he returned to the same area nine months later, in April 1831, when he was appointed Commander, Deal Coastguard District. He served there until 1836 and again from 1838 to 1839 after which time he was promoted to Captain and remained as such, on half pay, until his death in 1848 at the age of 62.

Another doughty officer, Lieutenant William (Hellfire Bill) Lilburn left the war against smuggling when he retired, with a decent pension, from the revenue cruiser *Lively* in 1830. Unlike their counterparts in the Royal Navy, officers on revenue vessels were eligible for superannuation. During the 24 years he had commanded the cruiser Lilburn had certainly seen some changes, not only in those who controlled the fleet of revenue vessels but also in the levels of smuggling. The comparatively quiet spell towards the end of the Napoleonic wars had been followed by the explosive years of the Coast Blockade which now, in 1830, showed no signs of abating.

The spring and summer of 1830 saw considerable unrest in the rural areas of Kent and Sussex. The poverty, unemployment and hardship that had been rife in the early 1820s were still around at the end of the decade. Attitudes were hardening amongst farm workers but at first there were only isolated incidents where a barn was set alight or a meeting of farmers stormed by local protesters. These minor, spasmodic outbursts were easily contained within the parishes but then came the hard winter of 1829 where many crops failed. The prices of corn and bread remained high; they showed no signs of dropping and attitudes hardened amongst the protesters. In 1830 the agitation became more organised when members of Radical groups addressed large crowds of men many of whom had families living barely above starvation levels.

Across the two counties written demands and threats were sent to farmers and landowners in the name of a mythical Captain Swing. Few threats were against the person, they were usually concerned with machinery and property. Except in Rye, where attempts were made to demolish a sluice and a bridge, rioters usually burnt barns and ricks and smashed the job-destroying threshing machines. Nevertheless the threat to public order grew so great that the Coast Blockade Service was called upon at times to provide civil security against rioting mobs, particularly in Sussex. The Swing Riots started in Kent but spread quickly through Sussex which was still the poorest county in Britain. The first report of a threshing machine being destroyed was at Lower Hardres near Canterbury on 28 August 1830, but four months before, as mentioned in the next chapter, there was a serious riot in Rye when a Blockade officer and 27 of his men had to face a mob of around 1,000.

In his reports Captain Pigot made only one reference to a request for the Kent Blockade Force to provide assistance against riots, although there were probably others not logged. On 15 November 1830 the Town Clerk at New

Romney said a body of labourers was about to cause a disturbance and the magistrates sought the help and assistance of the Coast Blockade. Pigot ordered Divisional Lieutenant James Stuart to '. . . so arrange . . . provided the beach remains guarded . . .'

Riots or not the smuggling still went on. In October the *Kent Gazette* reported 'a smuggling transaction at Shellness when Lieutenant Autridge and his party caught Thomas Brown, James Hall, Richard Keen, Henry Coltrup and Thomas Wood. They were later taken, under a Blockade escort, before the magistrates sitting at the Dover Castle Inn. The guards . . . had strict orders to be watchful of the prisoners. Notwithstanding this precaution one of them, Thomas Wood, actually walked away unobserved . . . and regained his liberty to the infinite joy of the bystanders . . .'

Five years had now passed since the separate Kent Blockade Force had been established and in that time it had expanded by adding nine new Stations to those shown in the 1825 list of Appendix C, against the loss of three closures. In the Left Division new Stations at Milton, Conyer, Faversham, Castle Coote and Sea Salter Cliff were opened and those at Harty and Graveney closed. In the Centre Division Westgate, Sandwich and *Pelter* (Eastware) were opened and Hougham closed, whilst the Right Division had a new Station at Galloway, west of Dungeness. Plans were afoot for further improvements. At Lydden Spout, for instance, Mr Marsh agreed to take £12 a year for the rent of half an acre of his land and the use of a 9ft wide track to the main road. It was proposed to move the watch house there at a cost of £50.

Everything seemed to point to a sure and steady future for the Coast Blockade. In December 1830 Captain Pigot authorised William Peche, Purser of Right Division, to contract the supply of fresh beef for the year commencing 1 January 1831. Contracts were made with George Green to supply Dover District at 37s-6d a cart, Thomas Mitchell to supply Hythe District at 41s-0d a cart and James Smith to supply Romney District at 41s-0d a cart.

Unknown to all in the region – traders and Navy men alike – the Coast Blockade Service had only a few more months before it would be abolished. The demise was not far off as they entered 1831 but, as Chapter Eight shows, there were still one or two more vicious fights to be fought with the smuggling gangs before the naval sentinels stood down.

CHAPTER SIX

The Sussex Coast Blockade, 1825–30

Early in March 1825 Captain William James Mingaye moved from the Oriental Club, his temporary abode in London, down to Newhaven to rejoin his ship and take command of the Sussex Coast Blockade. As with many of his colleagues, Mingaye's early years in the Royal Navy had taken him to stations far and near although his service in home waters had been longer than that of either McCulloch or Pigot. He entered the Navy as a Volunteer in 1798 and made Lieutenant quite rapidly in 1805. Then came twelve years of sea service in the East Indies, Mediterranean and home waters before he advanced to Commander in 1817 and was given command of the revenue cruiser *Cameleon* (10) based at Portsmouth.

Some four years in command of *Cameleon* gave Mingaye ample experience of preventive work in the Channel. In 1822 his successor on the revenue cruiser was engaged in the acrimonious correspondence with Captain McCulloch mentioned in Chapter Four, but by then William Mingaye had moved on and 'made post' in 1823 as the acting Captain of the yacht *Royal George*. In July 1824 he took command of the troopship *Romney* (50), fitting out at Chatham, but was moved to command *Hyperion* (42), then at Sheerness, with a commission dated 8 January 1825.

H.M.S. *Hyperion* was a frigate, a fifth rate man-of-war, that had seen service in South America, the Pacific and the West Indies. With a harbour crew of around 250 men she would be the depot ship for the Sussex Blockade but, unlike the arrangements at Deal, there was no Navy Yard close by to provide naval stores, most of which had to be brought by tenders from Portsmouth, although Blockade galleys were still built and repaired at Deal.

H.M.S. *Viper* and H.M.S. *Highflyer* were assigned as tenders to the Sussex Blockade in March 1825 but within weeks Captain Mingaye had his eyes on a third vessel. His men in Rye had just seized the *Dart*, an 18 ton sloop, with a cargo of spirits. Back in 1820 Mingaye remembered seizing her sister ship, the *Diamond*, only to see it sold by Customs at public auction for a ridiculous £100 and, as usual, returned promptly to the smuggling trade. The *Diamond* had continued her nefarious work until the day in November 1824 at Rye when Lieutenant Dicken bored those holes in her to find the clever concealments of four lines of tubs below the ballast.

The *Diamond* was then destroyed because she had those concealed spaces but the *Dart* had only a cargo hold with no hidden places. In the normal way she would have been auctioned but Mingaye said she would be a useful tender. The Board of Customs agreed and the *Dart* served the Sussex Blockade at least until September 1830. She seemed a particular favourite with Captain Mingaye and he used her from time to time for visits to stations.

In the fight against smuggling Mingaye was equally as dedicated as McCulloch if not quite so eloquent and informative in his reports. At the start he acknowledged his main problems were shortage of men and the perennial matters of discipline – particularly bribery and desertion. In an early report to Vice Admiral George Martin at Portsmouth on 12 June, Captain Mingaye explained that the Sussex Line was some 98 miles long, exclusive of harbour shorelines. Along the line he considered the greatest problem was bribery, which had reached alarming proportions '. . . with only 2 men per mile bribery may be successful but not so if there are 4 men per mile – it is our most serious evil'. Thus, quite neatly, he used the mounting incidence of bribery to support an increase in complement and asked for a total of 1058 officers and men. This did not include the ship's company of *Hyperion* which dropped from a full crew of 304 to a harbour crew of 248.

The new Blockade complement was endorsed by John Croker and agreed by their Lordships. Mingaye could now set about finding the 54 petty officers and 222 other ratings needed to bring the Line up to full strength. He sent his two tenders away on recruitment voyages and stationed two Blockade officers for some months at the *Perseus* recruitment rendezvous in London. This soon produced results; by August the deficiency had dropped to 54 and by the end of the year the Sussex Blockade was at full strength, a situation that prevailed throughout 1826.

During the summer of 1825 Mingaye decided that the existing titles of his three Divisions – Fourth, Fifth and Sixth – were inappropriate now that the Sussex Blockade was a separate entity. He changed them to East (Camber-Langney), Centre (Tower 71-East Shoreham) and West (West Shoreham-Chichester Harbour). At that time the Divisional Lieutenants were Mr Barton (East) at Hastings, Mr Chappell (Centre) at Newhaven and Mr Dickson (West) at Littlehampton but over the next five years there would be several changes amongst the officers who held these posts.

The new Blockade commander also brought fresh ideas on other matters and within weeks of his arrival Mingaye produced his own initiative to combat bribery. He sent an order to all officers and men announcing that henceforth the Party involved in a seizure would receive 10% of the gross amount of the reward plus 10% of Mingaye's share in addition to their own individual share and any 'head money' due from the capture of smugglers. Head money at that time was £20 if the man's conviction resulted in impressment and £15 if he went to prison.

A few weeks later Captain Mingaye was reporting, with obvious pleasure, that the measures taken to combat bribery appeared to be working. Cornelius Kehely, a Landsman at Hastings was offered a bribe of £40 but reported it to his officer. At the event the smugglers landed their goods and,

Clockwise from top left (1) a water tank fitted with two compartments for hiding spirits. (2) tubs roped in pairs for ease of handling (3) a sectional sketch of a vessel fitted with secret spaces full of tubs.

as dastardly as ever, gave Kehely a few sovereigns bulked out with silver coins so as to appear in the darkness to be the promised sum. The Blockade men swooped and captured all the tubs; unfortunately the boat got away because one of the Blockade men in the pursuing galley 'lost his stroke'. Honest Cornelius was not only allowed to keep the money, he was also promoted to Ordinary Seaman.

A report from Lieutenant William Jones, Felpham District on 18 March 1825, just after Mingaye had taken up his post, showed the friction that existed at times within the Navy between the Coast Blockade and the men-of-war engaged on preventive work in the Channel. H.M.S. *Brazen* was on a preventive patrol when she sighted a large white lugger at anchor off Elmer and launched a boarding gig. Whereupon a galley, already loaded with tubs, put off from the lugger and made quickly for the shore. The landing '. . . to the east of the cottage on Elmer Station' was seen by Sentinel William Connally when he was some distance away. He ran towards the landing spot and the eleven men in the galley, realising they were in danger of being caught between the sentinel and *Brazen's* gig, made off across the beach.

Connally was the first to reach the galley and its intact cargo of tubs. He stood there to claim it as his seizure, but when the gig landed a Lieutenant jumped ashore, drew his pistol and threatened to shoot the sentinel unless he backed off! That was one seizure the Blockade did not get; it seems the officers of *Brazen* would not countenance sharing the credit (and the reward) with their service colleagues in the Blockade. Divisional Lieutenant Dickson felt sufficiently annoyed to write a strong report protesting about the unwarranted threats to Connally, but no further action was taken.

Less than two months later *Brazen* moored in the Downs off Deal. Her commander, Captain Willes, was senior to Captain McCulloch and, as mentioned in Chapter Five, took great exception when the latter failed to pay the customary respectful visit on board, even though the poor man was seriously ill.

The first report from Captain Mingaye on a smuggling incident said briefly that one smuggler had been arrested at Ecclesbourne on 15 March, had been fined £100 and despatched to Horsham Gaol in default of payment. No name, no goods, no details of the landing. Unfortunately, this was typical of some of the early reports from the Sussex Blockade.

Captain Mingaye's particular interests seemed to be in matters of equipment, weapons and clothing. Within weeks of his arrival at Newhaven he placed an order with local coppersmiths for 500 cartouches – pocket cases made of copper to carry shot – and one was to be issued to every sentinel as he went on watch. Later that year he requisitioned 1,058 short pistols and 136 muskets. The new smaller pistols were easier to hold under a sentinel's coats and so could be better kept dry on a wet night.

In his early days in the Blockade Service Captain McCulloch had derided the quality of cloth used in his men's uniform trousers. Some ten years on, it seems nothing had changed; in 1825 Captain Mingaye condemned '. . .the very poor uniform trousers of blue cloth. Particularly for this service they are of no use after a few days wear . . .' On a later occasion, still concerned over the quality of clothing, he informed the Navy Board that '. . . on the coast where there is marshy ground I have found it necessary to issue 3 flannel waistcoats to every seamen to wear under their shirts . . .' His report was, in effect, seeking retrospective authority for the issue, made out of slops, otherwise the Captain would have to pay the full cost himself!

The Blockade Station at East Elmer provided quite a few problems during 1825. On 8 April 30 new men arrived at Littlehampton to join nearby stations and some were due to go to East Elmer. But four men had deserted from there in the past few days. Obviously suspecting the cause to be harsh discipline Captain Mingaye asked for the officer in charge, Lieutenant Newnham, to be transferred but the Admiralty refused. Somehow or other he was moved because on 23 June the East Elmer Party, now led by Lieutenant James Carter, was involved in a violent fight with local smugglers and one, Charles Horne, was shot dead by Carter.

Next month one of those early deserters from East Elmer, Richard Harrison, met up with his old pal Sentinel Jim Sullivan and tried to persuade him to come and have a drink. Sullivan refused and told Lieutenant Carter who went to the inn, the Black Horse, and found the deserter playing skittles with a corporal and two lancers of the dragoons. Carter demanded the dragoons help in securing Harrison as a prisoner but the orders were ignored and the deserter slipped away once again.

That year it seems harsh discipline was endemic at East Elmer. On 21 October Captain Mingaye was called quickly to the station to investigate a case of mutiny. Lieutenant Carter alleged that Quartermaster Jeremiah Wilkins had threatened him with a cocked pistol but Mingaye soon found that Wilkins was at the end of his tether. Carter had been assaulting him frequently for months and the Lieutenant subsequently admitted striking and abusing the other men in the station. The Admiralty ordered that Carter be discharged forthwith without waiting for a replacement. Poor Wilkins, then 42 years old, was also discharged for outrageous and unjustifiable conduct – and lost his wound pension of £10-12s.

The injustice suffered by Quartermaster Henry Isum at Hastings was more of the traditional kind meted out by belligerent magistrates with a hatred of the Blockade. On 9 June 1825 Isum was walking near Castle Cliff at Hastings when he surprised a gang of smugglers. In the ensuing fight he was shot through the hand and beaten badly before other Blockade men arrived; they rescued him just as he was about to be thrown off Castle Cliff. Five men were captured: James Campbell, (the leader), Tom Mann, Tom Bumstead, James Roper and James Dugdale (the master of a pleasure boat). The five were duly prosecuted at Hastings on 30 June but, according to Divisional Lieutenant Barton, only one man, not named, was convicted. The charges against the others were dismissed but Isum was committed to Horsham Gaol on a charge of attempted murder! Henry spent a miserable month in gaol, loaded down with leg irons, before his trial at Lewes assizes on 3 August. There he was acquitted and returned to the comforting care of his wife and five children. Henry was transferred out of the Blockade Service nursing, no doubt, not only the marks of his imprisonment but some acid thoughts on the standards of justice in Hastings!

The various domestic problems that had beset Captain McCulloch from time to time were still around in later years. Nothing seemed to be built or repaired with any urgency. The construction work he had pressed for at Newhaven during 1824 was modified and the building opened as a barracks for 32 men in May 1825. It included a hammock room for only 24 men, presumably because some would be out on duty each night.

After a similar delay a permanent station was also built at Cuckmere for one officer and sixteen men. This released *Congo* and she was moved to Rye to be moored 'on the river bank near the town'. Again she acted as a watch vessel but only remained until March 1826 when she was sold and replaced by two vessels H.M.S. *Adder* and H.M.S *Dwarf*. At Rye Harbour *Enchantress* remained beached as a separate station.

That summer the Haddocks Watch House, near Fairlight, was reported by District Lieutenant Dyball '. . . to be falling apart because of the poor foundations, the building is moving in many different ways, there are many leaks and recently the front porch has moved 7½ inches . . .' At Kingston Station the men complained about the rotten meat supplied by William Martial, a Worthing butcher. When he made his next delivery there was a heated argument and Lieutenant Routledge frog-marched the abusive butcher off the premises; he retaliated by taking out a summons for assault.

At Brighton the Blockade Service encountered difficulties in finding a suitable Watch House. The town was now an important cross-Channel port, not so eminent as Dover but nevertheless thriving and ambitious. By 1820 sailing packets carried around 5,000 passengers per year on the

Brighton to Dieppe service against 35,000 between Dover and Calais. At Brighton the shallow beach forced the packets to moor off shore and their passengers had to be ferried to and fro in rowing boats. All this changed soon after the steam packets arrived. The first across the Channel, the *Rob Roy*, worked out of Dover from 1821 and the *Liberty* used Rye. But the next year a similar craft was operating at Brighton and in 1823 the town's Chain Pier opened as a prestige landing stage for the steam packet service. Brighton was then the busiest cross-Channel port in Sussex but, not to be outdone, Newhaven started a similar service in 1825 and Shoreham followed in 1826.

As well as all this passenger traffic there were also many fishing boats landing their catches on the shore at Brighton to supply the busy fish market on the town's beach. This hive of activity created ample opportunities for smuggling, right on the doorstep of the town, and the Blockade Service needed a Watch House close by. Ideal premises were found '. . . in two casemates in front of the town . . .', possibly near the new carriage road that had been built at the base of East Cliff to provide access to the Chain Pier. Alas, the owner of the two casemates, Mr Crunden, was adamant in his refusal to rent them to the Navy Board and the Blockade Service had to settle for two other casemates '. . . not so well adapted'.

By September 1825 the Naval Coast Blockade may still have been a fairly new innovation in West Sussex but the attitude of the locals to any preventive force -naval or otherwise – was unchanged. James Whittington, well known to Customs and Blockade men as a local smuggler, was caught red-handed attempting a run near Bognor and brought to trial at Chichester Quarter Sessions. The judge directed the jury to convict the man, but they discharged him.

Similarly at Shoreham the magistrates were just as hostile to the Blockade as their counterparts at Hastings. On 7 December Lieutenant Henry Leworthy of West Worthing Station had seen a cutter with a boat in tow hovering off the beach. As soon as it became dark he launched his galley and quietly laid her alongside the cutter unseen by her crew until the last moment and six men and 92 tubs of spirits were taken as well as the cutter, the *Mayflower* of Brighton. The men were subsequently prosecuted in the Shoreham Court before magistrate John Wakefield. Five of the six were convicted and given light fines but John Wilkinson, who admitted owning the cargo and being on board the *Mayflower*, was freed because he claimed he suffered from fits.

Wilkinson, a Shoreham man well known to all and sundry as a smuggler, was examined physically prior to the court hearing by Mr Peins, Blockade Surgeon, and pronounced fit for naval service. In his defence Wilkinson produced nothing by way of medical evidence to show he was epileptic, but he did have letters vouching for his good character from nine citizens of Shoreham. Eight of these worthies were dismissed by Captain Mingaye, in his report, as '. . . all brothers in the Trade . . .' The one exception was Mrs Anro, landlady of the 'Royal George', but according to Mingaye that hostelry was 'nothing more than a pot house in a nest of smugglers'. Word of Wilkinson's release soon spread around Shoreham and magistrate John Wakefield was cheered through the streets.

In modern parlance, the Coast Blockade Service generally had a bad press; any comments or letters that did appear in local papers were usually derogatory. Sometimes, however, there was the occasional note of praise. Someone (who may, of course, have been a Blockade officer) wrote anonymously to the Brighton Gazette about bribery '. . . this has been tried by a gang of smugglers in this town as a means of corrupting the officers and men of this formidable Blockade system . . . alas, in this too the poor fair traders have lamentably failed. Palm oil it seems has not the same mollifying effects on the Blockaders that it used to have on the custom house officers and riding officers of the old regime'. On reflection the praise is so favourable to the Blockade it seems highly likely it *was* written by one of the officers!

Bribery featured in two smuggling runs in November 1825. Sentinels Tom Lyons and Richard Harrington of Camber Station told Lieutenant Brown that a local gang was attempting to bribe them. A trap was set and two boats plus 112 tubs were taken together with seven men: William Somers, Barlo Mathieu, William Ashdown, William Mortley, William Morris, William Boxall and Thomas Clark. During that same month, at an unnamed Station, Sentinel William Colson accepted £2 to allow four tubs

In the 1820s this inn at Alfriston was said to have 21 rooms, 47 doors and 6 staircases plus secret cellars.

to be worked on the understanding that a larger sum of money would be forthcoming if a boatload was landed successfully when and where he was next on duty. The time and place were subsequently fixed but somehow or other the petty officer, Quartermaster Peter Copeland, found out just as the smugglers left for a rendezvous out in the Channel where the contraband would be transferred from a waiting ship. Copeland disarmed the sentinel and forced him to go through with the operation as if nothing had happened. Colson was told to take up his watch position on the beach whilst Copeland hid nearby. As the smuggler's boat came ashore Copeland ran out and captured it with the cargo of spirits and two men whilst Colson seized a third man! Surprisingly, the report from Captain Mingaye to the Admiralty suggested Colson was due a reward of £15 'head money' for capturing one smuggler – should he be paid? To which their Lordships replied '. . . certainly not . . .' and discharged him forthwith for bad conduct.

Divisional Lieutenant Edward Chappell pinpointed one substantial source of bribery in his Division when he asked for proceedings to be instituted forthwith against Thomas Wood '. . . a most indefatigable and notorious agent for smugglers in Eastbourne and Hailsham . . .he frequently attempts to bribe Coast Blockade men'. But Customs were wary of such prosecutions because attempted bribery was difficult to prove at times, even before unbiased magistrates.

Many prosecutions for smuggling offences were conducted by local solicitors appointed by Customs with Blockade officers and men appearing as witnesses. During 1825 it seems there was lack of attention and contact at times between the solicitors and the witnesses. Captain Mingaye became most annoyed when he found some lazy solicitors were leaving his officers to prepare and correct witness briefs '. . . it is most definitely not part of their duties . . .' Lieutenants at stations were issued with reference books on Customs law and each officer must have groaned anew when the latest heavyweight edition of 'Hermes Laws of Customs' was issued to the Sussex Coast Blockade late in 1825.

The saga of the capture of smuggler John Wicks near Tower 50 on 18 December 1825 could be sub-titled 'Surrender? – never!' The preliminaries are not mentioned in a report by Sentinel Michael Mallowney which starts:

> I was chasing John Wicks and saw him drop two tubs. I called stop but he still ran. I drew my pistols and called him again but he still ran. I got in front of him but he still closed me. I tried to turn him inland towards the towers and gave him a stroke from my cutlass but he did not stop and still came at me. I knocked him down but was afraid to hold him in case his men arrived. There were no Blockade men to my assistance. I pointed a pistol close at him and directed him stop but he shoved the pistol away. Finding this to no avail I used my cutlass on him again and the last blow was harder than the others and caused him to fall. I then stood over him and fired my pistol in the air to call other Blockade men to me. After about 20 minutes from the start of this chase Lieutenant West and the Party came to my assistance.

John Wicks, who lived at Westham, was carried to Tower 50, near Bexhill, and held prisoner whilst his wounds were treated by an Assistant Surgeon. Other men taken at that time were prosecuted before magistrates, by order of the Board of Customs, for offences that brought maximum penalties of £100, but Wicks was not charged. Perhaps the Board considered he had suffered enough. Whatever the reason, John Wicks spent a sombre Christmas in Tower 50 and was released on 31 January 1826.

It seems that Lieutenant Charles Moss at Tower 71, Eastbourne, had decided to start his Christmas celebrations early that year. He was visited by his Divisional Lieutenant at 11am on 22 December 1825 and found to be very drunk. A check of the Station's rum store revealed a shortage of 3½ gallons! Moss had only made Lieutenant that year after passing the examination back in 1814 and had been at Tower 71 just 13 days! Captain Mingaye ordered his immediate suspension and reported that it was for Lord Melville (the First Lord) to decide whether Moss should be struck off the List. The Captain suggested a court martial might not be required as the offence was committed on shore. His Lordship agreed and Moss's punishment was confined to be superseded – sent home on half pay.

Metaphorically Captain Mingaye's own spirits were high that winter. His Blockade Line was at full strength, the measures against bribery had shown some limited success and these two factors combined to produce results. On 10 February 1826 he reported with some relish that the French lugger *Eugene* had been caught off the Owers, south of Selsey Bill, by H.M.S. *Scorpion* a tender to H.M.S. *Victory*. The lugger had been trying to land her cargo of 360 kegs of spirits and 2 bales of tea for twelve days. Hunger amongst the crew of nine Frenchmen and six Englishmen had eventually forced them to run in for provisions and so she was caught.

Captain Mingaye was pleased to point out to his Vice Admiral this demonstrated '. . . the effectiveness of the Coast Blockade . . . it shows the officers and men are not asleep at their post . . . this has been a good week with two other seizures, 428 kegs in one galley with 12 men and 92 kegs in the Mayflower galley with 6 men'.

He did not say whether this was the same *Mayflower* as operated before by the 'epileptic' John Wilkinson – then she was described as a cutter – but the number of kegs carried was identical. The same Lieutenant Leworthy at West Worthing was also involved with this seizure and some days later he received a letter from Thomas Churcher, one of the six men taken aboard the *Mayflower* and now in Horsham Gaol. The writer said he wished to give useful information and when the Lieutenant went to Horsham he found Churcher ready to tell all. Out in the Channel the 92 kegs had been transhipped from the *Watchful Shepherd*, a Shoreham cutter, into the *Mayflower* which was owned by Richard Wicks of Worthing. The sketchy records of the case stop there unfortunately, but it is interesting to see the Lieutenant's expenses for the day in Horsham were '. . . hire of coach 18s, coachmen 2s, other expenses 10s . . .' Normally for visits such as this to attend court or convey prisoners a daily expense allowance for food and drink was paid by Customs at the rate of 15s to Lieutenants, 10s-6d to petty officers, 7s-6d to seamen – and 1s to prisoners!

Divisional Lieutenant Edward Chappell left the Blockade Service in April 1826 on promotion to Commander. After 15 years in various ships he had joined the Blockade in 1819 and spent most of his time on the central part of the Sussex coast, around Eastbourne. In February 1822 for his valiant efforts in rescuing passengers and crew from the East Indiaman *Thames* (see Chapter Seven) he received a plate worth 100 guineas. Chappell subsequently became a Captain in the Post Office Steam Packet Service when it was a naval command. Later, in 1840, he was given a special naval project to circumnavigate the British Isles in the steam vessel *Archimedes* and report on the properties of the 'screw propeller'.

With just one exception, accidental deaths were not entered in the 1825-1831 records of the Sussex Coast Blockade but they must have occurred at roughly the same level as they did in Kent; the same gales and heavy surf battered the Channel coasts of both counties. The stretches of coast either side of Seaford are particularly exposed in bad weather and four Blockade men were lost off there in December 1824 when their galley capsized. That was before the Line was divided into two commands and thereafter the only accidental death shown in Sussex Blockade papers was that of Lieutenant Roger Aitken, from Tower 74 (Seaford) who drowned on 14 March 1826 after falling overboard from his galley then some three miles off the coast.

Accidental deaths of Blockade men in the Newhaven parish between 1825 and 1831 are recorded in the parish register of burials. During those six years there were entries relating to 16 men, two women and 13 children, each shown as 'from Hyperion', that being a shorthand description for Blockade Service families living in the parish. Five of the children died of smallpox during the autumn of 1826. Two men, George Sayer and John Hewett drowned in November 1826 and February 1827 respectively and the following April William Faulkner died after 'falling over the cliff'. In April 1828 John Hicks, James Morris and Thomas Brown 'died at the mouth of the river'. Elsewhere in coastal parishes along the Sussex Line

Sussex County Gaol, Horsham c. *1830*. Horsham Museum

there must have been similar fatalities but burial records often lack adequate descriptions.

The regular supply of fresh water to some Blockade stations was quite a problem at times. At Littlehampton a local contractor, Mr Tupper, charged £30 just to dig one well and a Mr Sensier threatened to cut off the supply to one station unless he was paid two guineas per year. Later, at Cuckmere, there was trouble with the well near the new Watch House whilst at Thorney Watch House the farmer wanted another £1 a year to continue the 'emergency' supply; the well there became contaminated with sea water at high spring tides. Where a Watch House stood on a vast shingle bank, such as at Winchelsea, water had to be delivered in barrels rolled across the wide expanse of pebbles by contractors. As Mingaye said '. . . this is an evil under which we have to labour . . .'

Another evil was the increased use of firearms by smugglers in Kent and East Sussex in the spring and summer of 1826. On the Kent Line it brought the death of Richard Morgan on 30 July and Sam Hellard's consequent pursuit of the Aldington Gang in October and November. In Sussex it also started in the spring of 1826 and some of the armed runs may have been by the Aldington men. On 4 May the *Brighton Gazette* published a report headed 'Dreadful affray at Rye between Sussex Coast Blockade and smugglers' which described how:

> On Thursday last the guard boat off Rye Harbour observed a smuggling galley a short distance off and chased her. The smuggler made for the beach and reached there just as the guard boat got alongside. There was an exchange of small arms fire and the smugglers were driven out of their boat. The firing had brought the Blockade men over from the Camber Watch House and a petty officer took one smuggler into custody. At this instant a body of armed smugglers not less than 200 rushed from behind the sand hills to rescue their people and firing heavily on the Blockade killed one man and dreadfully wounded another. The Blockade however captured the galley, 42ft in length rowing 10 oars with some tubs of spirits in her and drove off the smugglers who carried away their wounded. A Coroner's inquest was held on the body of Patrick O'Sullivan, sentinel, and a verdict of wilful murder was returned. The body was found to have 5 shots and 30 slugs.

The action took place on what is now Camber Sands at about 2.30am on 27 April and the petty officer was John Jackson, Captain of the Top. The Blockade galley ('the guard boat') from *Enchantress* came under a considerable amount of fire from pistols and muskets as it came in to capture the smuggling galley and 15 tubs. There is nothing to show this was the Aldington men but it had all the marks of their organised and ruthless operation. And this affray was only a short distance from where the Battle of Brookland started in February 1821.

Another run by a large smuggling galley was made just over two weeks later on the night on 12 May near Tower 50. Sentinel Daniel Huoy thought the long white galley just off shore was a Blockade boat from a nearby station and hailed her, but there was no reply. As the boat got nearer he realised it was making a run and fired his only pistol as an alarm. Before he could re-load Huoy was set upon by the boat's crew and floored after his cutlass had been knocked from his hands. He was rescued just in time by Mate J.P. Wheeler, Quartermaster William Hunter and two other Blockade men but they in turn were soon fighting for their lives on the beach surrounded by some 200 men many armed with bats and some using firearms. Wheeler knew another Blockade Party was coming and was determined to hold out. When it arrived the smugglers took fright and scattered with shouts of 'Home! Home!', but not before Hunter had been knocked senseless and badly injured.

The galley and its complete cargo of 200 tubs were taken as were two of the crew, both French. It was believed that four smugglers had been killed and six injured against two Blockade men wounded. In its next edition on May 18 the *Brighton Gazette* gave a report of the run and added '. . . in this instance Blockade behaved in a most humane manner, having received a full volley from the smugglers before the officers gave orders to fire. But we have just heard that five smugglers were killed in the affray'.

For his bravery and the injury he received that night William Hunter was given a special pension. Mate J.P. Wheeler received a commendation for 'his initial check on the smugglers to enable others to arrive' and was promoted to Lieutenant, having passed the examination in 1816. Captain Mingaye took heed of Daniel Huoy's difficulty in having one pistol and promptly ordered another 500 short pistols so that every sentinel on the Sussex Line could carry two when on watch.

The defeat of the Aldington Gang in Kent brought only a short respite in the use of firearms against Sussex Blockade men, but in any case there were always the ubiquitous bats plus knives and any bricks or stones that came to hand. On a dark November night in 1826 Sentinel Jas Forster was walking along Black Horse Lane, near his station at East Elmer, when he was ambushed by three men wielding knives and stones. They managed to break two of his fingers and cut off part of one ear before Forster was able to draw a pistol out and fire an alarm. He was also stabbed in the chest but that was a minor wound thanks to the thick layers of clothing he wore on that cold night.

Lieutenant Moriarty believed the attack to be revenge for the death of Charles Horn, a smuggler shot by Lieutenant Carter the previous year; in January Lieutenant Ward and George Thorn, Captain of the Top, had been beaten up in Newnhams Lane, probably by the same men. Some months later two local men, Thomas Sadler and Jas Gorsech, were prosecuted at Petworth for these attacks and given twelve months hard labour.

Signal stations and accommodation in general occupied some of Captain Mingaye's attention in the summer of 1826. The signal stations set up by Mr Goddard in 1820 were still operating at 31 Tower (Pett), Fairlight, Galley Hill, Kewhurst Hill, Tower 55 (Pevensey Sluice), Langney Point and Beachy Head but they only relayed messages between themselves or from Deal and there were no stations west of Beachy Head. Mingaye wanted further signal stations along the coast to Portsmouth to give the Sussex Line a complete system and proposed a further 17 stations from Seaford Hill east to Southern Point at Chichester. A contractor gave an estimate of £60 to construct each building plus a further £30 for its mast and machinery. The papers were sent to the Navy Board but there the matter ended; there is no record of these signal stations being built during the existence of the Blockade.

The long stretch of sandy beach east of Camber was notorious for smuggling runs but, in Mingaye's opinion, it lacked adequate cover. The Kent Blockade had its most westerly station at Jews (later (Jurys) Gap just by the county boundary but then to the west, in Sussex, there were two miles of sands before Camber Watch House. That building had been designed to hold 21 men, but under Mingaye it housed 33. There was a need for a further station and, in the summer of 1826, a 'Boundary watch vessel' (no other name) was beached on that stretch of shore about a mile from Jews Gap.

Further west there was another stretch of coast with a difficult problem that also required attention. In a letter to the Navy Board dated 30 June 1826 Captain Mingaye explained that between the Watch Houses at Bearhide and Salt Dean (east of Brighton), at a spot known as Porto Bello Gap, there was a hidden valley with just one house sited some 50 yards from the cliff. The occupants were an elderly couple '. . . who take every opportunity to corrupt the Blockade men. More men are drunk at their posts here than any other part of the Line, due to the old woman's cunning . . .' Mingaye knew the house was up for sale at 270 guineas and considered '. . . another 80 would put it in fit state to take a Mate and ten men. The proprietor's solicitor in Lewes is not aware of our interest otherwise the price would double. Admiral Sir George Cockburn has already visited the locality last Saturday'.

The Navy Board ordered the purchase of the house but, as with Fish House at Sea Salter in Kent this took some time to complete, probably because of the clandestine nature of the negotiations, and possession was

The Blockade Watch House at Rye Harbour had only 2 Petty Officers and 6 seamen in June 1825.

not obtained until 25 March 1827. Unfortunately for Lieutenant Digby this was not soon enough. One night in January he and some of his Party were attacked near the house but both the first sentinel and his petty officer were unable to sound the alarm because their pistols 'snapped' and failed to fire. Contrary to a specific order from his Divisional Lieutenant, Digby did not check all fire arms prior to the sentinels going out on watch. When the attack came the men had only one good weapon between them. Digby himself was disarmed and severely beaten by the attackers; the Admiralty considered whether he should be superseded but settled for an admonishment. The Board offered £100 reward for information on the attackers and this eventually produced an informant and a conviction.

Further west still, at Pagham, the problem with the Watch House was that it was 1 1/2 miles from the harbour! Captain Mingaye was given approval to rent a house from Mr. Adam at £8 per year; this was only 50 yards from the harbour and would take a Mate and two boat's crews.

That hostile magistrate, John Wakefield, had to deal with more smuggling cases on 5 and 6 October 1826, this time at Worthing. On the first day he sat with Sir Richard Jones K.C.B. when three men, George Baker Clarke, Jonathan Banyard and Nathaniel Hilman were convicted for smuggling and given five years impressment. The next day, apparently sitting alone, Mr Wakefield heard a case where four men were accused of flashing and a fifth of carrying contraband. One man named Barnard was found guilty and four; Evans, Dyer, Steers and Jupp were acquitted. It was not the verdicts that upset Captain Mingaye overmuch but the attitude of Mr Wakefield '. . . he is extremely hostile to Blockade witnesses and always in favour of the accused. He called Able Seaman Murphy a liar saying he remembered him from before'. Mingaye's report to the Admiralty and Customs was supported by a letter from Mr Cooper, the Brighton solicitor who had prosecuted on behalf of Customs. Ending with a final burst of exasperation Mingaye suggested the Admiralty '. . . should aim to remove this magistrate from the list'.

The Selsey peninsula featured in more than a few reports during the winter of 1826 and 1827. On 30 December four smugglers: James Robinson, William Cook, William Bartlett and Edward Wade were caught by the Selsey Party. No details were given of the run but 'all were sentenced to impressment and their fine Cowes sloop seized'.

A few months later Mr Wilson, the new Divisional Lieutenant, was complaining bitterly about the interference of the Reverend Edward Goddard, vicar of Sidlesham. In the next parish of Selsey the Reverend Barr-Phipps had confined his protests to a concern for the spiritual welfare of the Blockade officers and men (see Chapter Three). At Sidlesham the Reverend Goddard was openly hostile and took every opportunity to defend his parishioners vigorously against any wicked accusations that they were smuggling. As Lieutenant Wilson said '. . . he has interfered with the duty of our officers on several occasions, for example taking the part of a notorious smuggler and the Reverend shows every disposition to encourage litigation in opposition to established laws laid down for the prevention of smuggling'.

Although the Blockade Service was despised by many local folk they were happy to enlist its support if something threatened their livelihood and the Lieutenant at Selsey Station was drawn into a serious local issue that had nothing to do with smuggling. Contractors boats from Chichester and Pagham had started to remove stone from the Mixon Reef, a rocky bank off Selsey Bill, for building work in Chichester and Bognor. For centuries the reef had provided shelter for fishing boats based at Selsey and local fishermen were incensed at this wanton destruction. As the local Navy officer 'in residence' the Lieutenant gave his active support to the protest campaign and, in March 1827, he sought Admiralty authority to stop the removal. His letter was passed to the Treasury for a decision but nothing had happened by November when memorials (petitions) from Selsey pilots and fishermen were laid out at the Swan Inn, Chichester for persons to sign '. . . if it (the removal) continues it will no longer provide shelter . . .' Sad to say it did continue and today the reef is barely visible at low spring tides.

Lieutenant Henry Leworthy of West Worthing Station was in action again on 25 March 1827 when around 10pm he and his men encountered a large gang near the Tarring Road. About 30 armed men and perhaps 200 others '. . . many with bludgeons 4 to 5 feet long . . .' were gathering for a landing and the appearance of the Blockade Party brought brisk volleys of fire from the smugglers. Lieutenant Peake and his men from another station then arrived and the firing continued for five minutes or more from both sides. The smugglers then scattered but 39 were reported to have taken refuge in the George and Dragon at Tarring, now part of Worthing. Leworthy placed a cordon of men around the inn to prevent anyone escaping and rode to the residence of the only available magistrate to obtain a search warrant – but he was not at home! Although on the ride back some teeth must have been well and truly gnashed, the Lieutenant had no alternative but to lift the cordon. He was, however, able to report that nothing was landed that night '. . . just before the firing started a lugger had appeared off shore with her masts struck but when the firing began she upped with her masts and stood off to the westward'. He believed that one smuggler had been shot dead that night and another badly wounded. For once there were no Blockade casualties.

According to O'Byrne's Naval Biography Henry Leworthy was born in 1792 and entered the Navy as a Volunteer 1st Class in July 1803 at the tender age of 11. The following year he was serving on board the gun brig *Grappler* when she was wrecked off Granville. All the crew were taken prisoner and Henry was held in France for the next ten years during which time he made three unsuccessful attempts to escape. The fourth attempt was successful and he spent the next two years serving in the Navy in the Americas. When the Blockade was stood down in 1831 Henry transferred, as a Lieutenant, to the Coast Guard.

During 1826 and into early 1827 the Sussex Blockade's complement remained at, or very near, full strength but that only lasted until April when a draft of volunteers went to H.M.S. *Sybille*. In the summer of 1827 other drafts were sent to men-of-war preparing for the Battle of Navarino which was fought in the Mediterranean in October to prevent Turkish hegemony over Greece.

The draft in April took a number of men away from the Rye area. The locals soon got to know and a smuggling run was made on the night of 13 April close to Tower 38, east of Fairlight. Quartermaster McLean gave the alarm but he was quickly surrounded and had to shoot his way out, killing one smuggler. Depleted Parties led by Lieutenants Bramwell, Wheeler, Harris and Holbrook and Mate Shearman took part in a running fight that moved inland. As had happened so often in the past they were unable to prevent most of the tubs being carried away and managed to seize only 15. Two more smugglers died that night, one near Fairlight and the other as he was being carried to Icklesham. The Blockade suffered five wounded, three from Tower 38 and two from Fairlight.

When Blockade men were sent to a man-of-war they could find themselves working alongside convicted smugglers who had been impressed into the Navy. Perhaps one or two old acquaintances were revived and scores settled! In June 1830 when *Sybille* was in action off the African coast against Brazilian slave traders, the 13 convicted smugglers on board acted with such gallantry and good conduct they were all ordered to be released on return to Britain.

Some of the Blockade Party at Hove were involved in a short, sharp action on 18 October 1827 when around 11.30pm Sentinel John Jones saw a boat coming in to the beach just opposite Wick Lane. A group of men who had been hiding nearby rushed out intent on reaching Jones before he could sound an alarm, but he managed to fire his pistol before being knocked and kicked to the ground. Sentinel Dennis Riorden ran over to assist but the gang were waiting and set upon him with their clubs. Lieutenant Williams was sitting in one of the rooms used by the Hove Party '. . . opposite Regency Square . . .' talking to Quartermaster Tom Wardel who had left Jones only ten minutes before the alarm. On hearing the shot both men ran over to Wick Road and it took them about three minutes to reach the two wounded sentinels. There they saw smugglers running away carrying at least one wounded man 'but as we entered Wick Lane, which was totally dark, shots were fired at us'. In the short period of time between the alarm and the arrival of Lieutenant Williams at the landing spot the gang had managed to whisk away most of the boat's cargo leaving just four tubs to be seized.

The officers at Tower 71 (Eastbourne) certainly seemed to have had difficulties maintaining their stock of rum. Mention has already been made of Lieutenant Moss being 3½ gallons short just before Christmas 1825. He was replaced by Lieutenant Parker who, on a subsequent inspection, was found to be 7 gallons short! The Admiralty superseded him onto half pay and from it deducted the cost of 5 gallons. Still on matters of discipline, Captain Mingaye became really exasperated with the conduct of some pensioners in the Sussex Blockade. As an example he quoted John Mincham, a senior petty officer at Felpham Station who was reported for being drunk and three hours late on duty. It transpired that he drank regularly at the 'Fox', a public house owned by a notorious smuggler. Mincham who was 44, was ordered to be dismissed from the Service and his pension of £27-8s, for 21 years service, reduced by £5.

According to Mingaye, pensioners were unsuited for Blockade work. He had 133 in the Sussex Blockade costing £1864 per year '. . . they find duties far more arduous and irksome than they expected and are constantly giving trouble . . .' He was firmly against their further employment. He set his argument out in a letter to the Admiralty and, in support, attached a list of 'Thirteen who had received corporal punishment or black listed and dismissed from 6 March 1825 to 27 October 1827 . . .' for crimes such as drunkenness, mutiny, theft of rum and disobedience.

The Admiralty passed the papers on to Captain Pigot of the Kent Blockade for comment. In his reply he explained that the Kent Blockade had 182 pensioners, of whom 93 were petty officers, and only 9 had received corporal punishment. 'In general they are sober, obedient and faithful . . . the purchase of their fidelity places them beyond the smugglers bribery. In many instances the pension is more than pay . . .' He was against Mingaye's proposal to discharge them. Captain Pigot's argument won the day and pensioners remained with the Blockade Service much to the annoyance of Captain Mingaye who continued to give vent to his feelings from time to time.

By December 1827 the diligent Captain Mingaye had brought his Line complement to full strength again after his tenders had made voyages to Cork and to *Perseus* in London. This was just as well because in January 1828 there came 'the Bexhill and Eastbourne battles' – as Mingaye described them in his reports. The first battle started on Friday 3 January 1828 on a clear moonlit night when small boats from a lugger landed around 150 tubs on the beach about a mile east of Bexhill, between the village and the desolate spot known as Bo-Peep. The initial action was described in the next edition of the *Sussex Weekly Advertiser:*

A landing at Bo-Peep. Drawn by Paul Hardy

> The inhabitants of Bexhill on this occasion were greatly alarmed at 2 o'clock in the morning to be woken by the sound of shots. Even they, who must have been accustomed to the frequent scuffles between smugglers and revenue men, can scarcely have believed the ferocity of the battle, for no other word will suffice, which took place near their town that night. The Blockade men

> had been expecting a run to take place since early the previous evening and had kept a close look-out. They were not disappointed, for at the time stated the boat landed with a cargo of 150 tubs of brandy at the spot where tower No. 45 had previously stood. At this time there were only four Blockade men on duty, against a 'company' of nearly seventy, with an additional twenty or so 'batmen'.

The four sentinels had fired alarm shots but were held at bay by the determined efforts of the batmen and could only trail the gang as it made off through Bexhill with the contraband loaded on horses and carts. Lieutenant Taylor of the Galley Hill Tower Station heard the alarm shots and, mustering his men, made to intercept the gang at the Well Field cross roads in Sidley Green, just north of Bexhill. There a pitched battle took place, at close quarters, between the Blockade men and the smugglers. The well laden carts and pack horses were sent on their way and the batmen and the rest of the gang, perhaps 50 in all, made a stand to protect the rear. At first the Blockade men held their fire but they suffered heavy injuries as the determined smugglers laid about them with long clubs. Quartermaster Collins died when his skull was beaten in and in the first volley of fire from the Blockade men a batman, Hokkey Smithurst, was shot dead. Come daybreak his body was found still holding a bat that had been almost hacked to pieces by naval cutlasses. The fight rolled around Sidley Green for some time as the smugglers fought on doggedly and ceased only when the gang dispersed leaving just five tubs behind.

According to Captain Mingaye there were 21 officers and men present at this battle – not the 40 mentioned in contemporary newspaper reports. He also reported that 'Lieutenant Taylor, Quartermaster John Brenan, Able Seaman Edward Mitchell and Ordinary Seamen Jeremiah Higgins and Peter Welch were wounded in the fight and incapable of further pursuit'. From his days aboard *Cameleon* on preventive work, Mingaye believed he knew the leader of the gang to be an old adversary, one Thomas Underdown of Rye. Some years before the man had been captured by Mingaye as the master of *Diamond* of Rye – the selfsame craft that ended its smuggling days when Lieutenant Dicken bored those holes in the ballast compartment back in 1824.

Tucked away in Admiralty archives at the Public Record Office is a real gem of smuggling history – a contemporary account of the Bexhill battle by two smugglers who must have been closely involved. Sitting uneasily amongst elegantly written letters from Admirals about 'the firing of the Great Guns' and 'the Disposition of the South Atlantic Squadron' is a letter from home to a seaman written in a rough hand, full of spelling errors and devoid of punctuation, but brimming with news. It is accompanied by a note, dated 11 January 1828, from Vice Admiral Blackwood, C-in-C Sheerness, to the Admiralty. This explains that the attached letter to James Pope, a convicted smuggler impressed on board the flagship H.M.S. *Gloucester*, was intercepted by Captain Horton and forwarded '. . . because it will throw light upon and lead to the detention of some of the persons involved in the affair at Bexhill'.

The first part of the letter gave family news that came with 'the well wishes of your mother and father'. It then went on:

> But now my boy this comes from your old mates James Brown and Richard Sims informing all that we now of at present – will make your eyes sparkle to read it concerning . . . partly at Backshill wich happened last fryday morning about two o'clock – moonlight as day the boat come in with about 150 tubs – 70 men in a lump at the spot and 20 skouts – but they was on the beach before the skouts could get clear and followed them over 2 miles and took the hind cart but the skouts took that away so thear was only 4 tubs lost and not a man taken thear was ten Hythe men and ten of thear own men no Dymchurchers and the Hythe men run away except old Hokkey and he was stopped with a ball in his throat never to rise no more your old friend Mac . . . had a ball in his right side and out of his left breast – walked 1/2 mile and lived 40 mins they buried he and Hokkey at Backshill on Sunday and Coset had 2 balls thro his hat and one struck his fase but got clear – all others got clear to your uncle John at No.4 Brook Street new Road London Tilbys stable cach fire and burnt down wiles men at supper and burnt four horses – we heard Horney Cook and 2 of is mates are got home and left on Board for another opertunaty at Portsmouth.

As the letter shows, on this occasion amongst the batmen or 'skouts' were ten local men and ten from Hythe including Hokkey Smithurst. Uncle John had probably kept a safe house for smugglers for some time, but the safety ended when his address appeared in the letter.

A few days after the inquest on Collins a local girl, Mary Easton, came forward to give information about the attack. For her own safety she was held on board *Hyperion* and shortly afterwards her boyfriend, Charles Hills, was arrested for being a member of the gang and joined her on board. There was some suspicion that Hills had arranged this so that both could be held in protective custody because then he too started to name some of the gang. Another man named Buffard was arrested in Pett and he offered to identify those members of the gang who came from around that area, being men unknown to Hills.

After the North Kent Gang had attacked and killed Richard Morgan at Dover they showed their arrogance by making another armed landing shortly afterwards. And so it was with the Bexhill battlers. There they had used clubs but on 24 January, just three weeks later, Captain Mingaye was at Eastbourne to report another battle that morning. This time the gang had left their clubs at home and brought muskets. Sadly for the record there is no information about this battle other than Mingaye's own brief report '. . . they were headed by the same person who conducted the affair at Bexhill – Thomas Underdown. They came in strength this time armed only with muskets so as to overpower our people. Thomas Reynolds seaman was severely wounded. One smuggler was found dead at Wilmington and two wounded were seen at Hailsham'.

Thanks to the experience and sagacity of Mingaye and his officers the local Blockade Stations were expecting this second battle. The casualties were surprisingly light in a fight where both sides were well armed and it is likely that Underdown and his men soon realised the Navy men would not be intimidated by a show of arms and made a hasty getaway.

As a result of information given by three informers 67 warrants were issued, within a week or so of the Eastbourne battle, for the arrest of members of the gang. The hunt was on and the task of leading the pursuit fell to Divisional Lieutenant John Green. It was a task unlike that undertaken by Sam Hellard when he hunted the Aldington men; he caught 16 of the leading members of the gang in and around the one village. John Green had to pursue 67 many of whom, on hearing news of the hunt, left their homes and scattered far and wide.

On 1 April 1828 the *Times* gave a detailed account of the Bexhill battle and said Lieutenant Green and his men'. . . were out scouring the country night after night for weeks in search of the accused persons and many houses were broken into by main force. The villages around Hastings for a circuit of 20 miles were continually in a state of terror . . . the distress occasioned is beyond conception. A great number of men have absconded leaving no other resource to their families but the workhouse. In Bexhill alone 23 families have been thrown on parochial funds . . .'

Within days John Green had arrested six men and despatched them to Horsham Gaol, but despite the extensive hue and cry only four more were caught; the remaining 57 had disappeared. At the Spring Assizes at Horsham the ten were indicted for trial at the Old Bailey and there on 10 April, Spencer Whiteman, Thomas Miller, Henry Miller, John Spray, Edward Shoesmith, Will Bennett, John Ford, Stephen Stubberfield, Thomas Maynard and William Plumb were found guilty of armed smuggling. Eight of them had been in the fight at Bexhill, seven at Eastbourne and five had been at both. All of the ten were sentenced to death but this was later commuted to transportation for life. Some six months later Captain Mingaye reported he still had 57 warrants 'for men known to have been in the Bexhill fray including Thomas Underdown, George Whiteman (Rye), John Bennett and Francis Pillegan (Bexhill), John Cathcart (Ninfield) and Thomas Waters (Hastings)'. There were no subsequent records to show that these men were ever caught, at least by the Blockade Service.

As in the Kent Blockade, Royal Marines were used in some Sussex Stations, both for guard duty and as emergency reserves. A Sussex Blockade return of 1829 shows 2 officers, 3 sergeants and 47 other ranks; of these *Griper* (Chichester Harbour) had 5, *Adder* (Rye) 4, *Enchantress* (Rye Harbour) 5 and Littlehampton 2. There were probably more at the east Divisional office in Hastings with the remainder stationed on board *Hyperion*. From the Blockade's point of view Rye was a town that warranted close attention, but this also meant Blockade officers had to be on their guard at all times whether on or off duty. Lieutenant Dicken had been beaten up by two assailants in November 1824, one being William Collins. In April 1828 a Daniel Collins of Rye (and perhaps of the same family) was prosecuted for assaulting Lieutenant McTavish from *Adder* and given 21 days hard labour on bread and water.

Again, as with the Kent Blockade and *Ramillies*, an officer of the rank of

Commander was appointed as First Lieutenant on *Hyperion* early in 1828. Commander W.J. Hood had been a senior Lieutenant on the ship when she came to Newhaven and was probably her First Lieutenant before being promoted in situ.

Captain Mingaye was able to maintain the Blockade at near full strength through the early months of 1828 but that changed in the summer when on 4 July 310 men, together with Commander Hood and one Lieutenant, were 'lent' to H.M.S. *Britannia* at Portsmouth. Commander Hood returned with in a matter of weeks but there was no indication that all the others came back and once again Mingaye was sending his tenders, particularly *Highflyer* and *Wolf*, to *Perseus* for recruits.

The uniform that had to be mustered by each of those 310 men at the time of transfer gives some idea of the clothing they used; this was a typical list for an Able Seaman: 3 Blue jackets and trousers, 1 bed (hammock), 6 shirts, 1 blanket, 2 pairs of shoes, 1 duck frock, 3 pairs of stockings, 3 flannel waistcoats, 2 black hats, 2 flannel drawers, 3 Guernsey frocks, 3 white trousers, 2 plates, 2 'basons', 1 knife, fork and spoon. The black hats were round with a flat top and brim and made of leather or japanned canvas. Around their necks men wore a black kerchief, introduced after Nelson's death in 1805. Pigtails, a fashion for some years, were banned from 1823.

By 1828 the Coast Blockade system was 11 years old and it would be reasonable to suppose that the demarcation in work between Customs and the Blockade had become well defined. Customs dealt with vessels bringing freight and passengers legitimately from foreign parts and the Blockade was concerned with all others. However, as the 1821 incident on the Rye packet *Liberty* showed, there were demarcation problems at times over the years. It seems matters really came to a head somewhere along the Line in July 1827 because, at the request of the Board of Customs, the Admiralty ordered Blockade staff not to go on board *any* vessel that would be dealt with by Customs.

The order annoyed Blockade officers in stations close to the ports staffed by Customs. The Navy officers had problems with bribery and corruption amongst their own men but it was said the Customs tide-waiters were not only corrupt but downright lazy. Lieutenant Couch on *Griper* in Chichester harbour was adamant that Customs staff were not searching the vessels they boarded. And Divisional Lieutenant Wilson had information that because of this slackness '. . . the Sarah has succeeded in running a large cargo of contraband into the harbour . . . on 22 June (1828) . . .' It must have indeed been frustrating for those naval officers, with their rigid and brutal code of discipline, to see such indolence creating gaps in what was supposed to be a Blockade Line, but there was nothing they could do.

Another 34 Blockade men were drafted to H.M.S *Revenge* in September 1828. Some went from Hastings Stations and the news prompted local smugglers to organise a run on to the town beach, within yards of the Customs House. For some time the locals had become proficient in organising 'grab-and-dash' operations on the town beach. A few thugs would be on hand to silence any sentinels but speed of unloading was the essence. As soon as the boat touched the pebbles it was unloaded swiftly by men who ran out from the cover of the net shops and the boats beached around the Fish Market. With one man per tub for a speedy discharge they could whisk away over 80 tubs into the dark streets and alleyways. It was all over in minutes; on this occasion there were no sentinels anywhere near and by the time Lieutenant Owen arrived in his galley everyone and everything, including the smuggler's boat, had long since disappeared.

In December the Blockade men at Felpham were more successful, they captured a smuggling craft and her cargo of tubs. She was the *James*, a six ton sloop from Selsey and Captain Mingaye obtained approval to attach her temporarily to *Hyperion* for Blockade use. That same month Mingaye was giving vent, once again, to his exasperations with naval pensioners serving in the Blockade. Ordinary Seaman Owen Daly was not only found drunk in a stable with two notorious smugglers but he had left his cutlass outside! Mingaye had previously reduced Daly from Able Seaman '. . . I have to repeatedly admonish these pensioners and an example should be made of him . . .' The Navy Board agreed and Daly, then 38 with 14 years naval service and 21 months in the Blockade, was discharged and also lost his pension of £7-8s.

By March 1829 the shortage of Blockade men was well known to many smugglers along the Sussex coast. Anyone in ignorance was soon informed when the *Sussex Weekly Advertiser* reported 'Blockade forces having been lately much reduced the smugglers are again on the alert and Thursday evening last a considerable run of contraband goods was effected near Kingston, only the empty boat falling into the hands of the officers'. More seamen were transferred away in August, this time to H.M.S. *Melville* and the total strength of the Sussex Blockade, including officers, was down to 870.

The local gang at Hastings made another run onto the town beach at about 4am on 9 November but on this occasion there were sentinels nearby. The boat came in '. . . opposite the capstans in New Town . . .' and about 100 men were hiding close by to whisk the tubs away. There was a fierce fight on the beach and four Blockade men; Armourer Thomas Brown and Able Seamen Adam Guy, William Ripon and George Grinstead were injured before Blockade Parties arrived from the two Watch Houses in the town. Lieutenant Grant Raymond commended all four of his injured men for their courage and for playing a major part in the capture of the boat and 130 tubs.

Those four Blockade men spent some time in hospital and this weakened the Line locally still further. Another landing of spirits came on 4 December near Tower 34, east of Fairlight, and for this the gang had first gathered in Iden churchyard, north of Rye. With obvious annoyance and frustration Divisional Lieutenant John Green admitted '. . . the weakened strength of the Coast Blockade made it impossible to muster enough men to attack a smuggling party of 80 to 100. As usual the batmen divided into two groups east and west of the boat to protect the tub men, first attacking the sentinel on the spot then keeping the others at bay as they arrived by which time the tubmen, with their usual expertness, were able to unload the boat. Four Blockade men were wounded and one smuggler was found dead on the beach'.

In December 1829 Captain Mingaye referred to '. . . five recent attempts to break through the Line and land goods, three of which we have succeeded in seizing all goods and some smugglers and in two they (the smugglers) were entirely successful'. Again, sadly for the record Mingaye does not give any details except those of one landing at Copperas Gap (East Shoreham) which was stopped by Mate Richie and his men '. . . after the smugglers had teased us a great deal a large quantity of spirits and some bales of tobacco were seized. Mr Richie showed courage and zeal seizing the boat and cargo although a large party of smugglers was just two fields away'. One smuggler was killed and three Blockade men received slight wounds. After the fight an Excise officer found two piles of loaded muskets in the field where the smugglers had been. Seven months later, in July 1830, Mr. Richie was promoted to Lieutenant.

The health of Blockade officers and men seemed to create more problems in Sussex than in Kent. From 1827 onwards there were cases of '. . . prolonged fever, including typhoid . . .' at various stations due possibly to the problems, already mentioned, concerning supplies of fresh water. In February 1830 medical officers from the Navy Board inspected the Sussex Blockade and noted that three additional hospitals had been established including one in the grounds of Camber Watch House. As ever, these so-called hospitals were nothing more than one or two rooms staffed by an Assistant Surgeon and some Blockade wives. By 1830 there were Blockade hospitals at Camber, Towers 32 (Pett Level), 41 (Bulverhythe), 51 (Cooden) and 72 (Eastbourne) as well as Porto Bello, Pagham and Cockbush. These were in addition to hospitals at the three Divisional offices in Hastings, Newhaven and Littlehampton where the Surgeons were based. Towers 32 and 72 were not manned as stations and seem to have been opened just as hospitals.

At Cockbush, later known as East Head, at the entrance to Chichester Harbour, the hospital – possibly one or two rooms in the station building – catered for naval families living between there and Pagham West. When the Blockade Force was at full strength there were 140 officers and men and probably at least the same number of dependants in the Selsey area. Some officers had large families; Lieutenant Wallington lived near Cockbush with his wife and nine children whilst along the shore at Thorney, just west of Selsey, Lieutenant Wilkinson shared a three room apartment with his wife and six children.

The local inhabitants in and around Selsey were already hostile to the Blockade but feelings ran close to boiling point for a while in February and March 1830. Lieutenant Carr, who was in charge of Selsey Station, was far too officious and zealous for local comfort, particularly in ordering his men to search boats and buildings. Local smugglers, accustomed to a spell of fishing in between runs, were being harassed day and night by this eager

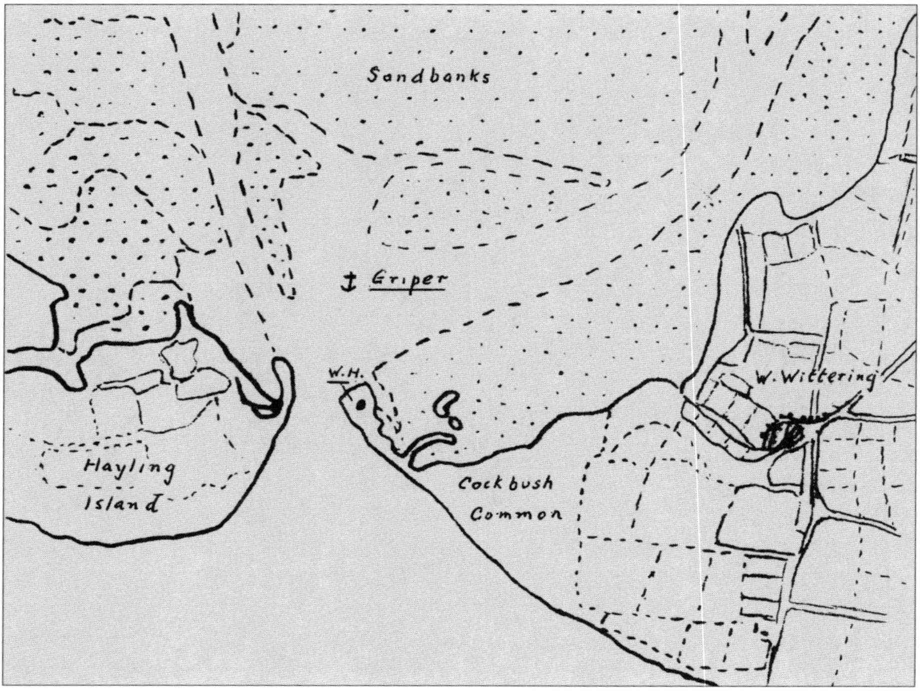

The entrance to Chichester Harbour c. *1830 showing the probable location of the Cockbush Watch House and the watch vessel* Griper.

officer. It was all very unsettling and, without doubt, Lieutenant Carr took care to avoid dark lanes and alleys during his night inspections. Added to this were the rumours flying around the Selsey area about the death of poor Mrs White, the wife of the Quartermaster at Cockbush. It was said she died because of mistreatment by her husband, but the Divisional Surgeon reported she had 'been on the sick list since April (1829) for pulmonary, hepatic and rheumatic affections . . . she being of most intemperate habits'.

Felpham, just east of Selsey, was a favoured spot for smuggling runs at this time. In February 1830 a newspaper reported '. . . a run of 30 casks of spirits from a boat near Felpham Sluice. The coast blockade succeeded in taking one badly wounded man and 8 tubs . . . several pistols were discharged. Another smuggler was believed to be badly wounded . . .' On 23 June Lieutenant Kortright of Felpham Station, out on patrol in his galley, caught the *Venus* of Cowes after a long chase and took the vessel, her contraband and four crew.

Joe Robinson, a Selsey man born in 1820, was involved in local smuggling from his early years; his reminiscences were recorded by a relative and are now in the West Sussex County Record Office. He recalls how local men would chip in £5 or £10 to finance a run by giving the money to a trusted friend, nicknamed 'Will Watch' from a traditional song, and he would sail over to Fécamp to make the arrangements. The boat would be a galley, perhaps 60ft long with two small auxiliary lug sails, built in France just for

Worthing Esplanade near the pier c. *1820*. Worthing Museum

the one trip and hence expendable. This type of craft, developed originally for smuggling on the short Channel crossing to East Kent, had now become popular all along the coast even well west of Sussex where the crossings were much longer. Such a crossing may have been a routine event for the crew but even so these men showed admirable courage in bringing their heavily laden and roughly-built expendable rowing boat across the Channel for perhaps a twelve hour crossing on a dark night.

Joe remembered a fine run in 1830 that brought a large cargo of tubs into one part of Pagham Harbour after the 'preventives'(Blockade men) had been lured by flashes and lights into another part. He also recalled how the preventives in their galleys would spend hours patrolling off shore in cold and stormy weather. To keep their legs and feet warm they filled tarred canvas bags with straw and packed them along the bottom of the boat.

At Fairlight, on the night of 22 March 1830, Blockade officers and men from several stations succeeded in capturing a substantial run, mainly of tobacco. The all too brief report mentions an affray in which 8 smugglers were taken and one other, named Stoneham, died. With the magistrates' approval the prisoners were held in Towers 37 and 38. The *Mary* of Rye was seized together with her tub boat and their combined cargo of 36 bales of tobacco and snuff and a chest of tea. It seems this was a joint operation, possibly with a Blockade tender, because the report concluded '. . . the remaining part of the cargo of 70 bales was taken from the smack *Neptune* of Dover 2 miles at sea . . .' The story is not completely clear but it seems the *Neptune* was acting as the supply boat for several runs that night, a practice known in the old Customs jargon as 'coopering'. The *Sussex Weekly Advertiser* reported the affray at Fairlight and added '. . . the next night at Bexhill there was another affray where only 3 casks were taken after one smuggler was shot, and has since died, and six taken prisoner . . .'

Within a few weeks of these runs Captain Mingaye had to switch his attention away from preventive work and on to more serious matters when he received a request from a county magistrate for assistance to put down riots in Rye. The agitation and torment amongst agricultural workers for food and better wages, that led to the Swing Riots, had spread quickly from Kent and Sussex.

Writing on 28 April 1830 Captain Mingaye said he had received a request from Mr Herbert B. Curteis, county magistrate and, as a consequence, ordered 15 marines and 12 Blockade seamen, all from *Adder*, into the town. This unit was later re-inforced by another 41 marines sent to *Adder*, all placed under the command of Divisional Lieutenant Jager '. . . to stop the destruction of property of the Scots Float Sluice, one mile east of Rye', but this was prevented by the arrival of the Blockade unit. As Mingaye said, '. . . if it had been destroyed 9000 acres of valuable land would have been flooded'. In his letter of thanks to Captain Mingaye Mr Curteis commended 'the conduct of Lieutenant Francillon and the few men under his command faced with a violent and threatening mob of about 1000. The Lieutenant withdrew his men at my request to prevent loss of life and on a promise from the leaders of the riot to do nothing till next morning. Two troops of dragoons are now under my command'. Those 'few men' were probably the initial 27 from *Adder*.

There were no further reports of Blockade men being employed against rioters in Rye, but the local agitators were still bent on creating major damage. On the night of 30 May Sentinel Fred Divorce came across '. . . four armed men drilling holes in the bridge to the west of the town to blow it up . . .' ('it' being the bridge and not the town!). They offered Fred a drop of gin to move on but when he refused they fired shots in the air as an alarm and several parties, who had been hiding nearby , ran off into the darkness.

By the late summer of 1830 a general pattern of incendiarism, machine breaking and threatening letters had spread throughout Sussex. Fire insurance companies suspended their insurance cover and the *Weekly Advertiser* carried notices offering rewards for information about arsonists in Lewes, Ringmer, Hailsham and Henfield. In just one instance, labourers from Bersted, Arundel, Bognor and Felpham came together to demand money, food and a wage increase from farmers otherwise all the threshing machines in the area would be destroyed. By then Mingaye had units of marines stationed at Rye, Fairlight, Newhaven and Littlehampton – all placed on 'immediate response'. County magistrates requested formal arrangements for Blockade assistance and Mingaye agreed advising the Admiralty 'Last night 3 loads of wheat ready for market, 2 barns full of wheat, some hay and calves at Southover were totally destroyed and a barn full of corn at East Dean . . .'

On 21 November a local Worthing magistrate, Captain George Pechell R.N., wrote to the Navy Board on behalf of the Worthing Division of Magistrates requesting 'the assistance of the Coast Blockade . . . in quelling any riotous assembly which is expected hourly in this part . . .' The Board copied the request to Mingaye and asked him to 'afford whatever assistance may be in his power if called upon'. Their Lordships were happy for marines and seamen to be used as a quick military response to quell riots, and perhaps help over-stretched fire brigades, provided the action was close to the coast and did not detract the Blockade from its prime task. When, however, a request came for a detachment of marines to be sent to Hailsham to quell riots their Lordships said 'No marines are to be sent from the coast into the interior'.

The normal work of the Blockade continued through the summer of 1830. In June there was a tragic disciplinary case involving William Welsh, Ordinary Seaman, who was given 48 lashes on board *Hyperion* for drunkenness and seizing arms with intent to murder. Six days later he died from inflammation of the lungs. The punishment had, of course, been ordered by Mingaye and any criticism by a coroner would have been reflected badly on the Captain. In the event the jury found the punishment had been administered correctly and cleared Captain Mingaye of any blame.

On the smuggling front an interesting case concerning Henry Stubberfield is recorded in papers that passed between the Admiralty and the Treasury. A petition, dated 8 June 1830, from the parish of Hove said that Henry 'of that parish' had been accused of violently assaulting seamen of the Coast Blockade at the sluice in the parish of Bexhill. He had been charged and imprisoned, leaving a wife and five children destitute and on parochial relief. The parish also had the cost of defending Stubberfield at the trial and this would be more than £50, not including the costs of briefing witnesses in London. The petitioners believed him to be innocent and they asked the Treasury for '. . . some small allowance towards expenses, particularly as the parish is for the most part very poor and quite unable to pay the expenses because there was a general failure in the agricultural crops last year . . .' The Admiralty passed the petition on to the Treasury where, needless to say, it received short shrift because they knew that many smugglers already claimed parish relief as a matter of routine. On 22 June 1830 Henry Stubberfield was tried and acquitted when the jury decided it was a case of mistaken identity.

The surname Stubberfield cropped up on more than one smuggling occasion during those years. Stephen was one of the ten sentenced in April 1828 for the Bexhill and Eastbourne battles and in August 1828 Captain Mingaye strongly opposed a petition to convert the sentence of five years naval service for Edward Stubberfield into a £100 fine. '. . . he is a leading Sussex smuggler. We have been years attempting to get hold of him. Even if the fine were £1000 it would be paid by his backers and employers'.

Following the pattern of previous years there must have been a fair number of smuggling runs during the summer of 1830 but Mingaye only mentioned two in his papers. On the night of 16 September the local grab-and-dash gang at Hastings were in action again. Thomas Latham, Captain of the Top, and William Lippet, Seaman, were on the beach near the Fish Market when they saw two boats making for the shore. From a distance the two looked to be a local Customs galley with a seized craft in tow, but as the Blockade men moved closer to the landing spot they realised their mistake when they were ambushed by two groups of smugglers. Latham and Lippet were knocked unconscious and their pistols stolen. Lippet was the first to recover and he ran to the Watch House to give the alarm but, once again, by

The Blockade Watch House at Cuckmere Haven, built in 1825.

then everyone and everything had disappeared from the beach – except for poor Latham. Later there were stories circulating in the town of how, within minutes of the arrival of the boats, nearly 100 men carrying tubs and sacks had disappeared like quicksilver into the side streets and alleys off the High Street.

The following night there was an attack on the Line near Tower 53, west of Bexhill. A Quartermaster and three sentinels were injured during the fight and were subsequently commended for their bravery by Captain Mingaye. However the Station Officer, Lieutenant Goodridge, did not appear on the scene until the smugglers were beaten off. He had already been warned by Mingaye for slackness and now received a further reprimand. As a result the Admiralty decided to supersede Goodridge and replace him with Lieutenant Pennington who had petitioned Sir Henry Hotham for a post in the Coast Blockade. Pennington, with 17 years service as a Lieutenant in the Royal Navy, considered the Blockade Service to be an attractive posting.

As with its counterpart in Kent, by 1830 the Sussex Blockade Force had made some changes in the deployment of stations, shown in Appendix D, that existed at the time of separation. Six Martello towers were paired off – 44/46, 48/49, and 59/62 – to operate as three stations whilst four others: 35 and 37 (Pett Levels), 39 (St Leonards) and 42 (Bulverhythe Salts) were occupied as additional stations. There were three vessels at Rye for use as stations: *Adder* and *Dwarf* at the Town Quay and *Enchantress* at the Harbour, whilst a 'Boundary watch vessel' was beached further east near Jury's Gap.

In October 1830 the Admiralty sent Mingaye a questionnaire calling for a detailed analysis of the Sussex Blockade's organisation and its achievements from early 1825 to July 1830. A similar questionnaire probably went to the

Kent Blockade but does not appear in Admiralty records. The first questions, with Mingaye's answers, were:

Number of land stations?	15 West Division, 21 Centre and 31 East
Number of tenders and vessels?	4 tenders. 4 vessels at Rye. One vessel at Chichester.
Approved complement?	Was 1,325 now 1,207 with 117 officers and 1,090 men.

Asked which vessels were the most dangerous Mingaye replied 'those with concealments' but added pointedly '. . . since July 1827 the Coast Blockade have been restricted from boarding vessels consigned to the Custom Houses or with passengers'. On the question of the cost of the Blockade he answered, diplomatically, 'see Navy Estimates'.

On the matter of achievements over the five and a half years the Sussex Blockade Force had seized 8,404 kegs of spirits, 255 bales of tobacco, 260 yards of silk, 40 packages of tea and 15 packs of gloves. The numbers of vessels seized were: 16 (1825); 31 (1826); 14 (1827); 19 (1828); 18 (1829) and 8 (1830).

The tally of smugglers caught and convicted is worth a closer look:

Year	**Captured**	**Convicted**
1825	82	49
1826	38	21
1827	23	14
1828	33	19
1829	30	28
1830 (to July)	20	20

The number captured was high in the first year but then dropped as the separate Sussex force, at full strength, made its impact. Some smugglers made their runs further west, away from the Line, taking their chance with the less effective Coast Guard. Others changed from fighting their way through the Line to more subtle methods such as 'sowing' tubs or concealing goods on board a cargo vessel. Apart from other considerations such methods involved far fewer men.

Notice also how the conviction rate rose in 1829 and became 100% in 1830 as magistrates, now in need of Blockade assistance to quell riots, looked more favourably on smuggling prosecutions. During the winter of 1829-1830 there were indications that this anxiety had even persuaded Hastings magistrates to drop their long-held belligerence to Blockade witnesses.

The total number of kegs seized, which averaged about 130 a month, was bound to be low when so often in a fight the heavily outnumbered naval men were held off by batmen whilst most of the contraband was taken away inland. Perhaps a more realistic indication of the impact of this naval campaign would lie in the number of casualties suffered on both sides and particularly in the number of fatalities amongst smugglers. But this can never be assessed with any accuracy; an attempt at estimates is made in Chapter Eight but the true figures will never be known.

In November Mingaye, like his fellow commander in Kent, was sufficiently sure of the future to authorise advertisements in local newspapers inviting tenders for the supply of fresh beef to the three Sussex Divisions for the year commencing 1 January 1831. But the completed questionnaires were now with their Lordships at the Admiralty and the Treasury and the answers given, no matter how they were analysed, could not disguise the simple fact that the entire Coast Blockade, from Sheerness to Chichester Harbour, was a very expensive campaign.

Dramatic changes in both Palace and Parliament had occurred during 1830. King William 'The Sailor King' was now on the Throne and the short and stormy administration of the Duke of Wellington had come to an end in November. Lord Grey was now Prime Minister and there was a new First Lord at the Admiralty; the future of the Coast Blockade Service was under scrutiny and by the end of May 1831 it would be dis-banded.

CHAPTER SEVEN

The Coast Blockade as a Rescue Service

For centuries the fate suffered by those shipwrecked on the shores of Britain was, more often than not, that of a watery grave. Rescue was dependant upon the ability and willingness of anyone watching on shore. Given reasonable conditions the traditional brotherhood of the sea might induce some local boatmen to make courageous attempts to reach the stranded ship; Deal luggers and galleys made many rescues from vessels caught on the dreaded Goodwin Sands. But that was in an area with a near unique combination of hazards and busy maritime traffic. Elsewhere along the coasts there were those who barely scraped a living in their poor parishes and for them a shipwreck was an answer to their prayers. As they gathered to watch the vessel founder their thoughts were more on the plunder to be had rather than on the poor souls trapped on board. Life was cheap in those hard and violent times and, in any case, there was often little anyone on shore could do to make a rescue.

Even if those on board managed to get ashore there was always the possibility of encountering savagery rather than salvation. Around the more remote coasts there were tales of shipwrecked passengers and crew coming ashore only to be murdered for the possessions they had managed to salvage. Such tales may not abound in Kent and Sussex but in the mid-eighteenth century there were episodes of piracy off Hastings and, in the hands of such villains, who could tell what fate befell those on board if a vessel was driven ashore in bad weather?

By the end of the eighteenth century maritime traffic between Northern Europe and the many far-flung settlements around the world was booming and Napoleon's final defeat heralded an even greater increase in sea-borne trade. The English Channel became the busiest seaway in this part of the world, and remains so to this day. Ships bound into and out of London and the East Coast ports were joined on passage through the Channel by French, Dutch and Scandinavian merchantmen, all trading to and from the burgeoning territories in Asia, Africa and the Americas. There were also vessels from the Atlantic coasts, as well as English coasters and the busy packet boats, trading luggers and fishing boats that criss-crossed the Channel every day – and night.

Inevitably the ever increasing seaborne trade brought more shipwrecks and more tragic stories of lives lost. Sometimes in the early years at the start of the nineteenth century local folk would be moved to take positive action and a dreadful disaster could spur a nearby community to raise funds to build a lifeboat and man it with volunteers. But these early efforts were fragmented and localised without any central co-ordination.

At that time attention was often directed more to finding some way of getting a line out from shore to the stricken vessel so that those on board could be guided to safety. A major step forward in this direction came when an Army Captain named G.W. Manby adapted a mortar (a short cannon) for this purpose. Manby, a boyhood friend of Nelson, was born in Norfolk in October 1765 and joined the Army as a Woolwich cadet. In later years, with his consequent expertise in ordnance, he devised a $5^1/_2$" brass mortar, weighing 300lbs, that fired a 30lb shot with line attached some 275 yards out from the shore. This was first used near Yarmouth in 1807 to rescue people from a stranded vessel and after further successful trials the apparatus was adopted officially by the Board of Ordnance in 1810.

Some Preventive Waterguard Watch Houses were issued with mortars and those in Kent and Sussex were transferred to the Coast Blockade Service as it took over control along the coast progressively between 1817 and 1824. Blockade records, particularly for Kent, are sketchy as to which stations had sets of 'Captain Manby's Life Saving Apparatus' as it was known. In Sussex a set was expected at Eastborne in 1822 and two years on sets were available at stations in Hastings, Seaford, Brighton and Littlehampton. Others were later provided at Birling Gap, Blatchington and Saltdean.

By then Manby's apparatus had been in use for some fourteen years and during this time some modifications had been made by the Navy. The mortar remained unchanged but the shot now weighed only 24lbs, to give greater range, and carried a small iron bar fashioned into an eye. This took the end of 120 fathoms of $1^1/_2$" 'messenger' line (rope) which in turn was secured to 140 fathoms of $3^1/_2$" heavy tarred line. Later requisitions in the Blockade Service were for 'deepsea lines of hide'. In some instances a cradle of canvas and cork was used to carry a person ashore – a forerunner of the breeches buoy.

During 1823 one local newspaper had the good grace to acknowledge that, with the Blockade Service now established as far west as Beachy Head, '. . . it is certainly consolatory in a great commonwealth country, to reflect that there is not a spot, however remote and obscure, along the coast of Sussex and Kent, from Beachy Head to the Isle of Sheppey, on which a vessel might be wrecked but there are men stationed at all hours of the night ready to give the alarm in an instant and to render assistance'. With some hyperbole the paper went on to claim that hundreds of people owed their lives to the exertions of the officers and men of the Blockade, all of whom refused to accept monetary rewards for their service. Whilst there was some exaggeration here it did at least promote the otherwise dented and tarnished public image of the Blockade.

Captain Manby's apparatus was certainly used successfully time and time again but in one unfortunate accident in 1826, at Brighton's Chain Pier, a young lad was killed when a mortar was fired. Ruefully the local newspaper suggested henceforth it should be known as the 'Death Dealing Apparatus'.

A lifeboat was provided at Eastbourne in 1822, soon after the wreck of the East Indiaman *Thames*. A local committee raised funds and placed the boat in the care of the local Comptroller of Customs; later it seems it was transferred to the Blockade Service. By now the number of such lifeboats had increased considerably, still without any national body to co-ordinate them.

The next important step nationally in the whole business of saving life from shipwrecks came with the efforts of Sir William Hillary, a philanthropic resident of the Isle of Man. He came to London in 1823 determined to create a national life boat service and attracted sufficient royal and noble support to form the Royal National Institution for the Preservation of Life from Shipwreck on 4 March 1824. The Shipwreck Institution, as it soon became known, was a charity supported by donations and subscriptions that would oversee the care and maintenance of existing lifeboats and provide others where needed. In its early years the Institution also awarded gold medals to those who showed outstanding bravery during rescue work. Later that award function was taken over by the Royal Humane Society and this left the Shipwreck Institution to evolve into the Royal National Lifeboat Institution.

The Shipwreck Institution operated through local committees and in some districts these were newly formed in 1824. In one instance, however, it seems the care and responsibility soon became too onerous. On 17 October 1825 Captain Mingaye told the Admiralty that a lifeboat had been placed at Brighton by the Committee of the Shipwreck Institution. Local care and control had been vested in a committee of gentlemen residents, but they now wished to transfer everything, including Captain Manby's apparatus, to the Coast Blockade. Mingaye was happy to accept and the Admiralty agreed.

In the pages that now follow in this chapter those rescues made by the Blockade Service and shown in Admiralty papers, or local newspapers, are set out chronologically. It is by no means a complete record of what happened; some documents about one rescue refer briefly to another that was not reported. In other instances the only record is a letter of thanks from the owner or master of a vessel or their agents. Nevertheless, the accounts that follow are good illustrations not only of the rescue work carried out by officers and men of the Blockade Service, but also of their courage, dedication and seamanship.

1819

17 December. Brig *Acorn* out of London for Malta wrecked at Dungeness. A letter of thanks dated 28 January 1820 from John Friend and Co., Lloyds Agents, mentions '. . . the meritorious conduct of Mr Charles Newton, Masters Mate and his party of No.3 Battery, Dungeness and their assistance afterwards in protecting the property . . .'

29 December. Dutch brig *Kozak* wrecked off Margate. A letter of thanks from the Netherlands government pays tribute to the assistance given by Lieutenant Dore and his men as well as officers and men of the Blockade tender *Industry*.

December. Brig *Phoenix* of Deal wrecked near Beachy Head. The crew were saved by Midshipman Tom Caswell and two Blockade men 'under the greatest peril of their own lives'. Letter of thanks, dated 21 January 1820, from John Friend, Lloyds Agent, Dover.

1820

24 January. Brig *Brothers* wrecked near Beachy Head. A letter of gratitude from Benjamin Lewes, owner and master, acknowledges the services rendered by three Midshipmen, including Tom Caswell.

24 March. Goodwin, Curling and Co., Lloyds Agents, wrote seeking Admiralty approval to give ten guineas to Midshipman Norton Alexander at Eastware Bay for the services rendered by him and his party in going to the assistance of the *Sir Godfrey Webster* when she was in danger. The date was not given. Assistance was also rendered to the sloop *Drie Susters* on 21 January 1820 but no award could be made because she was not insured. In a note attached to the letter, Captain McCulloch advised the Admiralty that Midshipman Alexander declined to accept any reward '. . . because he considered such services were only in the execution of his public duty'.

14 May. Brig *Brothers* wrecked at Swale Cliff. William Ogilby, Esquire, presented Lieutenant Grandy with a piece of plate to commemorate the services given by him and his Blockade party.

1821

15 January. Bark *Prudentia* with salt from Ostend, wrecked at Dungeness. With four of his men Masters Mate Charles Newton twice tried to launch a galley into the heavy surf but each time some of his men were washed out of the boat and back on to the beach. The third attempt was successful, they managed to reach the vessel and persuade the eleven crew to get into the bark's one remaining boat and cut it adrift. The Blockade galley then towed it ashore just as the bark started to break up. All eleven crew were saved. Four weeks later Charles Newton put his life at risk again – in the fight against the Aldington Gang at the Battle of Brookland.

9 May. Approval given by the Admiralty for 'two handsome swords each valued at twenty guineas and two brace of pistols at five guineas each' to be presented to the officers of Margate Coast Blockade District for assistance given to the late sloop *Oakes* of London. Unfortunately no other details were given.

November. Unnamed Danish vessel wrecked near Tower 33 (Pett Levels). Three Blockade officers made two attempts to launch a galley through the pounding surf but each time it capsized. Then a man was seen to jump from the stricken vessel and start to swim for the shore. Taking a line already secured on the beach Midshipman S. Drake, braving the heavy seas, swam out to meet the struggling man and both were pulled to safety by helpers on the shore. There was only that one survivor, sadly nothing could be done to save the master, three crew, two women and three children left aboard the wreck and they all perished.

December. French fishing boat *La Julie* wrecked near Tower 33. A local newspaper reported that '. . . all the crew were saved through the prompt and humane exertions of some officers and men of the Blockade Station'.

31 December. Dutchman *Yonge Martha* wrecked in Rye Bay. Midshipmen S. Drake, H.S. Burniston and J. Burnett saved the life of H.S. Locke the ship's mate and then made repeated but unsuccessful attempts to save the rest of the crew. For their brave efforts, at the risk of their own lives, the King of the Netherlands awarded each Midshipman a gold medal valued at 25 ducats.

1822

January. French vessel *Jeune Fante* wrecked near Beachy Head. In a letter to the *Sussex Weekly Advertiser* Mr. J.B. Stone, Customs Comptroller, Newhaven described how four survivors were '. . . housed and fed by the liberality of the Officers of the Coast Blockade stationed at Birling Gap whose humanity in all cases of Shipwreck has been highly honourable'. In particular he commended Joseph Thomas and William Pearson of the Coast Blockade and Henry Miller, Henry Earle, Thomas Elliott and Thomas Shelley labourers of East Dean'.

3 February. East Indiaman *Thames*, outward bound from London weathered Dungeness, heading down Channel, but by nightfall was caught in hurricane force winds and driven in towards Eastbourne 'in great distress, firing guns and making lights'. Eventually she struck just off shore between the Round-House and the Martello Tower. Divisional Lieutenant Edward Chappell and two Midshipmen persuaded four fishermen to join in launching a fisherman's lug-boat. Chappell described the surf as '. . . the heaviest I have seen . . .' but they managed to reach the stranded vessel and put lines aboard to bring people ashore. Meanwhile three more fishermen were trying to launch a second boat and Midshipman Francis Smith, of Tower 71, ran forward to join them. Then, in Chappell's words, 'the boat over set on the beach, Smith was knocked under and swept out by the surf and drowned in the presence of some 500 townspeople. Six or seven of the crew of the Indiaman perished trying leave the wreck in a boat'. For their efforts in saving the remainder of those on board the Lieutenant and the others involved in the rescue received awards and medals. Those for Midshipman Smith were presented to his father who lived in Margate.

1823

12 February. French fishing boat *La Clarisse* wrecked the previous night off Rye Beach. At daybreak Masters Mate John Finch and Midshipman John O'Reilly, with four Blockade men, launched their galley '. . . from the Main through heavy surf and in a tremendous gale of wind . . . after repeated attempts . . . succeeded in reaching the two men who had lashed themselves to the mast. Five others had perished'. Those were the comments of the Mayor of Rye in the letter of thanks and commendation he sent to the Navy Board.

10 March. Fishing lugger *Hit or Miss* of Sandgate wrecked there at night in tremendous surf. Four of the five crew were saved, after great difficulty, by Coast Blockade men. The fifth was trapped under the floating up-turned hull '. . . .and local inhabitants swarmed around trying to raise the boat . . . Midshipman James Broomer ran over and realised their efforts were fruitless because it was trapped air that caused the trouble. He gave vent by knocking a large hole in the bottom then with the assistance of his own men, in heavy surf, righted the boat and went into the surf to rescue the man who was nearly dead but survived'.

1 April. Vessel *Philippa* stranded near Beachy Head. The letter of thanks from Jas. Madge, master, mentions how Mr Darby and Mr Bradley of the Coast Blockade assisted at first to get an anchor out from the ship so that she could pull herself off but 'the vessel filled with water in the bad state of weather . . . they then took us off to safety when our lives were in danger'.

11 October. Vessel *Nottingham* of Weymouth wrecked off New Romney in a violent gale. Lieutenant Clayton and Midshipman Read '. . . launched a fishing boat through heavy surf despite the importunity of spectators who urged the danger . . .' They were unable to reach the vessel, came back to shore and re-launched again. This time they succeeded in getting alongside and rescued all the crew. Their efforts were commended in a letter from John Friend, Lloyds Agent, Dover.

11 October. Swedish brig *Amphion* driven ashore near Dymchurch. The subsequent letter from Mr Morris, Swedish vice consul in Dover explained how '. . . Lieutenant Dyball and Midshipman Collins and their seamen launched a boat that overset first throwing four into the tremendous surf, the Lieutenant being badly bruised. Mr Collins righted the boat with three others, set out once again and nearly reached the wreck when they were overset again and lost 3 of the 4 oars. But by using one oar and one of the waste (presumably 'waist') boards they returned to shore. They tried again and were successful in taking off one seaman and one young passenger. The Captain and ten crew were rescued by the Sandgate boat that had been taken by land some distance for the purpose . . . none but those of the Coast Blockade being near the spot . . .'.

4 December. Galliott *Sophie* of Bremen driven ashore on Sandwich Flats. Lieutenant Mott and Mr Riley went on board as soon as possible and offered their services to dismantle the vessel and save the stores. In his letter of thanks John Friend, Lloyds Agent, said he was there much of the time and acknowledged the prompt manner in which the Blockade men accomplished their help '. . . the Captain and crew speak in the highest terms of their kindness . . .'

LIEUTENANT JOSEPH CLARKE R.N.

The chronicle of rescues is broken for a moment to make a special reference to the activities of this officer who, during five years at Birling Gap Station between 1824 and 1829, was responsible for saving the crews of ten vessels. Unfortunately details of only six rescues have been found but in all he received awards ranging from an ornamental sword, a brace of pistols and a gold medal – all from Lloyds – to a gold medal from the Shipwreck Institution and another from the King of the Netherlands.

Joseph Clarke was born into a truly naval family; five of his brothers died whilst serving in the Royal Navy. He joined as an Able Seaman in October 1807 and later became a Midshipman serving on a number of ships including *Barrosa*, the frigate later commanded by Captain McCulloch. Whilst on *Leander* (50) Clarke was wounded in the arm during the Battle of Algiers in August 1816. Promoted to Masters Mate he came to the Coast Blockade in 1819 and gained his commission as Lieutenant before moving to Birling Gap Station in October 1824. There he remained until he transferred out of the Blockade Service in 1829 and joined the Coast Guard in 1830.

The stretch of coast around Birling Gap, just west of Beachy Head and part of the Seven Sisters Cliffs, was a notorious graveyard for those vessels running up Channel before a sou-westerly gale that found, all too late, they were unable to beat to seaward to get around Beachy Head. When a ship struck the wide rocky foreshore there was little chance of the crew reaching the safety of dry land unless someone came to their aid. Even then any rescue through the shallow waters surging over those rocks must have been really hazardous at times. There was no lighthouse there in those days, the first, Belle Tout, was not built until 1831. Due to the efforts of the Reverend Jonathan Darby of East Dean a cave below Beachy Head had been enlarged as a refuge and was lit on stormy nights, but that was just one spot in cliffs that extended for miles.

During the early years of the Blockade Midshipman Tom Caswell featured in several rescues at Birling Gap. Then from 1824 the task usually fell to Lieutenant Joseph Clarke and he was never found wanting in displaying the bravery, seamanship and tenacity that mark the best traditions of the Royal Navy.

1824

November. Vessel *Juno* out of Jersey, with a cargo of apples, went ashore at Birling Gap just a few weeks after Lieutenant Clarke had arrived. With eight men, and operating under great difficulty at times, he managed to rescue all

Above *The rocky shore at Birling Gap, the scene of many brave rescues by Lieutenant Joseph Clarke and his men.*
Below *The same shore during a sou'-westerly gale.*

the crew. For his efforts he was later presented with a handsome dress sword by the underwriters and a gold medal from the recently established Shipwreck Institution. Each of his men received £2. Lieutenant Clarke also supervised the salvage of some 1,200 bushels of apples out of the 1,600 carried as cargo and these were later auctioned by Customs in Newhaven.

23 November. Vicious storms had battered the Sussex coast for days. At Seaford every building on or near the beach, except the Martello Tower, was reduced to a ruin. The lower walls of Seaford Battery had been swept away and eight Army men, with their wives and children, were forced to take refuge in the upper floors of the Forthouses. '. . . At great risk Mr Darby, Masters Mate, crawled along the broken walls until he could bring his boat to the assistance of those stranded and help them climb down out of the second floor windows. Edward Plummer, seaman, broke his left leg and right arm during the rescue . . .' These details were given in a letter of thanks sent to the Admiralty from all those who were saved.

23 November. The Rector of Selsey, the Rev. Barre-Phipps, was moved to make a special note in the parish register: '. . . the wind being in the south and south west a remarkably high tide accompanied by a violent wind burst over the Shingles Bank . . . and the Sea Wall maintained by the Rector and Mr George Copies . . . as part of the marsh belonging to both of them'.

24 November. Brig *Hazard* of Leith with dried fruit and cork out of Bordeaux was driven ashore on high water at Felpham during a gale. Lieutenant Mitcheson reported that the crew were saved by Mr Ainsworth, Mate, and his men. They also assisted in landing nearly all the cargo and passing it to Customs '. . . the road to Bognor was destroyed, stone piers, sluices and groins at Felpham likewise. The county was overflown (sic) for many miles'.

1825

11 March. Dutch brig *Antonia Ulrica* bound for Antwerp with coffee and sugar went ashore in thick fog about one mile east of Birling Gap. Later Mr James Hodson, Lloyds Agent, wrote how '. . . Lieutenant Joseph Clarke and his men went out in their boat to the brig over dangerous rocks on a very dark night. They took off the crew and a little Portuguese passenger boy and brought them to the watch house affording them every comfort the situation required'. The Lieutenant was also responsible for 'securing the cargo and preventing any plunder' and for this he was presented with a piece of plate, valued at £5, by the Comptroller of Customs.

30 August. Sloop *Ardent* out of Belfast for London with linen and corn, struck on rocks near Beachy Head. Lieutenant Clarke succeeded in getting her afloat again within a few hours and she was able to continue on her voyage. James Hodson, Lloyds Agent, wrote '. . . again I must praise this meritorious young officer who acted under difficult and dangerous circumstances and record the gentlemanly manner in which he proffered advice to the Captain . . .'

8 November. Brig *Abeona* out of Cadiz for London with wine. Driven ashore under the cliffs at Birling Gap in a hurricane. Lieutenant Clarke and three of his men worked from the broken edge of the cliff and eventually saved all the crew and passengers. James Hodson wrote again 'It is out of my powers to find words that will fully do justice to the exertions of Lieutenant Clarke and his men on these occasions. This is the fourth vessel within a year that has been on shore at this place and each time he has preserved the lives of the whole of the people on board'.

17 December. Letter of thanks sent to Captain Mingaye regarding the cutter *Busy* 'recently stranded near Tower 31' (Pett Levels). Mr Coleman, Lloyds Agent at Rye acknowledged '. . . the assistance and the active and persevering endeavours of Lieutenants Griffiths, Mold and Helby in going to the help of the cutter. Also our thanks to Lieutenant Henderson of Tower 38 near which the Busy's boat was upset'.

1826

9 April. Dutch vessel *Emanuel,* with 400 tons of coffee, sugar and cotton, ran ashore in fog close to Beachy Head. When Lieutenant Carter and his men reached her they found the crew had been taken off by a Dover pilot boat. The *Emanuel* later sank but not before the Blockade men had salvaged some of the cargo and transferred it to Customs. The letter of thanks to Captain Mingaye came from the Deputy Sergeant to the Lord Warden of the Cinque Ports.

15 May. Vessel *Elizabeth* of Glasgow with timber from Sierra Leone driven ashore between Littlehampton and Worthing. Captain Mingaye was visiting the area and joined Lieutenants Ross, Leworthy and Drew in organising efforts to refloat the vessel. 'There was a great deal of surf but the Blockade Parties gave all assistance and as the flood (tide) made she was hove off by the efforts of the Parties and with many thanks from the master'.

7 December. Vessel *Princess Charlotte* wrecked near Tower 50. 'Masters Mate Shellard and his men got their boats alongside with great difficulty, the vessel now being on fire and the flood tide making, but they were able to save all the crew'.

7 December. Vessel *Lord Cranstown* driven ashore 3/4 mile east of Birling Gap. Lieutenant Clarke and his men made a successful rescue and James Hodson, Lloyds Agent, wrote '. . . once again a Captain and crew owe their lives to his timely intervention and the owners are grateful for his protecting their property from plunder'.

1827

1 March. Dutch galliott *Johanna* out of Bordeaux for Amsterdam with wine, driven ashore at Birling Gap and quickly became a total wreck. All on board were brought to safety by Lieutenant Clarke '. . . who was as usual exceedingly active . . .' and five of his men. In October the King of the Netherlands, by Order in Council, awarded a gold medal to Lieutenant Clarke for his fine, brave efforts in this rescue. Silver medals went to each of the five Blockade men.

1828

January. Brig *Spring* wrecked off Pagham. A report mentions that Lieutenant Lean of Pagham Station was presented with a piece of plate by the owners and his men received £10 for their assistance '. . .particularly in preventing the cargo of bales of cotton and many smaller packages from being stolen . . .' The report concluded 'This happened so soon after the wreck of the lugger Ranger with a cargo of herrings'.

13 April. Vessel *Katherine Stewart Forbes* was in a perilous situation near the Goodwin Sands. Boats launched from *Ramillies* succeeded in rescuing all those on board the stricken ship. Later the owners and agents were given Admiralty authority to make presentations and awards to the officers and men involved. Lieutenant Henry Lawless received a letter of thanks for boarding the *Gull* Light Vessel and firing her alarm signals. Lieutenant John Prattent was presented with a brace of inscribed pistols valued at ten guineas. The thirteen men who manned the boats under Lawless and Prattent each received a guinea. Bosun James McCullum, who commanded another boat, was given ten guineas with a further twenty four guineas being shared by his twelve crew.

1829

26 May. Russian vessel *Nicholas the First* lost off Dungeness. All the crew were saved by the courageous efforts of Lieutenant Richard Nugent Kelly, Quartermaster John Flynn and seven Blockade men.

24 November. Brig *Mountaineer* from Cape of Good Hope for London. She had anchored in the Downs on the 23rd but next day the wind shifted around to the east and increased to a gale. A Deal galley, with four oarsmen, went out to put a pilot on board but capsized as it neared the brig. The pilot and one man were drowned but the other three were brought safely on board the *Mountaineer*. By 4.30pm, however, the brig had lost her anchor and was being driven ashore at Deal. Divisional Lieutenant William Johnson took charge of the rescue arrangements that were hampered because Captain Manby's apparatus was not to hand. By 5.30pm it was dark and Johnson ordered tar barrels to be lit to illuminate the beach, much to the jeers of the crowd that had now gathered. The rising tide backed by the high wind made rescue attempts impossible for some hours and by 11.30pm, at the top of high water, it was evident the ship was breaking up in an easterly gale that had lost none of its intensity. Lieutenant Johnson waited another hour and then, as the tide started to ebb, went into the pounding surf '. . . got a rope out to the brig and clambered aboard with it, to the cheers of the Deal men . . .' The master and ten crew, together with the three Deal boatmen, were lowered one by one down the rope and then used it to drag themselves through the surf to safety on the beach. Fourteen were saved that night but four lost their lives; two men from the brig and the two from the Deal galley. Lieutenant Johnson made a report of the rescue and Captain Pigot wrote underneath '. . .a very modest report by Johnson who

Ramsgate c. *1824*. Dover Museum

displayed the best examples of courage and bravery'. For his valour that night the Lieutenant was awarded a gold medal by the Shipwreck Institution.

1830

20 February. Large French lugger, unnamed, wrecked at Fairlight. The ship's boy was drowned but the remaining ten crew were saved by the efforts of Lieutenants Prattent and James and men of the nearby Blockade Stations. Subsequently the Shipwreck Institution presented gold medals to the two Lieutenants and sixteen guineas to their men.

1831

During the early part of this year the Naval Coast Blockade Service stood down and departed from the shores of Kent and Sussex. The Coast Guard, which had covered the remainder of the coasts in England, Wales and Scotland since 1822, now moved into the two counties. Since its inception the Coast Guard had made many rescues from shipwrecks and these traditions would continue in Kent and Sussex, but with far fewer men.

During the six years from early 1825 to early 1831, there were more Blockade men watching the coasts of Kent and Sussex than there were Coast Guard men around the rest of Britain. If the crews of revenue cruisers and Blockade depot ships are excluded the comparative figures for coast watchers were some 2,500 Blockade men between Sheerness and Chichester Harbour and 2,300 Coast Guard men for all other parts of the British coast.

It was, admittedly, no source of comfort for any poor soul who did perish in a shipwreck – and it was never presented officially as a prime virtue – but, during the years of the Coast Blockade, Kent and Sussex did have the benefit and consolation of this intensive coastal watch, by experienced naval officers and seamen, for shipwrecks as well as smugglers. As the local newspaper commented '. . . there was not a spot however remote and obscure along the coast of Sussex and Kent . . . on which a vessel might be wrecked but there are men stationed at all hours of the night to give the alarm in an instant and to render assistance'.

For the many who were rescued it was a welcome paradox that the 'national evil' of smuggling had been responsible, albeit inadvertently, for saving lives instead of destroying them.

CHAPTER EIGHT

1831: The Sentinels Stand Down

In February 1827 Lord Liverpool suffered a severe stroke and left office. Those were turbulent times in politics and the turmoil was still there the following year after the Duke of Wellington was invited by George IV to form a government. Although this was led in the Commons by Robert Peel – courteous and well respected – the autocratic attitude of Wellington antagonised some of his senior supporters in both Houses. Even so, there were many who did stand by him over the next two years, including Lord Melville and John Croker.

King George died, lamented by few, in June 1830 and was succeeded by William, the popular 'Sailor King'. A few months later a new Parliament was elected and in early November, shortly after it first met, the opposition to Wellington was strong enough to bring about his downfall. On 15 November his government lost a vote of confidence and he resigned. When the King invited Earl Grey to form the next government Melville and Croker were among those Tories who left office being unwilling to serve under a Whig Prime Minister. Lord Melville retired from politics having served as First Lord of the Admiralty from 1812-1827 and 1828-1830. Sir John Croker continued to sit as a MP for several years and threw himself into active support of his party's policies, particularly over the Reform Bill. Sir James Graham, the new First Lord, paid tribute to Croker who had served as Secretary to the Admiralty for 22 years and 'regretted the Admiralty will no longer have the benefit of his brilliant talents and faithful services'.

The third senior figure at the Admiralty and co-supporter with Melville and Croker of the Coast Blockade, was John Barrow, Secretary to the Navy Board. Within weeks of the start of the new government Graham gave Barrow the task of amalgamating the Board of Admiralty and the Navy Board, an exercise that would occupy much of his time for the next two years. Knighted in 1835 Sir John had, from his early years, maintained a deep interest in Chinese affairs and became a respected sinologist. The founder of the Royal Geographical Society he died, full of other honours, in 1848.

One of the first tasks of Lord Grey's Cabinet was to put down the Swing Riots that were now sweeping across the south from Kent to Dorset. It seemed the winter of 1830 was going to be a bad one for crops and there was every possibility the riots would increase. Swift action was needed and in December Lord Melbourne, the new Home Secretary, sent out special commissioners to make harsh examples of those already held on charges of arson and rioting. Many magistrates had shown leniency over such charges but the commissioners were not so disposed. Across the south some men were hanged, many imprisoned and well over 400 transported; the rioting ceased but the rural hardship and poverty continued for many more years. One legacy of the riots was the gradual introduction, over the next two decades, of county police forces; Sir Robert Peel had already formed the Metropolitan Force in September 1829.

Another early task of the new Cabinet in January and February 1831 was to present a budget, but the first was a failure and had to be recast. The new government's control of finance was not as good as it's predecessor's, there was an urgent need for cost-cutting and the expensive Blockade Line was a prime target. A note from the Treasury on 31 January 1831 announced that no further officers and men were to be appointed to the Coast Blockade and this soon became public. Two days later the *Sussex Weekly Advertiser* reported 'It appears evident it is now the serious intention of the Government to do away with the Coast Blockade. The Commanding Officer of the Royal Engineers has been instructed to survey the towers and redoubts and report on their state'. Shorn of influential supporters at the Admiralty the inordinate cost of the Blockade made it ripe for demolition by a hard-headed reformer such as Sir James Graham, the new First Lord.

Immediate budgetary needs were undoubtedly the prime reason for the decision, but it is possible the high cost of the Blockade had already invoked opposition from none other than King William himself, well before Sir James Graham took office. Nothing appears in naval records but it is worth remembering that the first thoughts on replacing the Blockade with the Coast Guard came in that proposal from Customs to the Admiralty in March 1828 when Prince William was Lord High Admiral. At the time the idea was demolished effectively by John Barrow and set aside, but then came the Admiralty questionnaire to Mingaye in October 1830 several months after William's accession and a month before Lord Grey's government took office. During the short time he was Lord High Admiral, from 1827 to 1828, Prince William certainly tried to cut naval expenditure, without success, and it is likely he still had the same attitude when he became monarch. In his early years he had served in the Navy and kept a keen interest in naval affairs during the short reign that ended with his death in 1837.

The cost of the Blockade Service was certainly far higher than that of the Coast Guard over the same 200 miles of coast but it is difficult to make an estimate because some of the figures given in the records are suspect. In 1821, for example, with 1,276 officers and ratings in the Blockade Service the pay and incidental expenses were said to be £89,151, roughly £70 per head. In 1825 the complement had risen to 2,784 with the same costs quoted as £162,740, about £58 per head. This is admittedly a crude analysis but by 1825 all Midshipmen had been replaced by Lieutenants earning much higher pay. One important omission from the records is the cost of providing two depot ships and the seven or eight tenders used in the

The bluff and salty William IV satirized as a preventiveman.

two counties. By comparison the Coast Guard had no depot ships and only a few tenders. It used revenue cutters to make some waterborne deliveries to stations where the men were, in any case, fewer in number than those in the Blockade. All that can be said with certainty on the matter of costs is that it was a very expensive operation to maintain a Naval Blockade Line from Sheerness to Chichester Harbour with some 700 to 800 sentinels on the Line each night.

Along the Line in Kent and Sussex the month of January 1831 was a fairly routine one with bitter fights with smugglers, some disciplinary cases and yet another complaint about the poor quality of uniform. This time it was footwear and Captain Pigot was moved to complain to the Victualling Board that he was 'concerned about the bad quality of beach shoes and the deplorable state of men's feet for want of them. I have been of necessity supplying naval shoes. Please supply a few hundred good quality beach shoes and allow those we have issued at half the original charge'.

The disciplinary cases included the periodic list of deserters from the Kent Coast Blockade, eleven on this occasion but in addition, most unusually, there was a charge of murder. On 6 January George Bradley, Able Seaman at Shellness Station was charged with the murder of Michael Ward, Captain of the Top, on 26 December 1830 but no details were given of any subsequent trial.

The last attack on the Kent Blockade Line came near the Casemates Station at Dover (where Richard Morgan was killed) and was reported by Divisional Lieutenant James Stuart on 13 January 1831. Twenty or so smugglers managed to overcome two sentinels simultaneously wounding one, Joseph Jack. The two were bound and carried away to the back of the town where they were later released. The gang then lay in wait for Lieutenant Thomas Ross as he made his rounds and tried to overpower him before he could draw his pistols. The fight took place about 9.30pm on Dover seafront in full view of some spectators. Ross put up a spirited resistance and clung to some railings yelling for help from the onlookers. Two eventually came to his aid and the assailants ran off but by now the boat *Success* had landed and been almost unloaded by the rest of the gang. Ross fired his pistols and, after some delay, two other sentinels arrived to help him search the abandoned boat. They found just one bale of silk and judging from its size Ross reckoned another 30 had been landed that night.

The last attack on the Sussex Blockade Line came on 5 January 1831 below Fairlight Hill and was reported by Captain Mingaye as 'a severe conflict against a hundred men armed with bats. From the early assembling of our men at Stations East and West the smugglers were driven inland. Their boat and its cargo of 109 tubs was taken. Two smugglers were shot dead and several wounded carried off'. William Nixon, Captain of the Top, and Sentinels Fred Divorce (the saviour of Rye Bridge), William Bocock, Dennis Murphy and John Ray were wounded. The inquest on the death of the two smugglers, George Harrod and Will Cruttenden, recorded 'justifiable homicide'. Times had certainly changed over the lifetime of the Blockade; in such an action ten or so years earlier a Blockade man would probably have been charged with murder and clapped in leg-irons in a local gaol.

Early in February the two Blockade Forces knew they were going to be disbanded but their size and complexity, coupled with the rigidity of naval procedures meant the process of hand-over to the Coast Guard would take some months. In Sussex on 23 February Captain Mingaye was told 'to acquaint the Petty Officers and men of the Hyperion that the whole coast will be occupied by the Preventive Service by the second week in April when the Petty Officers will be discharged from the service. Captain Bowles has been directed to take immediate steps towards taking possession of the western extremity of the Coast of Selsea and that every facility is to be afforded . . .' That part of the Coast Guard occupying coastal stations was still known as the Preventive Service.

On 21 March the *Sussex Weekly Advertiser* announced 'The Coast Blockade it is understood, will be abolished in April. The Coastguard are preparing to occupy the several stations. The measure is the reverse of that calculated to excite regrets in this part of the Sussex District'. Two weeks later it reported 'The Coastguard establishment under the regulations of the Customs has commenced its duties within the last fortnight at Hastings and on Thursday twelve of the horse police arrived for the performance of their interior duty for the prevention of smuggling; they are well-looking men and are accoutred in a manner calculated for the Service'.

The Coastguard started to take over Sussex Blockade Stations on 21 March but was not able to occupy all three Divisions until early May. Some Blockade officers went home on half pay but many, including 39 Lieutenants out of a total of 57, were nominated by the Admiralty for transfer to the Coastguard and they either stayed in their old stations or moved to others close by. The ratings, however, had to be taken by tender to Portsmouth to be paid off from the Royal Navy and enlisted in the Coastguard. Some who made the changeover at this time had already spent years in the Royal Marines before joining the Blockade Service.

In Kent the changeover also started during March but progress was slow because nothing could inhibit the prescribed programme of naval inspections. Despite the confusion that it must have caused, Vice Admiral Beresford spent the month of March inspecting the Kent Blockade Force and did not finish the task until 2 April. March also saw the departure of Captain Hugh Pigot to the command of *Barham* (50). His appointment was dated 9 March but he stayed on *Talavera* until his successor, Captain David Colby, arrived. Hugh Pigot signed his last letter on *Talavera* on 22 March and four days later departed for Woolwich on the tender *Grinder* accompanied by Lieutenant James Stuart who was leaving Right Division, also for *Barham*. Captain Pigot was awarded the C.B. (rather apt!) in September 1831 and in later years added the K.C.H. and K.C.B. as he advanced through flag ranks to become Admiral in 1853, four years before his death.

David Colby, a senior Captain who had 'made post' in 1802, came off half pay to take command of *Talavera* on 23 March and on the same day William Beckett was appointed Divisional Lieutenant, Right Division, in place of James Stuart. As it happened Beckett was in the post just over three weeks; he transferred to the Coastguard on 19 April and was joined around that date by some 50 other Lieutenants out of a Kent Blockade complement of 69 (see Appendix E). This patently facilitated the hand-over in the county. All Blockade Lieutenants were ordered to transfer horses, carts and harness forthwith, any surplus to be sold at best possible prices. Station stores, galleys, ropes and Captain Manby's apparatus were all to be passed over on pro-forma receipts.

On 1 March 1831 a Parliamentary Committee of Special Enquiry said it was '. . . looking at ways to improve the efficiency of the Coast Guard without extra cost now it is taking in Kent and Sussex'. The government was still ardently seeking cuts in expenditure and it soon became clear that the Committee's remit was to finance the transfer in Kent and Sussex, as far as possible, by substantial savings elsewhere in the Coastguard. To this end the Committee proposed to remove the Coastguard entirely from shore stations in Scotland, Wales and North Devon and cover the loss with a few more small revenue cutters. In Scotland alone at this time there were 265 officers and men in the stations and the surplus staff from all three areas numbered around 450. Those that chose not to transfer to Kent and Sussex would be dismissed. No complement was quoted for the Coastguard staff needed in the counties; it was probably around 500 at first in 1831 although during the next 15 years it would rise steadily to over 1,400.

The proposal had originally been put to the Committee by Mr. R.B. Dean, Chairman of the Board of Customs, but was opposed vehemently by its Comptroller General of Coastguard, Captain Bowles. He declared the Committee had been misled by Collectors of Customs '. . . they resent a system which interferes with their authority and emoluments and the same time increases their labour and responsibility in various ways . . .' There was obviously some friction within the Customs department between the Coastguard and local Collectors and some of the latter were seeking a drastic remedy! Bowles had two further objections borne of the knowledge that the eight revenue cruisers already patrolling Scottish waters had to be large vessels capable of weathering all but the most severe gales. He pointed out there were few safe harbours in the areas to be vacated and furthermore it would be impossible for the small revenue cutters, envisaged by the Committee, to keep stations all year.

Captain Bowles, however, was by no means the only objector. The Committee's proposal provoked a furore in Scotland. Angry letters giving vigorous opposition to the very idea of withdrawing any Scottish Coastguard men arrived in Bowles office and that of Captain Knight, his Inspector General in Scotland. They now lie in Admiralty archives in bundles with titles such as 'Distillers', 'Tobacconists', Noblemen', 'Wine and Spirit Merchants', Civil Authorities', Officers of the Army', 'Officers of the Navy', 'Clergy', 'Resident Gentry', and finally and grandly, 'All of Scotland'. In Wales and North Devon it seems there was no opposition to the withdrawal of the Coastguard, no doubt the pragmatic locals could see positive advantages!

Nevertheless, although the opposition was confined to Scotland it did succeed in forcing the government to change its mind and the proposal to remove all the men from the three areas was dropped. On 4 April Sir James Graham wrote to Mr. Dean recommending that six cutters; three from Scotland, one from the Irish Sea and two from the north coasts of Devon and Cornwall, be transferred to Kent and Sussex. In addition 'at least sixty Coast Guard men should be transferred experimentally from the same areas to Kent and Sussex'. Sir James also considered '. . . a small number of cruisers on a long line of coast with a few men onshore judiciously posted, forming as it were a double line, will be far more efficacious than a greater number of cruisers forming a single line without aid on shore – a line constantly broken by adverse and tempestuous weather'. Economy was now the order of the day and the Admiralty's views had certainly changed since John Barrow's spirited defence of the expensive Blockade system three years before.

The recommendations, all of which had been initiated by Captain Bowles, were accepted by the Customs Board and a note from Mr. Dean recorded 'the unanimous opinion of the Board of Customs that the revenue would be subject to no additional risk by the substitution of the Coast Guard in place of the Coast Blockade'.

By early May the hand-over in Sussex had been virtually completed and the final act would be the departure of *Hyperion* from Newhaven. After lying there for six years she was in no fit state to return to sea service and arrangements were made to tow her to Portsmouth. Departure was delayed a day or so until strong gales abated but at 11.30am on 12 May she was towed out of Newhaven by the steam vessel *Colombia* to reach Portsmouth by late evening; there to remain until she was broken up in 1833. Captain Mingaye went on to half pay for some years, living in Newhaven; he achieved flag rank on promotion to Rear Admiral of the White in 1852 and Vice Admiral in 1857.

The officers and men of the Coast Blockade Service had departed from Newhaven for good, but they did leave one unusual memorial. During the years *Hyperion* had been there those officers and men (from the ship and two stations) numbered nearly 300 in all and many had their families with them in a town with a normal population of perhaps 850. In those God-fearing days this must have placed a considerable strain at times on the capacity of the parish church of St. Michael and Captain Mingaye offered the services of five naval carpenters to provide it with a gallery. This was gratefully accepted by the church elders and they duly acknowledged this help in an Agreement which stated:

> On behalf of officers and men of Hyperion and others placed to succeed them in the service of the Coast Blockade . . . it is agreed to secure 50 sittings in the North gallery . . . in recognition of the liberal aid afforded us in the erection of the said gallery by the employment of five carpenters to assist in this work. The Captain and officers to pay £5 per year each for the rent of two pews erected in the gallery . . . and we assure him seamen and marines to the number stated (50) will have free admittance to the use of the said part of the church'.

The gallery subsequently disappeared during substantial alterations in 1854 when the present choir and organ gallery was erected.

Having been delayed by the Admiral's inspection, the hand-over in Kent took longer and it was not until late April and early May that the tenders *Antelope* and *Industry* were busy taking men from the stations to be paid off at Chatham. The last few men were taken there from Whitstable and Sheerness on 25 May in the steam vessel *Messenger*.

H.M.S. *Talavera* was still in sea-worthy condition but her sails and much of the rigging had been landed into Deal Navy Yard when she became a depot ship. During May the crew was kept busy making her ready for sea: painting the hull, staying the masts, setting up the rigging, 'exercising the Great Guns' and changing the heavy mooring chains to temporary cables. During the first week in June she took on three months provisions and 136 tons of water. Then, at 5am on Tuesday 14 June, the sails were loosed 'in light airs' and at 6am, with topsails hoisted and topgallants set, *Talavera* slipped the best bower cable from her moorings in the Downs and nosed out, on a starboard tack, past South Foreland into the Straits of Dover. By noon the next day she was moored at Spithead but the crew now had to set to and prepare her for inspection. On Monday 20 June she received the Lords Commissioners of the Admiralty, in company with Admiral Sir E. Codrington who, no doubt, wished to assure themselves that *Talavera* was fit to resume service as a man-of-war. And indeed she was so engaged until destroyed accidentally by fire in Plymouth in September 1840.

The departure of *Talavera* marked the end of the Coast Blockade and of the 14 years preventive campaign conducted by the Royal Navy. Navy officers would still be nominated for service in the Coastguard but for the next 25 years that service would continue to be managed by the Board of Customs. From the start in 1817 those in authority in the Navy knew the Coast Blockade would be a difficult campaign because, in effect, the Blockade Service would become an army of occupation along a hostile coast. But throughout the years of the Blockade the Admiralty and the Navy Board showed, time and time again, their commitment to the campaign and made this known to all officers on the Line. A resolute approach that was in marked contrast to the weak and neglected management of the Preventive Waterguard elsewhere around Britain between 1816 and 1822.

As a campaign to prevent smuggling the Blockade only achieved a limited measure of success, but no armed force in the country could have actually stopped the flow of contraband. The Navy did succeed in curbing the Trade in notorious centres such as Deal and Dymchurch but large quantities of contraband came through the Line elsewhere. Essentially it was a war of attrition where armed service discipline and determination gradually turned the pattern of smuggling away from fights on the shores to concealments aboard vessels. The process had started before 1817 but the Coast Blockade did much to hasten it. Apart from other considerations fights so often brought death and injury whereas hiding goods away did not.

In addition to preventing smuggling the government was also keen to suppress the associated lawlessness that could pervade the South at a time when there was unrest elsewhere in the country. Any gang that became a small, permanent, army had to be broken as quickly as possible and in this the Navy was largely successful. Whilst in any fight the naval men were always heavily outnumbered they were never intimidated; there were always sentinels out on the Line the following night. And the officers, so often specific targets in any attack, were not only willing to take the lead in a fight but also to pursue any killers until they were brought to justice. As a consequence of this discipline the gangs were never able to maintain the domination enjoyed by their predecessors in the previous century.

The deaths of 58 naval officers and men are shown in this book, some killed in action whilst others died by accident or in unexplained circumstances. A further unknown number of deaths are believed to remain unrecorded, particularly in Sussex, and in both counties there were unknown numbers of those severely wounded, some perhaps maimed for life. How many smugglers died in what was acknowledged to be the bloodiest 14 years in the history of smuggling? So often a fight left Blockade men injured but one or more smugglers dead or dying. Any figure has to be a pure guess but a total of 150 fatalities over those years in Kent and Sussex is probably a conservative estimate.

By the end of June 1831 the Coastguard, which still comprised the Preventive Service, Mounted Guard and revenue cruisers, were stationed along all the coasts of Kent and Sussex. During the early years after it was formed in 1822 the popular concept of Coastguard Stations was summarised in *Punch* magazine as 'castles of idleness where able bodied men spend their time looking through long glasses for imaginary smugglers'. Captain Mingaye shared this view; in March 1831, obviously annoyed at having to stand down and hand over to this other force, he wrote to a colleague '. . . smuggling will soon be the best trade in Kent and Sussex and if those counties are not inundated when we leave I would venture to lose my commission'.

As it happened, Mingaye's commission would have been in jeopardy because Captain Bowles and his officers had created an effective preventive force that, despite suffering from the aftermath of neglect and still being thin on some parts of the coast, had seized over 450 vessels in the first two years. The original complement of about 3,000 dropped to 2,500 during the Blockade years but rose to over 3,000 after the return to Kent and Sussex and would increase steadily over the next 18 years.

Up to 1831 the Admiralty had not obtained any real influence in the recruitment of men for the Coastguard despite the intentions of the 1822 Treasury report. Officers were appointed by the Admiralty from the Navy List but the men were recruited by Customs from all walks of life, many with no sea-going experience whatsoever. Captain Bowles wanted to remove this landlubber element and as early as 1826 had written to Lord Melville suggesting that '. . . instead of direct recruitment . . . previous service in the Royal Navy should be an indispensable requisite – say seven years'.

The Admiralty saw the return of the Coastguard to Kent and Sussex as an opportune time to introduce Bowles' suggestion. On 22 March 1831 Sir James Graham wrote to Lord Grey:

> 'The Government's decision to substitute the Coast Guard for the Coast Blockade in Kent and Sussex having been nearly carried into effect . . . we would make some suggestions to improve the entire system of Coast Guards:
>
> (1) We should consider it in all branches essentially naval. It will be more efficient to use naval men than civilians and will provide an effective naval reserve. It will also be cheaper because we are employing naval officers already on half pay.
>
> (2) All officers and men to be selected by the Board of Admiralty. To be held out as a reward for merit and zeal displayed in the Royal Navy. The advantages for recruits will be that they will be on shore with their families and have the opportunities of seizure rewards'.

The proposals were accepted by the Treasury and Customs on 31 May. The Coastguard as a whole remained under the management of Customs but the Preventive Service and revenue cruisers were now staffed by the Admiralty and available as a naval reserve. As such it was not popular with officers in the early years because their pay was less than that in the Navy and many left after their first three year appointment. But, before he left the Coastguard in 1841, on promotion to Rear Admiral, Captain Bowles succeeded in raising the officers pay scales to Navy levels and extending their appointments to five years.

Rigid naval discipline had been an essential feature of the Coast Blockade Service. For the Coastguard there were no depot ships, no prisoners held in irons and no floggings, but discipline still had to be strict when there were so many opportunities for bribery and collusion. The ultimate sanction was dismissal and between August 1825 and February 1829, for example, there were 215 dismissals for offences that included drunkenness, mutiny and accepting bribes.

It only took a few months before instances of bribery were reported amongst the newly arrived Coastguard staff in Kent. In the Deal Coastguard District alone in the latter half of 1831 two chief boatmen, two boatmen and two mounted guards were dismissed and they were followed by a chief officer in 1832 and another boatman in 1833; all for accepting bribes. Their departures were probably due to the presence of the redoubtable Blockade veteran Sam Hellard who was Inspecting Commander, Deal District, from 13 April 1831. The incidence of bribery here and elsewhere showed that although the era of confrontation was coming to a close there was still enough vigour in the smuggling trade to warrant the liberal use of 'palm oil'.

A less important, but nonetheless irritating problem was also inherited by those Coastguard Stations sited on the vast shingle banks such as at Dungeness and Winchelsea. The Coast Blockade Service had hired contractors to deliver fresh water in barrels rolled over the pebbles, but the Coastguard used donkeys to carry such deliveries. At times it seems these animals were being kept at levels of extravagance that were unacceptable to the hard hearts in Customs headquarters. In January 1839 the Board of Customs expressed '. . . disapprobation at the amount hitherto charged for the forage for donkeys in the (Folkestone) District . . . furthermore . . . the purchase of beans is wholly unnecessary and too many oats have been given'. Some time later the donkey at Lydd Station developed vicious habits (due perhaps to a shortage of beans or oats) and was replaced by a more peaceful animal that had become redundant from Tower 27.

A different sort of donkey was introduced by the Coastguard to help their men stay awake at night on watches that often lasted for 16 hours. They were allowed to use one legged stools, known as 'rumpstools' or 'donkeys', as props during the lonely vigils. If sleep came then the man literally dropped off and hopefully regained consciousness. One can only imagine what Captain McCulloch would have said about such pandering! In the Blockade Service 'asleep on duty' was punishable by flogging.

As far as the smuggling fraternity were concerned one set of preventives had been changed for another but now they were far fewer. In the circumstances it might have been expected that some new large gangs would form in Kent to fight their way through the beaches, but the fact that none did shows the Blockade Service had largely succeeded in wearing down many of its opponents. Nevertheless there were still a number of local gangs operating from towns and villages around the coast. In the Deal area all officers were told to '. . . caution their men . . . against surprise by not allowing anyone to approach till satisfied it is their officer . . . smugglers will attempt to seize them by assuming a false character. Chief Officers are to be properly armed and on guard when passing through plantations, turning corners or near cliff edges . . . each company of smugglers will be accompanied by . . . batmen whose first and grand object will be to secure the officer'. Those officers and men who transferred from the Coast Blockade needed no such reminders!

On 6 October 1831 a local gang in Hastings tried the usual grab-and-dash operation as soon as the boat touched the town beach, but some were caught by Coastguard men during the dash into the town. There was a fight and Coastguard men William Gruer and Francis Duff were left on the ground severely injured. The Board of Customs offered £500 for information on the assailants but, as so often happened, it failed to produce a result.

Along the north coast of Kent another local gang, the Seasalter Company, was still thriving in the 1830s after some seventy years of successful operations. Working quietly and with discretion it seems the Company was seldom involved in fights with preventive men. The riding officers, Preventive Waterguard, and Coast Blockade had come and gone and now the Coastguard were there but the gang weathered all the opposition and continued quietly in business through a combination of prudence, good intelligence in the close-knit village – and the occasional application of 'palm oil'.

There were local gangs in Sussex that had also been operating for some years and were still ready to put up a fight if need be. Typically headed by one or two part-time organisers, the gang at Alfriston was led by a local

Coastguard man, late nineteenth-century

butcher, Stanton Collins, whilst at Rottingdean another butcher, known as 'Captain' Dunk was deeply involved with the village gang. Another of its supporters, for well over 40 years, was the Reverend Thomas Hooker, vicar of Rottingdean who lived in the large house still known today as the Grange. Both gangs must have used the coast between Beachy Head and Brighton for many of their runs.

There was one such run on 26 January 1832 when, according to the Collector Newhaven, a gang managed to land 300 tubs at Cuckmere Haven holding off the Coastguard men until all that was left was the boat and 10 tubs – the same old tale as told many times before. There were no deaths reported that night but on 21 February, in a fight at Bexhill, two Coastguard men were killed by gun shots; Boatman David Watts died instantly and William Meekes was mortally wounded. Meekes was stationed at Tower 42, close by where the Battle of Bexhill had started in 1828. The two lie buried in Bexhill churchyard, further additions to the tragedies suffered over the centuries by preventive forces in Kent and Sussex.

Deaths among the smuggling fraternity also continued and indeed one died the following night at Worthing when a local gang planned a run that emulated the grab-and-dash tactic. Some 200 local tub-men together with 50 batmen, said to be from Bexhill, gathered in the houses and dark areas close by the town beach. The boat ran in with some 300 tubs but was seen by a Coastguard man at East Worthing. His alarm flare quickly brought out a Party led by Lieutenant Henderson but by then the gang had managed to unload over 250 tubs. Although they heavily outnumbered the Party, and despite the presence of 50 batmen, the smugglers took to their heels and were chased in and out of many a house in the High Street. When they reached the outskirts of the town some attempted to cross a narrow bridge over a stream but a gate was locked and they were forced to turn and fight. Lieutenant Henderson cocked his pistols and ordered them to surrender but in reply their leader, William Cowerson, struck with his bludgeon and broke the officer's arm , whereupon Henderson fired his other pistol and shot the attacker dead. This was the signal for a general set-to in which the batmen gained the upper hand at first but fled when another Coastguard Party arrived. William Cowerson, a young stonemason who had been working on Tarring church, lies buried in the churchyard at Steyning, his home village.

George Pett, chief boatman at Eastbourne was the last member of the Coastguard to be murdered fighting smugglers on this most violent stretch of coastline. On a January night in 1833 he was near the Wish Tower when a run was made. According to the *Times* 400 (?) tub men, flanked by armed men, rushed on to the beach as their boat landed. Two Parties of Coastguard men soon arrived and in the ensuing fight some smugglers and three Coastguard men were wounded but George Pett was the only fatality. The newspaper reported that, at his funeral 'almost 100 Coastguards followed the remains which passed through Southbourne towards the church. The most respectful silence was observed and the effect was impressive'. Despite a reward offer of £1000 there was no information forthcoming about his killer.

The last major running encounter with armed smugglers in Sussex took place on 25 November 1833 at Pevensey. As usual men carrying firearms and bats held off attacks by the Coastguard whilst the tubs were unloaded. The fight, so reminiscent of the Battles of Brookland and Bexhill, then rolled on for two hours across seven miles of the Pevensey Levels. Three smugglers died that night and five were taken prisoner together with 68 tubs, but no Coastguard men were injured. The five were held in Horsham Gaol and later sentenced at Lewes Assizes to transportation for life.

The revenue cruiser *Cameleon* once commanded by William Mingaye and mentioned several times in this book sank in a tragic accident in 1834 when, lying at anchor off Dover Harbour in broad daylight on a clear day, she was rammed by the naval frigate *Castor*. Thirteen crew, including the commander, were lost and four saved. Following a court martial a Lieutenant from the frigate was dismissed from the Navy.

When making those changes in the Coastguard during 1831 the Board of Customs had also taken the opportunity to reorganise the Mounted Guard and to remove the old riding officers, some of whom had been in service not only when the Guard was formed in 1822 but for many years before that. Henceforth all new entrants were to be between 20 and 30 years of age and drawn only from cavalry regiments. Their tasks were to scout out possible gatherings of smugglers inland from the coast and to act both as mobile reserves and messengers to Coastguard Stations. It took some time, however, to prise some of the old-timers out of their saddles. It was not until 1834, for example, that a report in the *Sussex Weekly Advertiser* announced three riding officers in the Arundel District had been superannuated on full

Revenue cruiser Vigilant *built 1901 and long forgotten now being restored by an independent charity formed by Customs & Excise staff.* – Vigilant Trust

salaries. Their ages were 84, 80 and 72 and they had served for 50, 54 and 54 years respectively!

The new Mounted Guard, which numbered just over 150 for the whole of Britain, was only in existence for 18 years and during this period the era of smuggling violence and confrontation in Sussex and Kent drew to a close. Any information about the deaths of smugglers was bound to be sketchy at times – some may have died weeks after a fight – but it seems the last to die in Kent or Sussex was Thomas Monk, a fiddler from Winchelsea, who was shot by Coastguard men near Camber Castle on 1 April 1838.

The incidence of smuggling dropped dramatically in the 1840s, thanks to changes in the duty tariffs introduced by Sir Robert Peel when he became Prime Minister in 1841. He inherited a disastrous financial situation but, being a keen advocate of free trade, his first Budget in 1842 brought major changes in taxation. Many duties of customs and excise were reduced with the overall deficit more than compensated by the re-introduction of income tax, previously levied in the Napoleonic wars, at 7d in the £. With a financial deficit now turned into surplus the Budgets of 1844 and 1845 completed the reform by removing many items from the tariffs altogether.

Many goods were wiped off the smuggler's list. No longer was there any profit in dry goods or in fine goods such as silk, jewellery or lace. There were small sums to be made in smuggling spirits, not enough to support a run of commercial quantities but a few men still carried on with minor, isolated runs over the years; old habits die hard and even a little profit is welcome at times. Runs of 20 to 40 tubs were reported occasionally in Kent and Sussex, involving perhaps up to a dozen men. In one instance, in March 1850, a Worthing fly (horse carriage) operator was caught with 25 tubs and fined £25. The next January some tubs that had been 'sown' off Worthing washed ashore and were seized by the Coastguard in what seems to have been the last such seizure on that part of the coast.

The only commodity worth smuggling in any quantity was tobacco but the days of bold runs and fights were over. Contraband now usually came into ports hidden aboard cargo ships and from a revenue viewpoint there was no longer a need for an intensive coastal watch. By 1849 the Coastguard numbers had grown to more than 6,000 in Britain and Ireland with 1,450 in Kent and Sussex. The Board of Customs decided cuts were required and the Mounted Guard was virtually disbanded leaving just one or two attached to districts such as Deal, Folkestone, Hastings and Littlehampton.

In 1856, after the Crimean War, there was still some international tension and Britain had to look again at its coastal defences. In addition to its other work the Coastguard now had to act as a 'trip-wire' to warn of invasion and in consequence the Service was placed under the complete control of the Admiralty, leaving the Board of Customs with only its staff in the ports.

Over the next three decades there was some occasional smuggling of tobacco in sizeable bales; some were found washed up on beaches in Kent and Sussex as evidence of failed attempts at the time-honoured ploys of 'sowing' or towing. This period of smuggling, a pale shadow of former days, peaked in the 1880s and then declined. By the end of the century the once great Trade, a substantial source of black wealth and employment in the two counties with roots deeper than many legitimate trades, had vanished.

A Preventive Waterguard Service was formed again in 1892, as the uniformed branch of Customs, to combat smuggling and apply Customs controls over ships and their passengers and crews. The departments of Customs and Excise were merged in 1909 and in 1922 the Coastguard was transferred from the Admiralty to the Board of Trade as a life saving service. Customs and Excise decided there was still a revenue need for a coast watch and formed its own Coast Preventive Service. In 1971 both this title and that of the Preventive Waterguard disappeared when the Customs and Excise was reorganised into the department it is today.

During the second half of the twentieth century commodities worth smuggling commercially have appeared then disappeared as the profit involved diminished. In the post-austerity 1950s many thousands of nylon stockings were smuggled in from the United States by passengers and crews on the great liners. In an echo of olden days some were even floated ashore in large waterproof bags as the ships approached Spithead on their way to Southampton.

In the 1950s and 60s large numbers of Swiss watches were smuggled, usually through the Channel ports in specially built compartments in cars or luggage. In recent years, tobacco smuggling is again proving to be a

Customs staff launch a RIB (rigid inflatable boat) the modern successor to the preventive boat and Blockade galley. – Portcullis

problem, often hidden in containers or lorries arriving from France. But, even so, this is a minor problem compared to what can truly be described as the 'international evil' of drug smuggling.

Commercial quantities of cannabis and cannabis resin were first smuggled into Britain in the early 1970s followed within a few years by heroin and cocaine. Now, as we enter a new century, the country is still deeply involved in the fight. Being part of the Single Market of the European Union we now deploy fewer Customs staff to maintain revenue controls over anyone or anything coming from other member states. The

The war against drug smuggling requires close co-operation at times between the Royal Navy and Customs cutters. In this operational exercise personnel are transferred from a helicopter to H.M.C.C. 'Seeker".

H.M. Customs Cutter Sentinel.

emphasis in modern anti-smuggling work has to be on detecting prohibited goods, particularly drugs, arriving here from anywhere whether inside or outside the Union. This work requires vigilance on the coasts and at all points of arrival, combined with the gathering of intelligence in close co-operation with many other enforcement agencies around the world.

Drugs can be hidden in many spaces on ships or aircraft and in cargoes or vehicles – even inside passengers! In yet another echo of the old days cargoes of drugs, from as far away as North Africa, are brought occasionally by yachts or other craft into quiet spots on our coasts. To assist in combating this traffic British Customs use fast, rigid, inflatable boats to patrol inshore waters – the modern equivalent of the old preventive boats and Blockade galleys. Customs and Excise also operate a fleet of fast sea-going vessels, still known as cruisers and cutters and manned entirely by Customs staff, to patrol off shore around the coasts of the United Kingdom.

The fleet, which includes vessels with names such as *Seeker* and *Searcher*, gained a new addition in December 1993 when his Royal Highness, Prince Philip, Duke of Edinburgh, named it *Sentinel.* A name that would most surely have met with Captain McCulloch's wholehearted approval, although not perhaps without that one final parting shot!

APPENDIX A

I. NAVAL RANKS, RATES AND UNIFORM.
II. RATINGS OF SHIPS

I. OFFICER'S RANKS

(Up to the eighteenth century the term 'naval officer' applied to dockyard officials and senior employees of the Navy Board; officers of the Navy were known as 'sea officers'. However, by 1817 and the start of the Coast Blockade, the term 'naval officer' was being used, at least in general correspondence, as it is today).

FLAG OFFICERS. For seniority the prime concept was that of the traditional battle order of naval squadrons – White(van), Red (centre) and Blue (rear). In seniority the squadrons ranked Red, White and Blue and within each there were three flag ranks – Admiral, Vice Admiral and Rear Admiral.

CAPTAIN. The commanding officer of any post (i.e. rated) ship. Known as post Captain to distinguish from the captain of a merchantman or the petty officer rate of Captain of the Top.

COMMANDER. A rank introduced in 1794. Usually in command of brigs, schooners and the like, smaller than post ships. Also appointed as First Lieutenant on large ships.

LIEUTENANT. Lowest commissioned rank at the time of the Coast Blockade. Regarded as a gentleman whatever his social background. Could command small vessels such as cutters or luggers. After eight years it was usual to acknowledge him as a senior Lieutenant and in 1914 this became the new rank of Lieutenant – Commander.

MASTER. Originally the navigator of a warship when the captain was a military man. Warrant officer with Trinity House qualifications who might also serve spells in the merchant navy. Equated for pay with Lieutenants but remained a 'dead end' warrant rank until given commissioned status in 1843.

MASTER'S MATE. Senior petty officer, assistant to a Master. The highest paid rating and the only rating allowed to command small auxiliary vessels such as tenders. Usually promoted to the rate after entering the Navy as Volunteer 2nd Class. Midshipmen aspiring to be Lieutenants needed to be navigators and they too sought promotion to Mate. In 1824 Mates were recognised formally as the promotion step to Lieutenant. Many in Blockade records are shown as Admiralty Mates, a prefix achieved after two years service that is not used in this book in the interests of brevity. In 1840 the rate was given commissioned rank status immediately below Lieutenant and in 1860 it became known as Sub-Lieutenant.

MIDSHIPMAN. Senior petty officer who was recognised as a potential commissioned officer. Even so, some in the Blockade Service were promoted to Mates only after perhaps twelve years as Midshipmen.

VOLUNTEER 1ST CLASS. The cadet entry of its day achieved through a sponsor or by the parents asking a post Captain to take the boy. Some, under Admiralty patronage, entered the R.N. College, Portsmouth as College Volunteers. After two years both groups achieved 'Admiralty' status and became Midshipmen.

From 1843 Volunteers 1st Class became known as Cadets.

SURGEON. Warrant officer appointed by the Victualling Board. When not in a naval appointment he could take employment ashore in surgery or medicine. Raised to 'wardroom rank' in 1808 but not to commissioned status until 1843.

ASSISTANT SURGEON. Warrant officer appointed by the Navy Board from those apprenticed to surgeons or apothecaries. Not raised to commissioned status until 1866.

PURSER. Warrant officer appointed by the Navy Board to manage the ship's accounts, provisions and slops. Not qualified professionally but had to give financial sureties. Promoted from Clerk, he was allowed to take commissions on issues of provisions and slops. A purser's pound, for example, was 14 ounces not 16 and so he made a good commission on stores issued. Many Pursers became rich men with reputations for various fraudulent ways to make profits. Given commissioned status in 1843 and renamed Paymaster in 1855.

WARRANT OFFICERS. As a body were ranked below the most junior commissioned officer and for general engagement were divided into those in:

'Constant Employ'	required to stand by a ship, e.g. Gunners, Boatswains, Pursers, Carpenters.
'Inconstant Employ'	those who may find work elsewhere, e.g. Masters, Surgeons, Chaplains.

INFERIOR OFFICERS. General term applied to Midshipmen and Mates (senior petty officers) and junior warrant officers such as Assistant Surgeons.

PETTY OFFICER RATES. At the time of the Coast Blockade there were over 40 petty officer rates in the Royal Navy but the following featured most in Blockade records:

Boatswain's (Bosuns) Mate. On board ship the most feared and most vocal petty officer. Supervised men working on or below deck. Wielded the 'cat' when a flogging was ordered.

Captain of the Top. Supervised men working aloft. Rated by each mast on board ship and so there were Captains of the Fore Top, Main Top and Mizzen Top. In the Blockade Service the rate was known just as Captain of the Top.

Quartermaster. On board ship supervised the helmsmen and was responsible for maintaining the steering gear. Kept the ship's time by hour glass and supervised issues of stores and provisions from the hold.

Armourer and Armourer's Mate. In the Blockade Service they repaired and maintained muskets, pistols and cutlasses often using mobile forges for intricate work.

SEAMEN RATES. In descending order: Able Seaman, Ordinary Seaman and Landsman – the lowest animal of all! When on watch in the Blockade Service all three rates were known as sentinels.

UNIFORM. Normal working dress for officers was a blue jacket, edged in white, with a high cut stand-up collar and blue lapels over a white cloth waistcoat. Three buttons to pockets and cuffs. Lieutenants wore a single epaulet on the right shoulder. The jacket for a Mate had a narrow white edge but for a Midshipman it was plain. Blue trousers replaced breeches in 1823. The high collar carried distinctions:

Surgeon	anchor with serpent twisted around the shank.
Purser	two crossed anchors.
Mate and Midshipman	gold button and button-hole.

Up to 1827 Lieutenants in working dress wore a tricorne hat whilst inferior officers had either a top hat or a round black hat with a lower crown. In 1827 a flat blue cloth cap with gilt band was introduced generally for every day use as was a single breasted greatcoat, carrying a stand-up collar lined in white, with cuffs bearing one row of narrow gold twist for Mates and Midshipmen, one row of gold lace for Lieutenants, two for Commanders and three for Captains.

For details of uniform issued to ratings see the descriptions in Chapter Six of that mustered by men drafted to *Britannia.*

II. RATINGS OF SHIPS

		No. of Crew
First rate	Ships of 100 guns or more	800/900
Second rate	Ships of 80 – 99 guns	650/700
Third rate	Ships of 70 – 79 guns	600/650
Fourth rate	Ships of 50 – 69 guns	350/450
Fifth rate	Ships of 36 – 49 guns	280/300
Sixth rate	Ships of 24 – 35	125/175
Sloops and bomb vessels		75/125
Gun brigs, cutters, schooners and other small vessels		Up to 65

Ships in the first three rates formed the battle lines in any major engagement and so were known as 'ships-of-the-line'. Those in the next three rates were used for reconnaissance, communications and supplies. Fifth and sixth-raters were often known as frigates and occasionally as corvettes. All rated ships were commanded by post Captains.

Unrated ships (i.e. below sixth rate) were commanded by Commanders, Lieutenants or Mates according to size. Blockade tenders and watch vessels were drawn from the lowest of the unrated categories 'Gun brigs . . . other small vessels'.

In this book the figures in brackets after the name of a naval vessel show the number of cannon carried. These varied in size, according to the weight of ball used, from 3 pounders to 32 pounders.

APPENDIX B

NAVAL AUXILIARY VESSELS USED IN THE COAST BLOCKADE

Adder	Watch vessel moored at Rye Town from 1826. Gun Brig (12), 85ft long. Built Topsham 1813. Wrecked near Newhaven 1832.
Antelope	Tender based at Deal 1823–1831.
Bathurst	Watch vessel moored in West Swale 1823–1831. Survey brig, bought 1821 at Port Jackson.
Beresford	Watch vessel moored in East Swale 1818–1831. Schooner. Replaced *Congo.*
Congo	Watch vessel. Moored in East Swale 1818; Cuckmere Haven 1819–1825 and Rye Town 1825. Sold there in March 1826. Paddle schooner. 70ft long. Built Deptford 1816 to survey River Congo but was unable to progress far up river. Never used under steam and engine removed 1818.
Dandy	Tender 1829–1831. In service around Swale and North Kent coast.
Dart	Tender based at Newhaven 1825–1831. Sloop of 18 tons seized from smugglers March 1825.
Dwarf	Watch vessel moored at Rye Town 1826–1831. Cutter (2). 52ft long. Built Cowes 1826. Sold 1862.
Enchantress	Watch vessel beached at Rye Harbour 1819. Sloop (14). 80ft long. Bought 1804. Broken up 1869.
Flying Fish	Tender based at Deal 1817–1820. Schooner (1) ex *Lady Augusta*. 62ft long. Bought 1817. Sold Antigua 1821.
Grinder	Tender based at Deal 1827–1831. Sold 1832.
Griper	Watch vessel moored in Chichester Harbour from July 1825. Gun brig (12). 85ft long. Built 1813. With *Hecla* formed an expedition under Rear Admiral Parry, May 1819–October 1820, to seek the North West Passage. First expedition to winter so far north. Converted to Arctic discovery sloop (2) in 1824 and sent again to North West under Captain Lyon. Returned early 1825. Broken up 1868.
Highflyer	Tender based at Newhaven. Built Woolwich 1822 as a tender (2). 56ft long. Replaced by *Resolution* 1829 and sold 1833.
Industry	Tender based at Deal 1820–1831. Transport (4). Built Eling 1814. 104ft long. Replaced *Flying Fish* and became the longest serving Blockade tender. Broken up 1846.
Pelter	Watch vessel beached at Eastware from May 1826. Gun brig (12). 84ft long. Built Bideford 1813. Sold 1862.
Pioneer	Tender based at Deal 1819–1823. Cutter (12). 83ft long. Built Upnor 1810. Sold 1849.
Raven	Tender based at Newhaven 1829–1831. Survey cutter (4). 61ft long.

	Built Pembroke Dock 1829. Sold 1859.
Resolution	Tender based at Newhaven 1829–1831. Replaced *Highflyer*.
Snapper	Watch vessel moored in West Swale 1823–1831. Gun brig (12). 84ft long. Built Redbridge 1813. Sold 1865.
Speedy	Tender based at Newhaven August 1829–1831. Cutter (6). 64ft long. Built Pembroke Dock 1826. Broken up 1866.
Viper	Tender based at Newhaven from August 1825 until broken up August 1828. Replaced by *Wolf*.
Wolf	Tender based at Newhaven 1828–1829. Cutter tender (8). 55ft long. Built Cowes 1801. Broken up 1829 and replaced by *Speedy*.

NOTES

1 The figures in brackets after the description of the vessel show the number of cannon carried.

2 At the time of the hand over in 1831 some watch vessels were taken over by the Coast Guard but the transfer details are not known. In June 1831 the Coast Guard scrapped two old tenders *Providence* and *Lee*; they were probably replaced by ex-Blockade vessels but again the details are not known.

APPENDIX C

KENT COAST BLOCKADE STATIONS : MARCH 1825
(The numbers at each station are the complements for Lieutenants – Mates – Petty Officers – Men)

FIRST DIVISION

Sheerness	1-1-4-20	Warden Point	1-0-4-16	Sea Salter	1-0-4-20
Queenboro'	1-0-4-20	Laysdown	0-1-3-12	Whitstable [2]	1-0-4-18
Bathurst	1-1-3-18	Shellness [1]	1-1-4-20	Tankerton	0-1-3-8
Snapper	1-1-3-18	Harty	0-1-3-12	Swale Cliff	1-0-4-20
Scraps Gate	1-0-4-20	Pioneer	1-0-3-18	Herne Bay	1-0-4-20
East End Lane	1-0-4-25	Beresford	1-1-3-18	Bishopton	1-0-4-20
Hensbrook	1-0-4-18	Graveney	1-0-4-20	Reculver	0-1-3-15

[1] Plus Divisional Lieutenant and 6 Support Staff.
[2] Plus Surgeon, Purser and 2 Support Staff.

SECOND DIVISION

St Nicholas	1-0-4-22	Pegwell	1-0-4-20	Walmer [1]	1-0-4-20
Epple Bay	1-0-6-26	North Shore	0-1-4-12	Kingsdown	1-0-3-13
West Brook	1-1-4-20	Shingle End	1-0-4-22	Oldstairs	0-1-3-13
Newgate	1-0-4-20	No.2 Batt. Sandown	1-0-4-18	St Margarets	1-0-4-20
Kingsgate	1-0-4-20	No. 1 Batt. Sandown	1-0-3-12	Cornhill ★	1-0-4-18
Broadstairs	1-0-4-20	Sandown Cas.	1-0-3-8		
Ramsgate	1-0-4-20	Deal ★	0-1-4-20		

[1] Plus Divisional Lieutenant, Surgeon, Purser and 12 Support staff.

THIRD DIVISION

Casemates Dover	1-0-4-16	Ft. Twiss	1-0-4-16	Romney	1-0-4-20
Townshend	1-0-4-20	Ft. Sutherland	1-0-3-12	No.2 Batt. ★	1-0-4-18
Lydden Spout	1-0-4-18	Ft. Moncrief ★	1-0-4-20	No.1 Batt.	1-0-3-18
Hougham ★	1-0-3-12	No.22 Tower	1-0-2-11	Redoubt	1-0-3-18
No.1 Tower	0-1-2-11	No.23 Tower	0-1-2-12	Dungeness ★	1-0-4-20
No.3 Tower	1-0-2-9	No.24 Tower	1-0-3-9	Lydd	1-0-4-20
Folkestone [1]	1-1-4-20	No.26 Tower	0-1-2-12	Jews Gap ★	1-0-4-20
No.4 Tower ★	1-1-4-20	No.27 Tower ★	1-0-2-11		
Shorncliff [2]	1-0-4-20	Littlestone	1-0-4-20		

[1] Plus Divisional Lieutenant and 3 Support Staff
[2] Plus Surgeon, Purser and 2 Support Staff

NOTES (TO APPENDIX C)

1 In the Kent Blockade as a whole at this time there were also 10 Assistant Surgeons at various locations.
2 The total complement of 1,480 included 43 support staff.
3 Blockade Stations also equipped as signal units to relay messages from Deal are shown as

*. The separate signal station at East Hill was manned by a petty officer from St Margarets.

4 At Deal and the Divisional offices there were some Royal Marines but they were not included in these complements.

5 From early 1826 the First, Second and Third Divisions were renamed Left, Centre and Right.

APPENDIX D

SUSSEX COAST BLOCKADE STATIONS JUNE 1825
(The numbers at each station are the complements for Officers – Petty Officers – Men)

EASTERN DIVISION

Camber	1-4-24	Haddocks	1-5-20	No.50/51 Towers (Cooden)	1-4-8
Enchantress	1-4-15	Fairlight *	0-3-10	No.55 Tower * (Pevensey Sluice)	0-2-13
Congo (Rye Town)	0-3-10	Ecclesbourne	1-4-15	No.57 Tower	1-2-6
Rye	0-2-6	Hastings Watch House	0-4-10	No.59 Tower (Pevensey Bay)	1-2-9
No.28 Tower	0-2-8	Priory Watch House ①	4-5-22	No.62 Tower	1-2-7
Winchelsea	1-1-7	No.40/41 Towers	0-1-8	No.64 Tower	0-3-6
No.31 Tower *	1-1-7	No.44 Tower * (Galley Hill)	1-2-9	Langney Point *	1-2-8
No.33 Tower	0-3-8	No.46 Tower (Bexhill)	0-2-8		
No.36 Tower	1-2-9	No.48 Tower (Bexhill)	0-2-6		
No.38 Tower	1-2-11	No.49 Tower	0-3-8		

(Nos 31-38 Towers on Pett Levels)

① Included Divisional Lieutenant, Surgeon, Purser and their support staff.

CENTRE DIVISION

<table>
<tr><td>No.71 Tower</td><td>0-2-10</td><td>Crowlink</td><td>1-2-15</td><td>Salt Dean</td><td rowspan="2">1-5-30</td></tr>
<tr><td>Eastbourne Watch House</td><td>1-4-22</td><td>Cuckmere</td><td>1-1-15</td><td>Greenaway</td></tr>
<tr><td>No.73 Tower (Wish)</td><td>1-2-11</td><td>Blatchington</td><td>1-2-13</td><td>Brighton</td><td rowspan="2">1-4-32</td></tr>
<tr><td>Holywell</td><td>1-2-15</td><td>No.74 Tower (Seaford)</td><td>1-3-13</td><td>Black Rock</td></tr>
<tr><td>Beachy Head *</td><td>1-2-13</td><td>Newhaven ①</td><td rowspan="2">2-3-30</td><td>Hove</td><td>1-3-21</td></tr>
<tr><td>Birling Gap</td><td>1-1-15</td><td>Bear Hide</td><td>Copperas Gap (East Shoreham)</td><td>1-3-21</td></tr>
</table>

① Included Divisional Lieutenant. The Divisional Surgeon and Purser and their support staff were part of *Hyperion's* complement.

WESTERN DIVISION

Shoreham West	2-3-20	Elmer East	1-2-15	Selsey	1-3-21
Lancing	1-4-15	Elmer West	1-2-15	Thorney ②	1-3-23
Worthing East	1-3-15	Felpham	1-2-14	Cockbush & Chichester Harbour Watch Vessel ③	3-7-43
Worthing West	1-3-17	Bognor	1-5-17		
Goring	1-4-20	Pagham East	1-2-9		
Kingston	1-3-20	Pagham West	1-2-15		
Littlehampton ①	4-4-34	Wallend	1-3-13		

① Included Divisional Lieutenant, Surgeon, Purser and Support Staff.

② On the western side of Selsey village; not to be confused with Thorney Island in Chichester Harbour.

③ The old unnamed vessel, replaced by *Griper* a month later.

NOTES (TO APPENDIX D)

1 In the Sussex Coast Blockade as a whole there were also 9 Assistant Surgeons at various locations.
2 The total complement in mid 1825 was 1,109 including support staff.
3 Blockade Stations also equipped as signal stations to relay messages are shown as *. The separate signal station at Kewhurst Hill, near Bexhill, was manned by a petty officer from No.49 Tower.
4 There were Royal Marines at Rye, Newhaven, Chichester Harbour and the Divisional offices but those men were not included in the complements.

APPENDIX E

LIEUTENANTS TRANSFERRED FROM THE COAST BLOCKADE TO THE COAST GUARD IN MARCH 1831

This was the main group nominated by the Admiralty. A few others may have moved before or after March but their names are not known. Many transferees remained at, or in the vicinity of, their old Blockade Stations.

KENT COAST BLOCKADE (H.M.S. TALAVERA)

BAKER	Gustavus
BAKER	Joseph
BATE	John
BATT	Henry
BECKETT	William
BENSON	John
BLISSETT	Charles
BROKENSHA	Samuel
BUTLER	Thomas
CAMPBELL	G.
CLEUGH	Robert
DICKMAN	W.H.
DOUGLAS	John
DREW	George
DUFFILL	John
EDEVAIN	R.T.
ELWIN	Joseph
EVANS	John
GRAHAM	George
HALL	Thomas
HENSLOW	F.J.
HUMPHRIES	George
HUNTER	Robert
HUNTER	Valentine
JEAYES	John
JOHNSTONE	Charles
JULL	Edward
KIDDLE	John
KNIGHT	John Ellis
KNIGHT	Alex
LANGTRY	Joseph
LASTOW	Samuel
LAWLESS	Henry
LEARY	George
LEWIS	William
MARSHALL	William
MIDGE	Zacharias
MORGAN	Richard
NICKOLL	Edward
PEARCE	George
PRICE	E. Howard
POYNTER	C.W.
PUCKETT	Charles
ROSS	Thomas
SEAWARD	William
SQUIRE	William
STAPLE	Arch.
STEPHEN	John
WINGROVE	Henry
WHEELER	Thomas
WHITFIELD	William

SUSSEX COAST BLOCKADE (H.M.S HYPERION)

ASHBY	William
BARDEN	John
COLLINS	Francis
CONSUET	John
CONNOR	Samuel
COURTNEY	Henry
COWEN	Maurice
CRISPIN	W.
CURTIS	W.
DAVID	L.
EARLE	E.
EVERSFIELD	Thomas
FERRAR	William A.
FOSTER	Henry D.
FRANKLIN	Edward
HILLS	John
HINE	Frederick
HOWES	George
JOACHIM	R.
JONES	H.B.
KORTRIGHT	Alfred
LEWORTHY	Henry
McTAVISH	Archibald
MOTTLEY	John
NICKOLLS	James
PALMER	George
PENNINGTON	Thomas
PRATT	James
PRATTENT	John
RAWSTHORN	James
RAYMOND	Grant
SERVANT	Charles
SHORT	Henry
WESTBROOK	George
WIGHT	Alexander
WILLIAMS	John
WILLIAMS	Thomas
WILLETT	William
WRIGHT	G.M.

APPENDIX F

'COAST BLOCKADE – A TALE'
Extract from 'A Naval Sketchbook' by Captain W.N. Glascock – 1832

It was late in the afternoon of a gloomy day in the latter part of November when , in consequence of a signal made that a suspicious sail was seen off the coast, as if waiting for the flowing of the tide in the dark, Lieutenant _ _ _ _ _ _ _ _ _ _ gave orders to man his favourite galley and proceed in quest of the stranger. . . . . The boat being shoved off the beach, after pitching twice in the surf, rose triumphantly over the third sea, which had now exhausted itself. In a moment the sail was hoisted; she instantly gathered way and stood-off in a lateral direction from the shore. . . . . Taking advantage of the next heavy swell he rose in the boat to catch a glimpse of the strange sail in the offing, which was discovered broad on the lee-bow. . . . . The bowman, just then looking under the foot of the lug pronounced her to be a large lugger, which he had seen before on the station, under similarly suspicious circumstances. The Lieutenant, putting up the helm, edged into her wake and followed precisely her track . . . (but) . . . she rapidly outdistanced her pursuer. In half-an-hour she was hull down; the haze of the evening growing every moment thicker, she became almost imperceptible to the view. . . . . A heavy swell had now set in from the same point in which the wind had continued all day . . . . . they had got so far to the leeward that to return with the lug was impossible and the crew shipping their oars bent their broad shoulders to pull her through the heavy sea which flung itself in sheets of spray over the bows, drenching every man on board. It was soon found the oars were unavailing to contend against the force of a sea like this . . . . . and the united strength of the men could barely keep her head to wind . . . . A heavy sea, which now struck the larboard bow, making in consequence a rapid accumulation of water every minute, soon decided the reluctant Lieutenant to run (though at the obvious hazard of her destruction) the boat ashore in the first situation which might offer a chance of saving the lives of his brave companions. 'Lay in your oars, my lads' cried he, 'step the short mast – close reef the storm-lug, we must run all hazards and beach her under canvas'. Whilst executing the order the bowman sung out 'a sail close aboard sir, if she don't keep her luff, she'll run us right down', 'Luff, luff!' exclaimed every man in the boat. The lugger's course, however, remaining unaltered there could be now no doubt she had seen them first and perceiving her to be a king's boat, the object was to run clean over the galley by taking her right abeam . . . . .as she neared the galley the Lieutenant rose, levelled his pistol at the steersman and fired; the hand which grasped the tiller relaxed its hold and the miscreant his life. The lugger instantly broached-to, passing to windward of the boat – 'Out oars my lads' said the Lieutenant 'we'll board the villains' . . . . . . (but) . . . . . . the intention to board being suspected by the smuggler she had no sooner paid-off, so as to get the wind again abaft the beam, then shaping a course edging in for the land she quickly dropped the galley astern . . . . . . The men were clamorous to hoist the lug and give chase; a sentiment in which the coxswain concurred, as he observed 'capture or no capture, we are more likely to find a smooth by following the lugger which clearly was herself making for the beach'. The lug was hoisted at all hazards and the Lieutenant putting the helm up she flew with inconceivable velocity in the lugger's wake . . . . . The roaring of the surf was now distinctly heard and soon the whole scene was lit by its luminous appearance. The bowman, alarmed, now vociferated 'Breakers ahead – hard down, sir, hard down!' Before the word was repeated she had entered the frightfully agitated element 'Down with the sail or we're lost!' exclaimed the crew – 'Hold-on! Hold-on everything!' cried the veteran, 'tis our only chance to beach her'. The surf now reared itself in boiling masses higher than the mast and as it fell thundering on the shore the wild din burst on the affrighted ears of the seamen like successive salvos of heavy artillery. An enormous sea, striking her on the quarter swept her broadside to the surf washing out the Lieutenant with one of the crew and the next, bursting with wilder fury, turned her bottom-upwards, burying beneath her the seven unhappy seamen in one common grave.

BIBLIOGRAPHY

PRIME CONTEMPORARY SOURCES

Public Record Office, Kew

Admiralty papers :	ADM 1	Admirals and Captains papers. Navy Board minutes. Correspondence with Custom House and Treasury.
	ADM 6.	Coast Guard appointments.
	ADM 51.	Ships logs
	ADM 106.	Coast Blockade letter books.
Treasury Papers :	T.9	Minutes on Orders in Council
Coast Guard Papers :	CUST 38.	Statistics
House of Commons Journals		

Royal Naval Museum, Portsmouth

The Navy Chronicle

Newspapers

Times; Sussex Weekly Advertiser; Brighton Gazette; Kentish Chronicle; Kentish Gazette

OTHER SOURCES

Albery, William	*Millennium of Facts in the History of Horsham & Sussex 947-1947*	1947
Beilby, A.	*Heroes all. The R.N.L.I. Story*	1992
Bishop, George	*Observations, Remarks and Means to prevent Smuggling*	1783
Briggs, Asa	*The Age of Improvement 1783-1867*	1979
Bullen, Mark	*The Sussex Coast Blockade for the Prevention of Smuggling* Unpublished thesis in library of Customs and Excise	
Clowes, W.L.	*History of the Royal Navy*	1901
Cooke, G.A.	*Topographical description of Sussex*	c. 1820
Cooper, W.D.	*Smuggling in Sussex* Sussex Arch. Coll	1858
Douch, J.A.	*Smuggling, Flogging Joey's Warriors*	1985
Edgar, J.	*Inshore Craft of Great Britain*	1970
Finn, R.	*The Kent Coast Blockade*	1971
Gash, N.	*Aristocracy and the People 1815-1865*	1979
Glascock, W.N.	*A Naval Sketch Book* (1st Series)	1832
Holmes, T.W.	*The Semaphore*	1983
Hufton, Geoffrey & Elaine Baird	*Scarecrows Legion, smuggling in Kent and Sussex*	1983
Laker, J	*A History of Deal*	1917
Lewis, M.	*The Navy in Transition*	1965
O'Byrnes	*Naval Biography*	1849
Rodgers, N.A.M.	*Naval Records for the Genealogists*	1988

Shore, Henry N.	*Smuggling Days and Smuggling Ways*	1892
Smith, Graham	*Something to Declare*	1980
	King's Cutters	1983
Smith, Horace	*The Worthing Parade Two*	1954
Sutcliffe, Sheila	*Martello Towers*	1972
Robinson, Joseph	*Reminiscences 1820-1917* (notes written by his son; in West Sussex Record Office)	
Teignmouth, Lord & Charles G. Harper	*The Smugglers* (two volumes)	1923
Trevelyan, G.M.	*British History in the Nineteenth Century and after (1782-1919)*	1944
Waugh, Mary	*Smuggling in Kent and Sussex* 1700-1840	1985
Webb, William	*Coastguard! An official history of H.M. Coastguard*	1976
Wilson, Geoffrey	*The Old Telegraphs*	1976

INDEX

(See also the Lieutenants listed at Appendix E)